MW01407781

CRUSHED, BUT NOT BROKEN

MELISSA BOSCH

WestBow
PRESS
A DIVISION OF THOMAS NELSON
& ZONDERVAN

Copyright © 2022 Melissa Bosch.

All rights reserved. No part of this book may be used or reproduced by any means, graphic, electronic, or mechanical, including photocopying, recording, taping or by any information storage retrieval system without the written permission of the author except in the case of brief quotations embodied in critical articles and reviews.

This book is a work of non-fiction. Unless otherwise noted, the author and the publisher make no explicit guarantees as to the accuracy of the information contained in this book and in some cases, names of people and places have been altered to protect their privacy.

WestBow Press books may be ordered through booksellers or by contacting:

WestBow Press
A Division of Thomas Nelson & Zondervan
1663 Liberty Drive
Bloomington, IN 47403
www.westbowpress.com
844-714-3454

Because of the dynamic nature of the Internet, any web addresses or links contained in this book may have changed since publication and may no longer be valid. The views expressed in this work are solely those of the author and do not necessarily reflect the views of the publisher, and the publisher hereby disclaims any responsibility for them.

Any people depicted in stock imagery provided by Getty Images are models, and such images are being used for illustrative purposes only.
Certain stock imagery © Getty Images.

Scripture quotations taken from The Holy Bible, New International Version® NIV® Copyright © 1973 1978 1984 2011 by Biblica, Inc. TM. Used by permission. All rights reserved worldwide.

Scripture taken from the New King James Version® Copyright © 1982 by Thomas Nelson. Used by permission. All rights reserved.

Scripture quotations marked (NLT) are taken from the Holy Bible, New Living Translation, copyright ©1996, 2004, 2015 by Tyndale House Foundation. Used by permission of Tyndale House Publishers, a Division of Tyndale House Ministries, Carol Stream, Illinois 60188. All rights reserved.

ISBN: 978-1-6642-5976-8 (sc)
ISBN: 978-1-6642-5977-5 (hc)
ISBN: 978-1-6642-5978-2 (e)

Library of Congress Control Number: 2022903960

Print information available on the last page.

WestBow Press rev. date: 04/19/2022

To The only man on this earth I would choose over and over again, even knowing what we would have to go through. You ground me and push me to be a better person.

To Ella, Eli, and Everett. You never signed up for this journey, but took every punch, letdown, and heartache with understanding. You are the heroes of this story.

To Emmy, how you went through what you did and never wavered in your love and faith in Jesus is a testimony. Your smile has the power to light even the darkest of places. Never forget that your joy comes only from the Lord.

And to the One and only One Who could take an impossible situation and prove that anything is possible—the God who is my Jehovah Jireh, my Abba, my more than enough.

ACKNOWLEDGMENTS

He has delivered us from such a deadly peril, and He will deliver us again. On Him we have set our hope that He will continue to deliver us, as you help us by your prayers. Then many will give thanks on our behalf for the gracious favor granted us in answer to the prayers of many.
—2 CORINTHIANS 1:10-11(NIV)

Words are power. We use them to send forth messages, to communicate our desires, always hoping for answers in return. We speak to let others know our joy, but also our pain and anguish. The words I wrote to keep our family and friends updated, first on Caring Bridge and then later on Facebook, ended up bringing thousands of prayer warriors to our aid. As I wrote every night in an abyss of despair, I knew you were all praying for us. Team #Emmystrong, your prayers and thoughtful words are what got us through those months and years of unanswered prayers, tragedies, and sadness.

Dr. Toor, thank you for being the first doctor we ever needed and the first one to show us what compassion truly means. Because of you, we knew what kind of doctors we needed surrounding us in Boston to get us through the most painful chapter in our lives.

To the nurses on the neurology, ICU, and transplant floors at Boston Children's Hospital, we will never forget you. While many of you were young enough to be one of my daughters, you carried yourselves with courage and strength as you fought alongside our family, looking for answers, relief, and ways to make Emmy as comfortable as possible. I will forever be indebted to you for not only loving Emmy, but also our whole family.

To the doctors who listened to me and trusted my mother's intuition, thank you. All Emmy needed was just one advocate, and many of you stepped up to the plate.

To Emily and Beth, you paved the way for Emmy to finally find a diagnosis and cure. CNS-restricted HLH was almost unheard of, but you fought for answers and fought doctors to send you to the NIH, which ultimately led to a diagnosis. Because of your relentless pursuit for answers, Emily and Emmy are finally cured and still alive, even though the disease took a portion of them with it. Thank you from the bottom of my heart.

To the women of God who listened to His voice and comforted me with His words, may you be blessed beyond measure. The simple act of a call or text, just to let me know that God was still listening to my prayers and reminding me to "be still" continues to be my source of strength in times of doubt.

To every single person who cooked for us, watched our children, cleaned our home, painted our walls, and drove all the way to Boston to pray for us, *thank you*! It truly takes a village. And to those of you who urged me to tell Emmy's story, even though the majority of it is filled with sadness and despair, thank you. Weeping may endure for a night (or possibly years), but joy truly does come in the morning (Psalm 30:5 NIV).

PREFACE

Beloved, do not think it strange concerning the fiery trial which is to try you, as though some strange thing happened to you; but rejoice to the extent that you partake of Christ's sufferings, that when His glory is revealed, you may also be glad with exceeding joy.

—1 PETER 4:12-13 (NKJV)

Life is hard and, all too often, completely unfair. Well, at least it is in our eyes. We did all the right things, gave up the bad, and tried hard to be the people we thought God wanted us to be. We went to church, prayed over our kids, and walked in a manner that would make any Father proud. But then it happened. The earth broke apart, and we fell hard into a deep cavern of tragedy. We cried and screamed and pleaded with God to help, but we felt alone, lost, and mostly betrayed. I thought Christians were protected from all this. But then the questions started. Did God do this? Did He allow it and not intervene? Did we do something to deserve this? Everything we believed about who God was came into question.

Learning about God is much different than experiencing God face to face. Preconceived notions, lessons taught in Sunday school, and guilt piled on from years of thinking God just waits around to punish us—that was all hard to overcome while struggling to pull myself out of the despair I was in. Eventually, all the walls of lies came crashing down, and the true character of God broke though the thickest of lies and chaos. God is love. God is good. God never fails.

I struggled for years over what it meant to be a faithful Christian. I found myself telling God I was ready to have my faith tested after watching a television program about Christians who found themselves dying from cancer. Their faith never wavered, even when modern medicine failed and miracles never came. I wanted that kind of faith. But how do you know you have it without being pushed into the greatest test of your life?

I quickly learned that being Christian isn't a magical cloak that protects us from pain and reality. It definitely doesn't mean we get to tell God how things are going to turn out or how He should take away our pain. Being Christian doesn't mean we get first dibs on healing, while unbelievers have to wait. Being Christian means experiencing all the hard feelings of pain, sadness, despair and even loss. Without those feelings and experiences, our faith would never grow, our character would be left untested, and our ability to relate to others would be almost impossible.

While fighting for the life of our daughter, I found God—not the god people try to put in a perfectly sized box who only reacts with anger and punishment. No, I found the One who holds all the answers and is working everything out for our good. I found the God who cares about us more than we can ever imagine; the God who doesn't desire perfection but, rather, relationship and communion; and the God who carries us through the valley, even if we are too blind to see Him holding our hand and dragging us through the mud.

While we lived in the ICU for nine months, I watched some children die, yet others would miraculously walk away like they had never been sick. Why some children die and others don't is so beyond my comprehension. All death is wrong. But that's just it. We live in this fallen world with sickness and death all around us. How we approach and respond to the pain and suffering are what ultimately matter. How we choose to fight matters. But most of all, when we ask God what He wants and submit to His answer, that is the life changer.

I fought for our daughter every way I physically knew how, except the way God wanted me to. I found myself blaming God, even hating Him, but God was already there, in the future, working it all out. It was me who was doing it all wrong. All I knew was that through all the pain and suffering, making everything harder than it really was, I finally gave up. I couldn't go any further and found myself crushed and hopeless. I became so hurt and so filled with despair, I was barely recognizable from the woman I was before. But God found me and put me back together.

The Creator of the universe picked me up and molded me into what He wanted for me all along—someone who would know God so intimately that not even death itself could separate my faith in Him. A faith so strong that I would never be intimidated by fear again.

Every single person involved in the fight for our daughter's life was changed. We all played a part, and we all experienced God's faithfulness differently. But this is my story. This is how I found the love of God deep in the Valley of the Shadow of Death. Every heartbreak, every disappointment, and every tragedy crushed me into a million pieces. But just like the jar of clay, I was crushed but not broken. Nothing is ever too far broken for God to restore—nothing.

PART I
VIRGINIA

I waited patiently for the Lord to help me,
And He turned to me and heard my cry.
—PSALM 40:1 (NIV)

1
CHAPTER

And not only that, but we also glory in tribulations knowing that tribulation produces perseverance; and perseverance, character; and character, hope.
—ROMANS 5:3-4 (NKJV)

Emmy was in first grade the year she broke her arm. Before the break, she was a typical girl who practiced gymnastics; tapped her little feet away in dance; and wore mismatched clothes, accessorized with a glitter vest and biker boots. She was a naturally gifted auditory learner and had memorized hundreds of facts, even before her older siblings, but she despised traditional learning with textbooks. With much persuasion, I taught her to read and write, and she was right on track for a six-year-old.

After the break, something switched in her brain. She said words were fuzzy and moving all around. When I tested her in May, one month after breaking her arm, she couldn't even read a small paragraph of sentences without quitting. I tried to ignore the signs, but something wasn't right, and worry overwhelmed my thoughts. I was trying hard to be the good Christian by "calling those things which be not as though they were." I had always been warned that, if I said something negative out loud, it would happen. Positivity, while ignoring reality, would ultimately be my downfall.

The previous month in April, we'd finally had the chance to take a stateside vacation after spending three years conveniently landlocked in the Pacific Ocean. Before moving to Virginia, Hawaii had been our home.

Randy was given a position at the medical clinic at Pearl Harbor-Hickam, and flying our family of six to visit family was not an option we could afford. This most recent Air Force assignment landed us at Langley Air Force Base (AFB), Virginia, and we were antsy to visit Randy's family in New Orleans.

When we arrived on Good Friday at my mother-in-law's house, the house was alive with aunts, uncles, and screaming cousins waiting to hug us. Everyone was eager to catch up with Randy, but the noise of kids made it impossible. I offered to pack all the little kids into the minivan and occupy them at the local park.

The air was heavy with humidity, and it was hard to breathe, but the kids insisted I join them on the playground. Still after the hard work of raising four kids, I loved playing with my kids. Ella, our oldest at twelve years old, didn't want to come to the park. She preferred hanging out with her Mimi and aunts. She was quickly turning into a little lady and loved adult conversation. Eli and Emmy, ages nine and six respectively, still loved playing with me. They were at such fun ages; I couldn't tell them no. Everett was the youngest. I never realized how much better you get at parenting the more kids you have. At three years old, Everett had no cares in the world. He had three older siblings who adored him and a mom who no longer worried about the small stuff. Having four kids was so much easier than just having two!

After a game of chase on the wooden play structure, an awful episode of dizziness from swinging, and trying to fit my adult-sized body down the scorching hot metal kiddie slide, I decided to take an adult time-out in the shade. I didn't miss the humidity and feeling of suffocation from the hot air, even after having spent quite a few military assignments in the South.

"Mommy!" I heard a scream right out of a horror movie. It was that scream that only parents understand. I looked up, and there was Emmy, lying under the monkey bars holding her arm. I just knew she'd broken something. Scooping her up while corralling the other kids, I quickly drove back to the house. It was two days before Easter, and we were supposed to be relaxing, but here I was already in panic mode. How could this happen just hours into our vacation? After examining her arm, hand, and wrist, nothing seemed broken, yet she still wouldn't move it. Thankfully, one of Randy's uncles is a nurse, so he did a quick check, said it just looked sprained and gave her a splint to wear. After thirty minutes, Emmy wasn't crying from the initial shock of pain anymore but crying because she didn't want to go to the hospital. After four kids, you don't overreact too much, especially if your child says she is fine and just wants to play with her cousins.

Easter Sunday came and went. By Monday, Randy and I didn't like how Emmy was behaving. She had barely slept, even getting a small fever the first night, and she still wouldn't move her wrist. Randy knew his way around New Orleans, so he decided to take her to a nearby emergency room. Sure enough, Emmy had a buckle fracture right below her left wrist. I felt so guilty for waiting two days before having her checked by a doctor, but the temporary cast didn't do much more than the sling. The doctor wrapped her arm up and said to just give Motrin for the pain.

Emmy was very uncomfortable and still wasn't back to her carefree, bubbly self. She was only six years old and bound to have some pain, but I could sense something else was wrong with her. She was miserable in every way and was now complaining of car sickness as we drove to visit Randy's dad an hour away.

French Settlement, near Baton Rouge, was just as hot and muggy as New Orleans, and the hot, itchy cast was making Emmy's arm her only concern. She kept begging to take it off and complained constantly. We decided to head back home a day early and get her to an orthopedic doctor. Then something unusual happened the night before we left. We were all settling down for bed with the kids piled up on couches and air mattresses in the living room, when all of a sudden, Emmy let out a scream and just puked. It was a puke scene right out of the movies. It just shot out of her all the way across the living room. Emmy was certain that her stomach didn't hurt, and she couldn't explain why she had puked. We chalked it up to a twenty-four-hour stomach virus and headed home with no answers to what was going on.

Three days later, we were at the orthopedic doctor, and Emmy seemed completely fine. That puke incident didn't sit well with us, so I mentioned it to the doctor. I was really worried we might have missed a concussion or something else. The doctor did a concussion workup and asked Emmy if she'd ever hit her head, to which Emmy firmly replied, "No!" The doctor finished up by saying she had no physical signs that she'd endured a concussion.

As the days and weeks went on, Emmy started to complain of painful headaches. They were short-lived and very random. The strange thing was she would fall asleep during them and wake up just minutes later completely fine. Sometimes, she would say she was going to puke, get a wild look in her eyes, and then walk away like nothing was wrong.

Randy and I were pretty concerned, but we never retreated to negative thoughts. When we went back three weeks later to get her cast taken off, I mentioned the new onset of headaches along with the nausea she was now experiencing more often. Once again, the orthopedic doctor looked into Emmy's eyes, pushed on her tummy, had her follow the light, and cleared her of any concussion. We just knew in our hearts something wasn't adding up. That broken arm had done something to her.

Over the next few weeks, Emmy's painful headaches and vomiting episodes were getting more frequent and painful. At the beginning of June, I piled all four kids into the car and took her to the pediatrician at the first available appointment. Her doctor did a quick check on her and cleared her of a concussion.

"Are you sure there isn't something else? Could it be a deep concussion? Why would she break her arm and then all of a sudden start getting headaches and begin puking? None of this is making any sense. She has never been ill a day in her life or ever complained of headaches," I intently told the military doctor.

"Let me go consult with another doctor and see what she says," the pediatrician said as she quickly went to the next room. "Why don't you keep a food log for one month and see if she is reacting to any foods she's eating. Food allergies can cause headaches and nausea. Call back in a few weeks to make a follow-up, and we'll see if she needs to see neurology for the headaches."

And that was that. A food log and a possible visit to a neurologist. That seriously made no sense to me at all, but I could handle keeping a food log more than I could handle dealing with a concussion. I prayed that was all it was, a suspicious food allergy she'd randomly developed five days after breaking her arm. Saying this out loud now, after all we know, makes me want to scream and shake that doctor. Doctors, especially pediatricians, are trained to look for two symptoms in children—headaches accompanied with nausea. But we didn't know that at the time. We also had never had any large illnesses or injuries happen, so we were not too worried about a child who had been perfectly healthy her whole life.

I started the food log and noticed nothing. We thought dairy was causing the nausea. Or maybe it was gluten? None of those changed the severity of headaches or randomness and force of her vomiting. One evening her headache was so bad, I rushed her to the ER. But like every other headache, she fell asleep in my arms, and when we were called back to see the doctor, she woke up, and the headache was completely gone. That night, the doctor diagnosed her with constipation.

I called to make a follow-up appointment with her pediatrician, but the next one available wasn't until mid-July. Choosing to not overreact, I ignored the obvious that something was terribly wrong with Emmy, and I packed up the kids and did what we loved most; we went swimming.

Right in the middle of Smithfield was a private pool. Once we were able to get a membership, we spent every single day swimming. It was there that it all was finally exposed—the unmasking of the disease that was causing Emmy to behave so strangely after her broken arm. It is that pool that reminds me of the life we once had. It was that pool that made me remember every accident, every weird coincidence, and every near-death experience that happened to Emmy. And then I realized, her life had been under attack long before she was even born.

2
CHAPTER

Deep calls to deep in the roar of your waterfalls; all your waves and breakers have swept over me.
—PSALM 42:7 (NIV)

Some people call it a "generational curse." Some call it happenstance or just possibly bad luck, but whatever name you give it, we had no idea it had been hiding in our past, present, and future. It was so hidden, so invisible, that if not for God, it would have never been discovered and brought to light. But long before its discovery, we could tell that something had been after Emmy's life from the start.

After thinking back, from the day I found out I was pregnant with Emmy after a family trip to Disney World, I realized nothing about Emmy's life had been normal. The first strange incident I remembered was while I was six months pregnant with her. I was walking across a street after an OB checkup, and I suddenly slipped and fell in the middle of the street. Thankfully, I was able to protect my stomach and walk away with just a scratched knee and sore hand. That was just the first thing that happened in a long, strange series of unfortunate events.

There was the time I had to actually hurt Emmy, to save her. I was carrying eight-month-old Emmy down our wooden stairs in Minot, North Dakota, right before going out for a spouse's night at the community center. I rarely wore heels and had just recently given up my flight suit and combat boots for more comfortable clothes like yoga pants and slippers.

Not being used to wearing shoes with a heel, I suddenly felt my right foot get stuck on my left pant leg. Realizing I would crush Emmy if we both fell down the stairs together, I slid her down my hip and dropped her on the top stair. I quickly leaped over Emmy and all seven stairs, leaping to the floor, landing in excruciatingly painful splits. I quickly turned and watched Emmy's small, chunky body go plunk, plunk, plunk down each step. Everyone just stood shocked, frozen in terror.

"Why on earth did you just drop her on the stairs, Missy?" Randy scolded me as he grabbed Emmy off the floor and cradled her.

"My foot got stuck, and I knew that if we both fell down the stairs, I would have crushed her!" I said as I tried to recreate the entire scene.

So many more things would happen to her—and only her. I felt like I had to be on guard every waking minute of every single day.

After living in Minot, North Dakota, for three frozen years, the Air Force must have felt pity on us because our next assignment was to Pearl Harbor-Hickam, Hawaii. With a waitlist to move into base housing, we found a rental house in the city Ewa Beach. It was one of the many blessings that did happen to our family.

I was new to homeschooling and hated every second of it. Wrangling two-year-old Emmy while trying to teach two different curriculums to Eli, a new kindergartner, and Ella, a second grader, was overwhelming. I screamed a lot—enough that Ella and Eli specifically said I was really mean that year. I had no idea how to get everyone working and was constantly trying to make homeschool like public school, which made it even worse.

I remember saying to myself, "There has to be a better way to teach all my kids without wasting the entire day." And just like that we were invited to join a homeschool swim team, where I was later introduced to a new homeschool program. One year later, I ended up directing the first Classical Conversations group on Oahu. That group eventually expanded and is now across many islands of Hawaii.

I was pregnant with Everett almost the entire time we lived in Ewa Beach. Morning sickness the first trimester and exhaustion from homeschooling was taking its toll. Emmy was a new two-year-old and always on my last nerve. She never obeyed, never listened, and was always on the go. I would find her in the yard, collecting geckos and hiding behind palm trees. She was the opposite of her older sister, Ella, who was as laid-back and as obedient as you could hope any child to be.

One morning, I was diligently teaching Ella and Eli math and fighting my nausea when we heard a loud *pop* right before our electricity shut off. I instantly looked for Emmy. At first glance, I evaluated it like a crime scene. A burnt wall, a metal hair clip, and a night-light halfway hanging out of an electrical socket was what I found first. As I looked around, I saw a guilty little girl's toes peeking out from under the bed. Somehow, she'd used her metal hair clip and made an electrical connection between the two metal prongs yet miraculously wasn't shocked and survived the whole ordeal.

That summer, Emmy also was quite clumsy and repeatedly hurt herself. Looking back now, I can see that she was my mini me—always on the go, always looking for something to do, and always in trouble. When she was bored, she would run around the yard, trek up and down the stairs, or jump on the trampoline until her pint-sized motor would just sputter to a complete halt. During those wild runs—for which we affectionately called her "wild child"—she would fall, sometimes directly on her tailbone. It would take weeks for her to recover, but we never thought she was left with permanent damage. We had no idea how much pain she was probably in until she had a full spinal MRI done just four years later, which showed multiple fractures on her coccyx and lower spine.

During our weekly practice sessions at the local swimming pool, I finally realized Emmy could not leave my sight. While the kids worked on swimming strokes, the moms would position their chairs in a circle and discuss the books we were reading together or just enjoy the fact that we were talking to other adults. While we talked, the toddlers and babies played around us with one another.

One day as we were chatting away, I felt a chill up my spine that something wasn't right. After faintly hearing someone say, "Turn around," I swung my head and looked toward the pool. What I saw was a tiny forehead bobbing up and down, with little blue eyes peaking over then under the waterline, as the water pushed her further from the stairs. The water was just deep enough, but also just shallow enough to keep her nose and mouth right below the surface of the water. Her eyes screamed for help.

In slow motion, I felt myself jumping out of my seat and yelling at the teens to grab her. None of them heard me, so I kicked off my shoes and ran toward the pool. My old lifeguard instincts kicked in, and my overly pregnant body jumped fully clothed into the pool and pulled Emmy out. She was unfazed. Nothing about that incident scared her in the least. Moments after catching her breath, she looked straight at me, and asked if she could play in the water again. Did she even realize she could have drowned? And who had told me to turn around, because none of the moms said they had?

Days later, we were back at swim practice, where I was cooling my swollen feet in the shallow end, as I often did. As I was talking with a fellow mom, I felt a small wave hit my ankle. If the water hadn't changed direction, I would have never even noticed that Emmy had quietly slid her entire body right into the water. I knew she loved the water, but why would she always be drawn to the deep end, even when she knew she couldn't swim?

By now, I rarely let Emmy out of my sight. She was fearless and loved to investigate everything. Not many parents like to admit it, but I even thought I lost her once. She, of course, said she always knew where she was.

After one of Eli's karate lessons, I was carrying Everett in his baby carrier, shuffling the other three kids through the doors, alongside the other families, when I lost her. I thought all three kids were following me to the car, so I opened the door to put Everett in the back seat. As I walked to the other side to open the door for Emmy, she wasn't there. It had not even been a minute from the time we left karate to when I opened the door for Emmy.

After pulling Everett back out of the car and retracing our steps, we couldn't find Emmy anywhere. All three of us started calling for her, but she never answered. I whipped back around to make sure no one had walked off with her, realizing how often child abduction happens in the United States. I knew most of the parents and they were all still walking to their cars. After five minutes of running into the building and then around the whole building and back to my car, Eli came running up to me with Emmy in tow.

"Mom, Emmy was just sitting up on the second floor by herself, laughing. She knew we were looking for her and didn't even come!" Eli's voice was filled with anger. He was almost as upset as I was. Eli was always overly careful. He never hid from me in department stores or let me leave his sight in public places. He was truly scared of being lost. But not Emmy. For Emmy to behave like this was so "irresponsible," Eli muttered.

It wasn't that Emmy wanted to get hurt or lost or even drown; it was that she didn't fully comprehend how painful the consequences could be. Or maybe she did, but something was pulling her toward life-threatening situations. Like the time I felt the ocean literally reached out and grabbed her.

It was our first Christmas in Hawaii, and I wanted the kids to pose near the ocean for our annual Christmas card. The local beach in Ewa Beach was never one we swam in because of the large waves that constantly pummeled the beach, but the white sand and ocean view were magnificent. Youngest to oldest walked along the water's edge, with Emmy the farthest from the water. Out of nowhere, a giant wave came and pulled Emmy underwater, ripping her from Eli's grasp. It was all so sudden and chaotic, but little five-year-old Eli swooped down, found her arm, and pulled her back onto the beach. Once again, she was unfazed and acted like it was no big deal. We just hugged her and immediately left. My fear of Emmy being hurt was at an all-time high.

To solidify that fear, one more occurrence near water would happen right before leaving Hawaii to our next assignment in Virginia. Ko' Olina lagoons was one of our favorite places to spend our days, and we would often take "staycations" there a couple times a year. We discovered early on that one of the lagoons was a sanctuary for rescued sea turtles that had been injured at sea. Emmy instantly fell in love with the *honu*, or sea turtles, and would feed them seaweed right out of her tiny fingers.

We asked our friend Nadia to take the obligatory Hawaiian family photo at the sea turtle lagoon. As our family lined up for pictures, Emmy slipped on the coral and hit her head. Randy and I quickly lifted her up, since we both were still holding her tiny hands. We had no idea how any of it happened. She was standing still one minute, then falling the next. We tried to finish up the pictures, but every photo after that showed a very sad little girl.

Besides the many water incidences, there were other accidents on land that left us stunned.

Thankfully Hawaii is a great destination place, because family was always flying in to visit. We were always driving to and from the airport, picking up one of our many guests. One time in particular, we were there picking up Randy's mom and step-dad. After finding our guests and picking up the luggage, we walked outside to head to the parking lot. As soon as Emmy popped out, she spotted Mimi, on the other side of the road. Faster than a blink of an eye, Emmy darted across four lanes of traffic. We don't know how or why, but all we know is the hand of God was all over Emmy that day. One by one, cars barely missed Emmy as she streaked across the lanes. Looking back, all I can picture is the movie *Final Destination* playing over and over in my head. It was like Emmy was marked for death, and every time she escaped, Satan was right there trying something else to get her. I prayed constantly over her little life, just like any mother would. But prayers for her became more intense the older she got.

3
CHAPTER

―❦―

For there is nothing covered that will not be revealed,
nor hidden that will not be known.

—LUKE 12:2 (NKJV)

It was almost three months since Emmy broke her arm on April 18, and July was proving to be more stressful than we had planned for. Randy was preparing for his first deployment overseas in over fourteen years, yet Emmy continued to get worse day by day. The doctor's appointment just couldn't come quickly enough. As we waited, we went swimming daily and even sent Ella, Eli, and Emmy to visit my cousin Sheri and her family in Maryland for a few days. Randy and I desperately needed some quality time together before he left for six months. We continued to think that whatever was wrong with Emmy would be solved at her next doctor's appointment.

I still can't believe we sent Emmy to Maryland with so many warning signs. Besides the headaches and nausea, the new dyslexia was hard to explain. But I found excuses for its new existence. Dyslexia was common among my mom's side of the family, so I brushed it off that we'd just happened to identify it at the exact same time her headaches and nausea started.

Then came Emmy's weird obsession with her stuffed animals. She would carry on conversations with them, like they were talking back to her. One in particular was her white bunny Daisy. Emmy would tell us that Daisy was telling her to disobey us and would make her do things she really didn't want to do. Ella and Eli were terrified and said the bunny was possessed and that we should throw it away. I didn't think much of it because Emmy was always overly dramatic. Singing, dancing, and making up wild stories were common for Emmy. She was always the center of attention. The strange behavior and talking to her stuffed animals were not exactly new. It was the sudden depression and erratic behavior that had my neighbor Sandra and I worried the most. My mama heart was all knotted up, and I just didn't know what to do, especially since the doctors didn't seem worried.

As we waited for the doctor's appointment, we tried vitamins and homeopathies, which did just as much as altering Emmy's diet. Nothing. The only thing that changed was the amount of time I was now spending on cooking special meals and looking up cures for headaches. I was starting to feel hopeless, and the planned upcoming deployment for my husband was adding more stress than any of us could handle. I tried to push the doctor's appointment up, but all I could do was get on a wait list.

The last deployment Randy had been on was when I was pregnant with our first daughter, Ella, in 2000. It was a typical deployment for us as enlisted communications specialists on the AWACs plane, so I wasn't too worried. Randy would only be gone forty-five days and really wasn't in much danger. He came back just in time for me to go into labor six weeks early. Even with the stress of being first-time parents and going home with a four-pound baby, that was nothing compared to the stress we would soon be feeling with her baby sister.

Somehow, Randy and I never deployed again after Ella was born. We left Tinker AFB, Oklahoma, for teaching positions at Keesler AFB, Mississippi. That was where we gave birth to Eli, just two years before we were slammed by Hurricane Katrina. That event pushed us to do something more with our enlisted careers.

Randy and I worked hard to earn our bachelor's and then master's degrees while we were in Mississippi. Randy used his newly earned master's degree and applied to become a commissioned officer in the Medical Service Corps. He was accepted at the same time I was accepted to fly Special Air Missions out of Andrews AFB, Maryland. The Air Force tried to station us together but was unable to and said they would try within the next two years. He had to go to Minot, and there were no positions there for my specialty as an airborne radio operator. The only choice they gave us was for me to be a single parent for two years at Andrews AFB. At first, we thought we could do it, since he had a year's worth of training anyway, but then they told me we would need to give someone temporary custody of our kids because I would be flying twenty-one days out of every month. That was not an option for me. There was no way I could leave our kids for that many days, let alone let someone else raise our kids for the next two years. I declined annual testing (which automatically allowed me to get an honorable discharge) and left the Air Force after nine years. In hindsight, God was working it all out for a future we never could have imagined.

As we moved to Minot AFB, North Dakota as a family of four, we were soon pregnant with our third child, Emersyn Elizabeth. At this point I knew I wanted to stay home with our kids, which had never been an option while in the military. I loved the new role of staying home and finally getting the quality time we all needed.

Deployments always seemed to pass right over Randy in his new hospital management role. Once, while in Hawaii, they talked of sending him somewhere, but it never happened. That was a huge blessing because I always say that Hawaii, which brought us our fourth child Everett, also brought us peace before the storm.

But the time had finally come that Randy was required to deploy. He spent weeks preparing mentally and physically for his six-month deployment to Southwest Asia. This would be our longest separation yet, and now we were pretty worried that he was leaving while Emmy was having mysterious issues no one could figure out.

The week before Randy was to deploy, out of nowhere, the sweetest thing happened. It was an early Saturday morning, and we were in bed cuddling with Emmy and Everett, who always snuck into bed with us in the middle of the night. As we lay there, Randy suddenly called for Ella and Eli to come join in the family snugglefest. Cuddled together, Randy had us all sing the song "Speak Life" by TobyMac over Emmy. It is one of the sweetest, yet most prophetic memories I have before it all happened.

July 15, just days before Randy was to fly out, I remember how hot the day was and how the kids begged to go swimming. Emmy had woken up feeling really, really awful, and so we spent the morning lying on the couch watching TV. After lunch, Emmy said she thought she felt good enough to go swimming, so we all piled in the Yukon. We stopped at the local gas station for an ICEE, which was a common occurrence. I clearly remember not letting Emmy have the cherry flavor because we were still trying to eliminate things from her diet that could possibly be triggering her headaches, and red dye was the next thing we were eliminating.

When you show up to your favorite pool and it is practically empty on one of the hottest days of the summer, you just know it's going to be a good day. We all jumped in and swam together, and I was even helping Everett learn to swim. I decided to take a break and read a book, but shortly after, I heard Emmy yell out, "Mom, Eli pushed me off the innertube, and I hit my head!"

I jumped into the pool and checked her head for any bumps and made Eli apologize. There were no bumps or bleeding, and Emmy said she was fine, so I swam back to the edge of the pool and lay back on the lawn chair to continue reading my book. As I was grabbing my book, Emmy screamed out that she was going to puke and started swimming frantically to the edge of the pool.

Puking was a common occurrence, but I quickly stood up and watched to see if she would make it to the bathroom. After pulling herself up the ladder, I noticed something strange; Emmy was confused. She looked to the left and then right and just started stumbling toward the bathroom like her legs didn't know how to walk. Running all the way around the pool would have taken way too long, so I dove into the pool and swam as quickly as I could to the other side. I continued following her with my eyes as I climbed out of the pool and ran after her.

The next moments are seared into my mind like a permanent scar. Nothing I have been able to do over the last seven years has kept me from having heart-wrenching attacks every time I think of that bathroom scene. No medication or prayer or sedatives can take away the pain I feel when I envision her standing by the sink, puking on herself, repeating over and over, "I'm OK, I'm OK, I'm OK" but with a slurred voice like she'd just had a stroke. A stroke. *A stroke? Why does she sound like she had a stroke?* That was what I kept repeating to myself over and over, and I washed up her face and scooped her up into my arms and ran her to the lifeguard station.

"Call an ambulance, call an ambulance, *now*!" I screamed as I ran as quickly as I could with my baby girl shaking in my arms. This was the moment I had known was coming, but I just hadn't known what it would look like. I lay her on the lawn chair, and the right side of her face slowly started twitching. The young lifeguards were not as fast as a scared mom, and I already had my phone dialed to 9-1-1 before they even reached the phone in their lifeguard shack.

"Nine-one-one."

"I am at the Smithfield Pool. I think my daughter is having a seizure. She was swimming and bumped her head on the side of the pool, but I don't think it's a concussion. See, she broke her arm three months ago and started having headaches. Oh no, her whole body is starting to twitch. Please, hurry!"

The next moments all seemed to happen so quickly. My other children were crying and asking what was happening. The lifeguards were trying to help as I frantically prayed for God to heal her. And then, within seconds, the ambulance was on the scene. They treated Emmy like a concussion patient, secured her head and neck, loaded her onto a board, and had her in the ambulance in under five minutes. It was like I was witnessing the most trained paramedics in the world. I am pretty sure God had a hand in that because, no matter how many paramedics we would soon meet thereafter, none of them worked as seamlessly as that crew.

What about my other kids? Who was going to watch them? What about my car? And Randy. Oh no, I have to call Randy.

"Do I have time to call my husband?" I asked the paramedics.

"Of course. We have to get her set up before we leave."

I quickly dialed Randy and held back my tears as long as I could.

"Hey, babe. What's up?" answered Randy.

"Randy, I don't know what happened, but Emmy was swimming, and she hit her head, and now she is having a full body seizure, and an ambulance is taking us to Riverside Hospital in Newport News. I have the other kids with me, and I don't know what to do. And my car is here. What do I do?"

"What? Emmy is having a seizure? OK, call Chris or Melissa to get the kids, and I will meet you there. Call me when you get in the ambulance and tell me what happened!"

I hung up with Randy, and Chris answered my call immediately. Chris was a single dad with two kids who lived directly across the street from us. He worked at the navy shipyard and was home earlier than most because they had swing shift hours. After I'd told him what happened, he was at the swimming pool parking lot within minutes gathering up Ella, Eli, Everett and all of our swim gear. He told me he would take care of my car and get the kids fed. Having good neighbors we could count on became one of God's greatest gifts to us.

Seizures—they have got to be one of the scariest things to witness in the entire world. I remember back when I was in junior high and a fellow student born with cerebral palsy had a full-blown seizure during our lunch break. Emmy's seizure was way worse than what I remember that girl having—probably because it was my daughter and not a classmate.

Emmy's started with small twitches in her right cheek, and then the twitches quickly moved to the entire right side of her body. Shortly after the right side was in constant movement, the left side started jolting. Thankfully, the paramedics were able to monitor her oxygen level, as none of the medicines they tried stopped the seizure. Then, due to the constant movement in her body, they tried over and over to put an IV in her very small veins and failed repeatedly.

The next fifteen minutes were a blur. Crying and praying and calling anyone I could think of to pray was all I remember.

4

CHAPTER

Have I not commanded you? Be strong and of good courage; do not be afraid, nor be dismayed, for the Lord your God is with you wherever you go.
—JOSHUA 1:9 (NKJV)

The freezing air blowing in the emergency room, my soaking wet swimming suit and cover-up clinging to my shaking body, the doctors cutting Emmy's favorite swim top off of her, and the constant beeping are all I remember. Randy was there before us, and I could see his eyes were filled with anguish, but neither of us could speak. We just knew. We knew that the broken arm was the cause of all of this. But what was *this*? What was wrong with Emmy?

Anticonvulsants and more sedatives were given, but the seizure was too powerful. The doctor was afraid that one more dose would stop her breathing, so they made a command decision to intubate her. The intubation took us by complete surprise and was very traumatic to see up close. The seizure stopped once they knocked her out, but would it come back?

Seeing our tiny daughter limp on a hospital table, covered in wires and then being forced to breathe through a tube was more than we could take. I was confused and speechless. I was shaking uncontrollably and crying, while Randy was just frozen in place, not taking his eyes off Emmy. No one could tell us what was going on. Once Emmy was stable, they took her to the CT scan. That, of course, showed the knock to her head in the pool hadn't caused a brain bleed or a concussion. The emergency room and hospital were not equipped for a pediatric patient, so they called an ambulance to take us to Children's Hospital of the King's Daughters (CHKD).

God orchestrated so many things for us this day. Randy just happened to be minutes down the road finishing up training when I called him. My friend Melissa was actually driving right by the hospital when I called her. She was able to drive to Smithfield, grab me a bag of clothes, and be back within an hour, along with our pastor Randy. We needed these people. Our families were thousands of miles away. How do we get through times like this without family to help? Our church family, that's how.

The timing of this seizure was probably the most obvious. The slight bonk on the head probably irritated her brain just enough to finally show what was brewing deep inside. If that seizure hadn't occurred on that day, just two days later, Randy would have boarded an aircraft and been stuck halfway around the world. Sometimes, perfect timing, even at the last possible second, is a bigger blessing than we could ever imagine.

The CHKD ambulance was there within an hour, loading Emmy and me back up. They kept Emmy intubated, just in case. It was late in the evening when we arrived at CHKD, but an ICU crew was waiting for us. Most children's hospitals do not like to keep kids intubated if they are breathing on their own, which Emmy was. They knew this because, once the sedative wore off, she would start fighting the tube.

The craziness that ensued once Emmy was extubated was more than Randy or I could bare. As Emmy opened her eyes and realized she was awake, she started repeating her last words, "I'm OK, I'm OK," but in that slurred, stroke-like manner. Then, she started thrashing around the bed and grabbing at all the tubing. She was belligerent and confused. Unable to hold her still from the side of the bed, I instantly jumped into bed with her and held her tightly. I was so afraid they were going to have to put the tube in her throat again. The on-call pediatrician kept watching her and calling her "the Hulk." The strength coming from Emmy was astonishing. Hours of Randy and I wrestling, praying, and crying with her started to take its toll.

The ICU doctor decided something more was going on in her brain, and they explained that she would need to be intubated again. They scheduled her for an early morning MRI, spinal tap, and another CT scan. They just couldn't understand why a healthy child, who was just swimming, would have a grand mal seizure if her CT scan was clear.

Randy and I stared at each other and just sobbed all night long. This had to be a dream, a really bad dream. It just had to be. Nothing seemed logical except the fact that we knew the broken arm had done all of this. But how could a broken arm cause a seizure? Our brains were on overdrive, trying to make sense of it all. The stress overcame us, and our bodies finally gave out. We passed out in reclining chairs next to Emmy, lulled by the synchronous sounds of the ventilator and heart rate monitor.

Rounds start early in an ICU. The number of specialists that come by to discuss the plan of care depends on why you're there in the first place. In every hospital, especially teaching hospitals, there are three levels of doctors, excluding short-coat medical students who randomly show up with other doctors. Residents, who are on the final phase of medical school, do rotations to learn each medical specialty before becoming a family physician or choosing to continue their education to become a specialist. Fellows are those previous residents who have chosen to continue with their education and are now learning a specific field, like neurology or cardiology. When they finally graduate, they become attendings. Those are the doctors you want to talk to, because they are the ones who have been doing their job the longest.

We had barely opened our puffy eyes before we had the resident asking way too many specific questions that we couldn't quite understand. About an hour later, the ICU fellow showed up and asked the same exact questions. When the actual rounds started, the attending asked the very same questions, while listening to the other doctors repeat what I'd told them. Teaching is important, except when it is your child being treated. We would learn this the hard way that too many errors and mistakes happen by students—at the expense of our daughter's well-being.

The team compiled our answers and concluded that Emmy must have had some hidden brain trauma from the pool incident. I quickly stopped them and told them, in detail, everything that had happened since Emmy had broken her arm. The broken arm didn't faze them, but the headaches and nausea quickly made them ask more questions.

"You're telling me that not one doctor ordered an MRI this entire time she has had headaches and nausea?" the ICU attending questioned. "Headaches and nausea at the same time usually mean one thing—a brain tumor. I am not trying to worry you, but we are trained to look for those symptoms in children."

Now my mind was all over the place! A tumor? No way. A broken arm didn't cause cancer, or could it? The team rushed Emmy to the MRI early, and Randy and I spent the first hour and half alone, which we would later deem our "date" time. These random hours of testing would become the only time alone we would get for the next few years. Brokenhearted and confused and questioning everything we had done over the last few months made our minds stuck in a reel of despair. Should we have known to get her an MRI? Who even thinks about getting their healthy child an MRI after a simple fractured wrist? Our minds were playing every event over and over until the primary neurologist snapped us back to reality. Emmy was out of the MRI, and we were patiently awaiting answers.

"Are you sure Emmy was swimming yesterday? I am asking this because there is no way she could have been possibly walking or even swimming; her entire brain is covered in lesions. Come look at her MRI," he said gently.

"*What*? What is a lesion? I have no idea what you are talking about," I cried.

"It's like a bruise, right, doc?" answered Randy.

"That is correct. These things can happen when the immune system begins attacking the brain. So now we are going to do additional tests to understand what is causing this to happen. We are going to do more specialized MRIs, take spinal fluid, hook her up to an EEG, and do more bloodwork to understand what is causing this. I am truly so sorry you have to go through all of this," the doctor said with compassion. As he talked to us, he showed us each splice of brain captured in the MRI picture. Almost every picture showed spots of inflammation.

My daughter's perfect brain was covered in bruises? I think at that moment is when I lost it, right in the middle of the ICU. I began crying uncontrollably, and all I remember is a chaplain appeared out of nowhere and pulled me and Randy into the hallway. He handed me tissues and instantly opened his Bible and asked if we knew of Joshua from the Old Testament.

"Yes," we replied.

"Good. I am going to share a verse with you that was once shared with me when I thought all hope had been lost. When I read something, I want you to repeat it after me, OK?"

Randy and I just stared at him.

"I don't understand what you want us to do," I questioned.

So, he explained he wanted to make us understand what the verse truly meant by having us say it out loud so we could relate it directly to our situation.

"Say your names out loud. Good. Now repeat after me," he said.

This is what everyone in the hallway heard as they walked past us: "Missy (Randy), have I not commissioned you? Be strong and of good courage; do not be afraid, nor be dismayed, for the Lord your God is with you wherever you go" (Joshua 1:9 NKJV).

My loud, guttural crying came to a silent stream of tears. I was no longer gasping for breath; his words calmed both of us down. I was still in shock, and I couldn't wrap my mind around how all of this had started from a broken arm. But now we had more real-world issues to deal with like whether the Air Force was still going to make Randy leave on his deployment. I couldn't do this without him. He was my rock, and I would crumble without him. And how would he survive in another country knowing his daughter was sick and intubated in the ICU? This was all too much for us to worry about.

When people meet the love of their life, I often wonder if they have the same kind of story as we did. Our paths in life were so similar it was almost unbelievable. It was like we were born for each other. Even though Randy is from New Orleans, and I am from Billings, Montana, our lives followed the same historical timeline and circumstances.

When Randy and I first started dating, we realized our childhoods were eerily similar. We were both raised by single mothers and then later had stepdads who we really didn't get along with. Once we were old enough to work, we both worked multiple jobs even working at a pizza restaurant at the same time. College after high school was put on hold for both of us as we tried to figure out what we wanted to do with our futures. Randy eventually took local college classes, while I attended cosmetology school, following in my mom's footsteps. But on a whim and in the middle of both our schoolings, we decided we were going to join the military. The navy was the first choice for both of us, but we each soon realized the open waters was not a place we could spend the next four years. At the very last second, we both enlisted in the Air Force and left for basic training within weeks of each other. Randy left for basic at the end of December in 1994, and I got to Lackland AFB, Texas, in February 1995. God was lining up our paths before we even knew each other.

Halfway through basic training, I realized that, even though my recruiter had laughed when I'd said I wanted to fly on airplanes, the opportunity to do so was offered to me because of my high electronic scores. Randy went to basic with a confirmed job as an airborne electronics specialist, and I became one during basic. Randy was from the south and I was from the north, but we met up right in the center of the United States at Tinker AFB, Oklahoma.

We became instant friends during training and eventually married just a couple years later. We quickly purchased a house and began starting our family. Our life together was pretty much how we planned it to be, besides allowing the Air Force to be our tour guide. Ella was born in Oklahoma, Eli was born in Mississippi, Emmy was born in North Dakota, and Everett was born in beautiful Hawaii. Our plans, our lives, and our dreams were perfect. We enjoyed every moment we had together. But now, here we were in Virginia, horrified and confused, lost in a sea of medical jargon, and wondering if our Emmy would even live through the week.

The Air Force quickly gave the deployment to someone else and put Randy on leave to stay with me and Emmy during the day and our other kids at night. This was the first of many times that the Air Force, specifically the Medical Service Corps, would step up and take care of our family like no other civilian job would have.

5

CHAPTER

*Now faith is the substance of things hoped for,
the evidence of things not seen.*
—HEBREWS 11:1 (NKJV)

Ten days—that was how long it took for the doctors to find the right cocktail of medicine that would stop Emmy's brain from actively seizing. Before that, they wouldn't take her off the ventilator. She was in a medicine-induced coma the entire time, which felt like she was never going to wake up. During those ten days, besides antiseizure meds, her doctors filled her little body with steroids, antivirals, and IVIG (intravenous immunoglobulin). Acute demyelinating encephalomyelitis (ADEM) was the diagnosis they kept throwing around, along with a possibility of herpes of the brain. Herpes was initially diagnosed because the part of the brain that was showing the largest seizure activity was where herpes attacks. Children can get herpes by being kissed by someone with a cold sore. This was all so new to us, but eventually the herpes test came back negative, so that diagnosis was quickly thrown to the side. Vaccination injury was the next new buzz word in the myriad of medical jargon that we had never heard of before.

For three days, we had to confirm over and over to at least five different doctors that Emmy had not been vaccinated in over two years. We learned that the MMR vaccination and the flu vaccine can commonly cause ADEM in patients. When vaccinated, the white blood cells are activated and start an immune response like it should, but sometimes it can cause a cytokine storm. That is where the immune system becomes overloaded and confused and begins attacking the body. Most commonly, it is the brain where those vaccines show the most damage.

The most mysterious thing of all was that Emmy's doctors couldn't definitively give her any of those diagnoses because her bloodwork and spinal fluid showed absolutely *zero* signs of disease or inflammation. No active inflammation of any kind could be detected anywhere in her body. That was unheard of. The spinal fluid should have been filled with white blood cells related directly to the active inflammation occurring in her brain. But according to the tests, she was a perfectly healthy kid, who just happened to have a brain full of inflammation.

Stumped, the doctors thought the tests had failed. So, they took more spinal fluid and bloodwork and sent them off once again. Still, the tests came back negative for any inflammation activity at all. Time was at a standstill.

During those ten days, we just stared at Emmy breathing on the ventilator. I couldn't occupy my time with anything else but staring at Emmy and praying. Randy needed to keep his mind busy to stay positive, so he found things to do. Randy is a gifted artist, so his creativity kicked into full gear. He began spending his days creating paracord bracelets as a symbol to pray for Emmy. He chose colors he thought represented Emmy and gave them away to all of our friends. We needed our healthy girl back. We needed to be a family again.

Later on, he created a symbol to help represent Emmy. While in Hawaii, Emmy had lived in a Super Girl costume for an entire year. She wore it everywhere—to the store, church, and while digging for cockroaches. Yes, she loved all creatures made by God! Eventually, we convinced her the cockroaches were dirty, so she began collecting roly-poly bugs instead. Eventually, that Super Girl dress had so many holes in it I had to buy her another. That was who we needed Emmy to be to get through this horrific series of events—strong. Replacing the *S* on the Superman emblem with an *E* and later printing it onto a shirt became a way Emmy's followers could show her they were praying for and thinking about her.

At this point, none of the other kids had seen Emmy. We'd thought she would only be asleep for a few days. But when it turned into longer, we allowed Ella to visit. Ella was thirteen, and we wanted her to know what was going on firsthand. As Ella spotted Emmy laying helpless on the hospital bed, she just wept. We all cried. Looking back wouldn't have let Ella see Emmy like that. It was a tough lesson on how hard and cruel the real world truly was. It was ironic how we'd spent this entire time shielding our kids from the ugly, hateful world, only to thrust them deep into a world of pain, disease, and sadness.

The time finally came to wake Emmy up. The seizures were lessened, and all the tests her doctors knew to perform were back. Emmy was not infected with some disease that could spread to others. Her brain was not filled with parasites. She didn't have meningitis. She had nothing known yet something damaging, but keeping her asleep was not the cure. This was the scariest moment of all. Would all of that brain inflammation and damage cause her to be someone else? Would she remember us? Would she be able to speak or even understand us? What if she was left completely mentally and physically disabled? The fear of the unknown was unbearable.

Before the medical team woke her, we were warned about how much sedation she had been on and that she would have to be weaned of the medication slowly for about a month with alternative medicines. Ten days is a long time to be given sedatives continuously. Morphine and benzodiazepines given twenty-four hours a day for ten days straight is equivalent to someone going on a drug binge for weeks at a time. If the body is addicted, the wean has to be slow. If the benzodiazepines were weaned too quickly, they could actually cause more seizures. That was not what Emmy needed. Randy and I had no idea how Emmy would react while withdrawing; nor did we know what to expect from the brain damage itself. What we witnessed over the next weeks and months left us shocked and confused.

I had never observed a person act the way Emmy did upon waking. Randy and I just stared in horror at first. She was slapping her head and kicking her legs up and down and laughing uncontrollably. Emmy couldn't speak. Or at least the sounds she made we couldn't understand. It took quite a few days for her to physically calm down before real connections were made. She did realize who Randy and I were instantly, but we needed to know she understood us. Randy asked her if she could give us a shaka sign like we commonly did in Hawaii, and she instinctually did it! That gave us enough hope that her memory was still intact.

A few days later, we realized that her body was affected by the brain inflammation. At first, we thought she was just moving weirdly as a result of having been sedated for so long and withdrawing. Then we noticed her left arm began curling tightly into her chest. A few days later, we also realized her left leg was not the same. It was stuck in a straight, pointed position, which made her ankle hurt all the time. Pain was now hard to assess, as she couldn't talk. It all seemed like a bad dream, but Randy and I were diligent and did our research and started believing we would see a full recovery. Even though blood and spinal tests didn't prove ADEM or any other inflammatory disease, that was the ultimate diagnosis she had been given; and that had a very high recovery rate.

The other thing that was hard for us to deal with was the emotional and mental damage that come along with brain damage. I noticed it the first time we held Emmy.

"Is there any way I can hold her? I know she is covered in wires, but I just need to hold my baby," I asked the nurse.

"Sure, let me get everything organized, and you and Dad can both hold her!" She said excitedly.

"Randy, what is Emmy doing?" I said with confusion on my face as I held Emmy.

As I was holding Emmy, she began behaving like an infant. She was drawn to my chest and acted like she was trying to nurse. This was the first time I remember being overcome with embarrassment.

"Emmy, stop, baby. It's Mommy. You're six years old, honey. And you don't do this anymore," I whispered over and over as I pulled her closer and tighter.

Not one article or book ever spoke of the weird behaviors that Emmy would go through. It took about a week, but we slowly witnessed her "grow up" mentally from infancy back to a six-year-old. The other thing we noticed was she was constantly touching her face. The touches resembled nervous ticks, like a drug addict would do. She hated her hair touching her face, and the hospital gown made her want to crawl out of her skin. I now had a full-time job of making her feel comfortable.

Emmy was transferred to a step-down recovery room about twenty-one days after being admitted into the ICU. The nursing staff was wonderful. They understood that, because of the amount of brain damage, it was more helpful to allow Emmy to sleep and only do cognitive/brain tests while she was awake. The room was newly renovated with a couch that slid open to a bed and also large enough for the entire family to visit. The ICU room was obviously nothing like this room. Not many of the ICU rooms were actually "rooms." The majority were spaces separated by a curtain, which was how we spent the first week. We were moved to a more secluded room for the rest of the ICU stay, but no ICU is pleasant. It was nice to think she was well enough to be moved out of the ICU and onto a regular floor.

At this point, I reflected on how relieved I was that we'd taught Emmy basic sign language when she was a baby. When Eli was born, he was an active little kid, walking at just eight months old, but he didn't speak a word until he was four years old. Those four years were very difficult for us to understand him, but siblings have an uncanny superpower and can read minds and understand baby-talk. Ella was Eli's interpreter. She would relay every grunt and cry to us in actual words. It was so frustrating he couldn't talk but also a blessing that it made us want to teach Emmy sign language.

Within a few days of waking, Emmy was signing that she needed a drink or was hungry. She would point to the pain scale and then her body parts. She understood what was going on and found ways to make us understand her through sign or pointing at objects. But after a month of this, I started becoming quite panicky that this would become our new norm. I never thought I would have to learn the entire sign language dictionary to speak to a child who had been talking with a very large vocabulary just a month ago.

Early one morning, after about five days in the new hospital room, I was woken up by a knock on the door. I'd started to sit up to say, "Come in," when Emmy beat me to it.

"Come in," Emmy whispered as she looked at the door.

It seemed so instinctual that I started clapping and laughing, and the nurse quickly joined in my celebrations. Emmy had not lost her speaking skills at all. It was there, but now we had to figure out how to teach her muscles to push the words out.

The ability to communicate through spoken word is something taken for granted until it is gone. My heart aches for those parents who have children who can't speak or have the ability to learn or use sign language. But I do know that children will find a way to let you know what they need. Emmy showed us that over the next few years as her speech would come and go. She taught us that the eyes are truly the window to the soul.

Once Emmy began to speak, we could barely understand her. It was like the words were there, but her mouth couldn't get them out. We desperately needed help. The rate of healing greatly depended on how quickly physical, occupational, and speech therapy were started and old abilities were revisited and practiced. The neurology team felt like it was time to move to the therapy floor and get her moving and talking again. Neurological connections were obviously damaged in her brain, but the neurologist kept reminding us that children's brains are "elastic" and can rewire and heal faster than those of adults. We truly hung onto that fact, even when we weren't seeing the healing we were hoping for.

During the month of August, Emmy fought daily to relearn basic skills. Her left hand would not open, and her left foot started turning in because of the intense pointing. The therapists worked on her muscle coordination and strength with the use of a walker, swings, and balance balls. Her body was weak, and the new seizure meds made her sleepy, but she worked harder than ever. Emmy managed to put a puzzle together with one hand, even though it took her over half an hour. Randy and I just knew she would be back to her old self, dancing and singing and doing headstands. She just had to. What would we do if she was left this way and we were now the parents of a physically handicapped child?

Prednisone and seizure medicines were new to us. What lasting harmful effects did they have on her brain? What were common side effects that we should look out for? No one really gave us those answers. I think neurologists see so many patients they forget everything is new to first-time patients.

Sleeping also became an issue, along with horrible pain from her tightly clenched left hand. Melatonin was added nightly, along with a benzodiazepine called Klonopin to aid her in relaxing and falling asleep. The Klonopin was great at relaxing her, but during the day, Emmy constantly complained of her ankle and wrist pain. Physical therapy created a makeshift orthotics ankle brace while she was in-patient, but said a permanent one would be made after we were discharged. We were also told of the benefits of Botox therapy. Botox, while used mostly for wrinkles, is a safe therapy for people with spastic or tight muscles. As soon as Emmy heard that this could help her with her pain, she begged for it. About four days before she was discharged, she had Botox injections in her left arm and left leg.

During this time, something changed in me. Maybe it was there all along, but it finally reared its ugly head and became obvious. Anger was my emotional response to the depression I was feeling. Each day that she didn't become noticeably better, my anger grew. My sympathy for Emmy started to wane, and I was short with her at every turn. I was just so angry she wouldn't stop moving or sleep longer than forty-five minutes at a time. Our life was not supposed to end up this way. Anger continued to intensify as I thought about the life Emmy was losing, the life that we were just enjoying and how much I missed Ella, Eli and Everett.

Anger never left my side. I faked the smiles as Emmy learned a basic skill. Nothing made me happy at this point. Physically, I was fatigued, and I had not slept since July 15. If Emmy didn't sleep, I didn't sleep, which made me angrier. Then during the day, I still couldn't sleep because I had become her "voice" and interpreter. I could read her mind and know what she needed by just looking at her eyes. It was the biggest blessing to know I could give her what she needed and when she needed it, but it was also a very heavy burden to carry. I was her everything. It hit me like a truck that I would have to be with Emmy twenty-four hours a day until she recovered.

"Homesick" was a word everyone could understand when Emmy said it. Since July 15, Emmy had been away from home for thirty-six days and could care less about therapy. She showed how much she wanted to leave by refusing to participate in any activity. Crying became the norm, which made me even madder. The nurses decided to call the staff members from Child Life, who were trained to help improve the emotional and physical well-being of hospitalized kids. They instantly realized Emmy needed to focus on making small goals that resulted in rewards and created a chart so she could see what she had accomplished. Emmy begged to be home by her birthday, so August 28 was set as the goal date. Emmy finally started working with the therapists again. Prizes and gifts were Emmy's only motivators, so they were always dangled in front of her to keep her on track. The chart was placed on the wall, and Emmy felt a sense of pride every time we marked off one of her accomplishments and gave her a prize.

Days before Emmy was discharged, we were given the opportunity to take her out for the day and see how we could handle having a child in a wheelchair. The stress of it all was overwhelming, but Randy, his mom and our kids all went out for a "fun" day. Friends from Hawaii were visiting Virginia and met us at Build-a-Bear. This was the first time I saw Emmy become very self-conscious over her new physical situation. She still had small "ticks," like touching her nose all the time, and her body was pretty wiggly. Her left leg stuck straight out in front of her, but she quickly learned that if she folded in half and laid her head in her lap, all of her muscles would relax. All of these things made her feel different. She *was* different, and there was no other way around it. Everyone's heart hurt. Our lives were changed, and it was a hard thing to accept.

We ended the day at a busy restaurant and soon realized it was a terrible idea. From needing to hold her up to eat to carrying her to the bathroom, our lives were going to have to adapt, or we were never going to leave our house again.

Three days later on August 27, 2014, Emmy was discharged. Emmy became stubborn and mean after spending the day with her family and she didn't want to be in the hospital one more day.

"Please take me home. I hate it here. I can practice walking at home. *Please!*" Emmy cried over and over all day long. Her mind was made up, so we decided to get discharged a day early.

We did not own a wheelchair, so a loaner chair was given to us. Everyone thought Emmy would regain her ability to walk very quickly, so there was no talk of getting our own. We loaded her up in a booster chair and packed the wheelchair, bags of books, and toys and headed home. Emmy was given a hot pink iPod from Child Life for her birthday, so she was just about as excited as any kid could be.

The whole neighborhood was waiting with signs and balloons welcoming the once vibrant and energetic Emmy back home. I could see the shock on everyone's faces as Randy carried Emmy from the car into the house. Emmy was stiff, laughing uncontrollably, and definitely not the same girl who'd left to go swimming on July 15. As her excitement increased, so did the number of slaps she kept giving Randy on his face and head. The look on her friends' faces made me ache with pity. They saw a different child. They looked at her strangely. Would they accept her as she now was? Would the kids still play with her? Would she ever be a normal kid again? The fear of the unknown was breaking my heart.

From the day we arrived home, Randy and I realized that Emmy was not progressing like she should have been. We really didn't know what to look for, but she obviously wasn't getting better, only worse and very sleepy. We kept using runaround logic like before, trying to make our minds stop worrying. *Was it the medicine making her tired? Maybe the brain gets tired as it heals?* But the signs were obvious.

We needed to make her one-week follow-up appointment, but it wasn't with the doctors from CHKD. Active duty military dependents have two options for medical care. One is to go to a military clinic as long as they provide the specialty that is needed. The other is to choose your own primary care doctor within network and pay deductibles and co-pays. We had never needed to think about the second option because none of our family had ever been sick or needed specialty care. Plus, Randy worked in the military clinic, and it just made life easier going where he worked. For Emmy, Langley AFB didn't have a neurologist, but Portsmouth Naval hospital did, so they made her go there. The neurologist was one of only three in the entire military in the United States, so it seemed like a blessing. Or so we thought. We were sad the doctors who'd cared for Emmy the last two months would no longer see her, but we were ready to start a new chapter of healing.

We should have known right away that having a military neurologist was going to be difficult when we couldn't even get a follow-up appointment scheduled. The first available was over two weeks away. During the month of September, as we waited for the appointment, numerous new conditions started appearing. The first noticeable issue was that Emmy started losing strength in her right arm. Upon leaving in-patient therapy, we'd seen nothing wrong with the right side of her body, but now she was dropping objects and refused to use her right hand. We continued plausible deniability and took her to *Frozen on Ice* with our neighbors. I tried to pretend she was fine, but as her body flailed all over as she squealed in delight, I knew she wasn't OK. Not even close.

The first neurology appointment was a waste of time. The doctor was brand new and just out of his fellowship. He had never seen this kind of case or a child who had such extensive brain damage with no real diagnosis. We told him how her right arm was losing ability and wanted to know if it meant her brain was healing or she was still sick. *Was getting worse before getting better even a real thing?* His answers were vague, but he did schedule Emmy an MRI for October 3, three more weeks away. During the weeks ahead, we sat day after day watching Emmy deteriorate. She became lethargic, stopped talking, and her right eye began winking and then suddenly became crossed. Frantic, I called the military neurologist, but his first thought was for her to see an ophthalmologist.

Our appointment was made for the next day, and Emmy was tested by one of the best eye doctors in Southern Virginia. After a battery of tests, he concluded that her optic nerves were just fine and had no inflammation. He did sound worried that it may be something else going on deeper in her brain causing her eyes to cross. This news crushed us. Her brain was still sick, and no one knew what it was.

The MRI was done a week later at the beginning of October and proved once again to be a waste of time. No new findings showed up on the MRI, partly because it was a less powerful machine than had been used in all of Emmy's previous MRIs. The military neurologist urged us to also do an EEG that month, just to cover all the bases. On Halloween, the military neurologist called with good news. Parts of her brain had actually improved. What a relief. So maybe the lethargy was just from her brain taking so much energy to heal. We celebrated by dressing up Emmy as a kitty cat and hauling her house to house in a red wagon. Candy always made Emmy happy.

But as the days went on, Emmy became so lethargic she looked like she was in a wide-awake coma. I looked up medical research on brain damage and convinced myself that it really was just a side effect of her brain healing. Just like a domino effect, her body started failing piece by piece. At first, her crossed eyes seemed to become glossy, followed by a horrible series of nausea bouts and headaches. Then, she began choking when she drank.

We instantly brought Emmy into the neurologist's office, and he behaved like nothing was wrong with her. We were so incensed that he didn't fully understand how much worse she was, even after just seeing her weeks ago.

"When regression occurs, the most common treatments are plasmapheresis, chemotherapy, and/or steroids. Do you know which one you want to try?" he asked us, like we knew what she needed.

"You need to call Dr. Toor at CHKD. Something is not right with her, and he will know which one to do," I pleaded with him.

He promised to bring Emmy's case up the next day at "Grand Rounds," where all the unsolved cases were talked about with the local neurologists from the area. After he talked with them, he said he would call us with what was recommended.

His call was later the next day, and he told us the recommendation was to try three days of high-dose steroids. We were told to come in on Monday, and it would be booked as an outpatient appointment, so we wouldn't have to spend the night.

During this time, my attitude was still deteriorating. I thought being home would make me feel better, but it only made it worse. I was still the primary caretaker for Emmy, since Randy had to work. Emmy never slept. She always cried. I was always angry. Something had to give. I went from living a normal, carefree life to staring at a child who I believed was still sick and possibly dying. The lack of sleep and the constant fear made my brain useless and unable to control the anger welling up inside me.

That weekend, a friend we had lived next to during our assignment in Hawaii stopped to visit us on her way to northern Virginia. When Jenn showed up and saw Emmy, she just sat in complete silence. What she saw was a little girl, barely strong enough to roll over, with crossed eyes that seemed to silently scream for someone to just help her. As I sat, talked, and prayed with Jenn, I realized that this was not good enough. This inexperienced doctor was not good enough. Emmy deserved more, and we were going to take her back to the lead neurologist at CHKD.

I called Dr. Toor at CHKD and told him of our intentions of changing Emmy's insurance. He said to follow through with the already scheduled steroid therapy and then come in to see him the day after. I already felt better knowing he was going to be part of Emmy's care team again.

Steroids are a miracle drug for inflammation. Emmy was so strong during the placement of the IV and seemed to perk up immediately after the first dose; her eyes even went back to normal. She was finally seeing straight! The only problem was the nurse decided to leave the IV in Emmy's arm to save her from being poked each day. During the night, the needle dislodged while she was sleeping. Emmy was not able to talk anymore since coming home, so she couldn't tell me what was wrong. She was already crying every single night, so I didn't even think to unwrap her IV tape and look at it. That night we didn't get even an hour of sleep.

When we returned the next morning, the nurse found the IV pulled out after she unwrapped the tape. It had wiggled all night long, poking her over and over. I can't believe how many little things like that would go wrong over the course of the next four years.

The last two doses of steroids were given over the next two days. It worked like magic. Emmy instantly gained back energy. We also noticed that the constant dilation of her pupils was gone. Her eyes had looked so strange since she became sick on July 15, kind of like an animal looking for something in the dark. I couldn't wait to see what advice Dr. Toor would have the next day.

6
CHAPTER

Blessed are those who mourn, for they will be comforted.
—MATTHEW 5:4 (NIV)

Being able to choose a specific doctor is an option every person should have. I am so thankful we realized early on that just making one simple change to our insurance could get us the care Emmy needed. There are so many doctors to choose from, but only a few have what it takes to be great. It isn't their race, sex, or even the college they attended that makes them different from one another. There is one thing that separates regular doctors from great doctors—compassion. Compassion moves unsurmountable mountains. Compassion creates appointments in an already full schedule for little girls who are fighting for their lives. Compassion keeps a doctor for hours past his regular work schedule to make sure everything possible is being done. That is who Dr. Toor was at CHKD.

As soon as Randy changed Emmy's insurance, Dr. Toor fit Emmy right into his schedule. The minute I wheeled her into his office, you could see the confusion on his face. Just two months earlier, Emmy had been able to sit upright, use a walker, and even pronounce her words. As I sat her on the table, she was now falling back, unable to talk loudly, and still pretty lethargic. He performed the normal neurological tests on her, took extensive notes, and finished by scheduling her another MRI for the next day. He was bound and determined to figure out what was still going on in her brain.

Randy and I took Emmy to the MRI appointment and had our "date break." Her MRIs always took longer than usual because she had to be sedated. There was still no way Emmy could sit still for an hour and a half. That time gave me and Randy plenty of time to walk downstairs, eat breakfast, stare silently into one another's sad eyes, and then silently march back to the waiting room. As soon as it was over, we drove Emmy home, and I couldn't shake the feeling that something bad was headed our way.

Emmy fell asleep that night, but her body seemed extra wiggly. Her wiggles always began in her right arm and would flail and dance around like a marionette puppet. With her right arm dancing, she would try hard to make it stop, which made the rest of her body move. It would frustrate me so badly that I would crawl in bed with her and hold her body tightly. This was a nightly routine, and I dreaded bedtime with her, which used to be my favorite time of the day. Cuddled next to my kids, reading a book and sharing stories was now a distant memory.

I just didn't understand how she could be looking better one day, especially after steroids, and then be so weak and shaky the next. Emmy slept OK that night and even woke up hungry, but in the blink of an eye, she spiraled out of control.

The wild eyes and puking began just an hour after she was awake. Then came the migraines. Once again, in between the bouts of nausea and headaches, she would pass out. The disease was back. I just knew it. But I had been briefed by the nurse on the effects of sedation, so maybe that is all this was. I rushed to get the "What to expect after your MRI" paperwork, and it said nausea could be normal, but if it lasted more than four hours after the MRI to call the phone number listed. I quickly dialed the phone number.

"Hello, CHKD," the nurse answered.

"Hi, my daughter Emersyn Bosch was just seen for a sedated MRI yesterday, and today she has been puking nonstop and having massive headaches. Is this normal the day after sedation?" I calmly explained to the nurse.

"OK, honey. Let me just look at her chart. Hold on." After a pause, she was back. "OK, she should not be having any side effects from the sedation, so let me send a message to her neurologist, and he will call you back."

Why is this still happening? I said to myself over and over.

November used to be my favorite month. It's the month of my birthday, of perfect weather, of trees showing how artistic God is and a reminder that seasons always change. We were finally on the East Coast where the trees turned every color of the rainbow, but now none of that mattered. It would be the first time I realized that, no matter what treatment options we chose, no matter the positive benefits of each one, this disease was always going to fight back.

Emmy's neurologist called within the hour with the bad news.

"Hello," I said calmly.

"Missy, this is Dr. Toor. I hate to tell you this, but we found another lesion on Emmy's brain," he began to say.

"But why didn't the images show this just three weeks ago when she had an MRI done at Portsmouth?" I quickly asked him.

"That MRI is a 1.5T, and the one we use is a 3.0T, which means ours is twice as strong as that one. It picks up greater detail. I want you to take Emmy directly to the ER. I already called them and told them you would be coming in. They are going to perform a spinal tap and get bloodwork to send away to be tested," he carefully explained to me.

"OK, should I leave right now? I have to get Randy home to watch the kids—" I started to say.

"Get everything situated and then come as quickly as possible. Emmy really needs to be given medicine to stop whatever is happening," he said urgently.

Just as he explained, the moment we walked into the doors, we were rushed back into a procedure room, and all the tests were accomplished. We waited for about an hour, and Emmy was once again admitted into CHKD.

What a blessing it was to have a hospital with a group of neurologists to help one another. I was definitely thankful we made the decision to change Emmy's insurance and get her back to CHKD. The team of neurologists had a round table meeting and decided what to do for Emmy. Dr. Toor brought us the news.

"Missy, all of us have discussed Emmy's MRI pictures and with the lack of disease evidence, we think we should use everything in our arsenal to hit this head on. First, we think we should do plasmapheresis. This will be done five times, every other day, over the course of ten days. Next, we will stunt what immune system is left with the chemotherapy Cytoxan. Finally, we will give her a dose of IVIG before heading home," Dr. Toor laid out simply.

"We looked up plasmapheresis when the other doctor mentioned it, and we aren't too sure about it. Is it safe?" Randy asked.

"Yes, it's performed all the time. She will lose no blood, only her plasma, which holds the majority of white blood cells. Emmy will have to go to surgery to get a port put in her chest, but even that is very quick and safe," he said confidently.

We really were out of options, and our daughter was dying before our eyes, so we agreed to the plan.

Surgery was quick and without issues, so plasmapheresis was started the next day. The premise behind plasmapheresis is that blood is pumped directly from Emmy's heart into a machine. The plasma, which contains a large portion of white blood cells, is removed, and the red blood cells are returned to the body after mixing with an anticoagulant agent. Red Cross handles this procedure because it deals with blood products, so a new nurse from Red Cross showed up and began prepping the machine. She explained how the process would take two to five hours, depending on how Emmy reacted to her blood flowing in and out of her body and how she would be prepped with Benadryl and Tylenol to prevent an allergic reaction to the blood products. She assured us this procedure was done all the time, and those side effects rarely happened. Emmy had nothing to worry about—or so she thought.

Emmy was prepped with Tylenol and Benadryl and the machine was turned on. We covered the large blood-filled tubes attached to her chest with blankets and did our best to keep Emmy occupied. And then, she fainted. It was so alarming to watch, but the nurse quickly stopped the machine, gave her a large bolus of IV fluid, and allowed her to wake up. After Emmy's blood pressure was back to normal, they restarted the machine at a slower rate. I was pretty scared that Emmy had to do this procedure four more times, but the nurse seemed confident it probably wouldn't happen again.

Emmy became very uncomfortable with everything happening to her. What seven-year-old would be OK with any of what she had been through? She had an IV sticking out of her hand and then two large tubes hanging out of her chest, which were filled with bright red blood during plasmapheresis. She still couldn't talk very well, but we managed to understand some of her words, and she had mastered eye gaze. Eye gazing works by the person looking at you, at the object needed, and then back to you. I am not sure at what point I mentally could read Emmy's thoughts, but God gave me the gift early on when we first moved out of the ICU. Not only could I understand her quiet mumbling sounds, but I could now figure out what she needed without her saying a word.

Emmy never became mean or resentful and was still the sweetest little girl. She would never throw a fit or fight back when she needed an extra IV or had to participate in the neuro checks. When we would say prayers at night, she always prayed for the children in the hospital or her daddy, who had a headache. If ever there was an angel on earth, it was Emmy.

The second plasmapheresis happened just like the first. She was prepped with the meds; the machine was started; then, within minutes, Emmy fainted. I can't believe this nurse seriously said it was no big deal. Watching mass amounts of blood pumping out of your sick daughter's heart was a huge deal, not to mention watching her faint. This was what nightmares are made of.

Two days later, we dreaded the third procedure. Oh, how I prayed Emmy would be safe, and she wouldn't faint again. Randy and I were nervous wrecks. She was prepped with meds as before, and the machine started up. Within two minutes this time, Emmy fainted. But when she woke up twenty minutes later, something was horribly wrong. Her big blue eyes looked up at me, and my heart stopped.

"Get the doctor, now!" I screamed to the nurse.

Everyone was just staring at Emmy's eyes and afraid to move. After completing a neuro exam, the neurologist on service calmly said, "Well, she seems fine."

"She seems fine? What part of one eye dilated while the other one is small seems fine? Her eyes don't even match," I snapped back.

"She had a large dose of steroids just a week ago, her eyes are reactive, and we just did an MRI, so we will just continue to monitor her. We have done and are doing everything we can for brain inflammation. We will finish the plasmapheresis and pray it stops the inflammation," he calmly said as his eyes showed all I needed to know. None of this was right. All of this was new territory, even for a veteran neurologist like himself.

Then an angel of God showed up on the fourth session of plasmapheresis. The first three times we had the same nurse, but for some reason the Red Cross sent someone new. As he was prepping the machine, he stopped dead in his tracks.

"How tall is Emmy? Is she really five foot eight inches tall?"

"*No!* She is under four feet tall. Why?" I said in shock.

"Well, whoever calculated the initial measurements said she was well over five feet tall, which meant she had enough blood in her body to prime the machine and didn't need us to add extra blood. But because she's under four feet tall, we should be prepping the machine with a whole bag of blood before connecting her. The machine has literally been draining Emmy of blood. That is why she kept passing out!"

I have never seen a nurse so mad. He was furious that professionals would make this kind of mistake, especially nurses who did this day in and day out. Sadly, more and more medical mistakes would happen over the next four years. The nurse left, quickly returned with a bag of blood, and primed the machine before hooking up Emmy to the tubes. For the first time, Emmy didn't pass out. She watched movies and played, which is what children should do. Why the first nurse didn't catch this critical error was beyond me.

By now, our whole family just wanted back some normalcy. This brain disease was affecting everyone. Everett was just four years old and still needed his mommy. He proved to be the most resilient and optimistic of our kids. He didn't see anything Emmy suffered as permanent and was always asking when Emmy would walk again.

Eli was only ten, but I felt like he didn't want to be a burden, so he kept any issues he had hidden. Eli was so caring toward Emmy and always looked at her with great pity in his eyes. They were very close siblings, and Emmy was always there to play when he got bored.

Ella was a brand-new teenager and was thrown into the new role of mommy and caretaker while I was gone. She coordinated with the food train started by our church and helped whichever grandparent was staying with the kids to make sure everything was taken care of. Ella also became a surrogate mommy to her baby brother, Everett. She comforted him when I couldn't. She would read to him, put him to bed, and cuddle him before bed. Besides all that she was doing to help us out around the house, Ella's body was fighting a silent disease that many girls and women have. But who could look for signs or ask questions when her mom was in the hospital, and she really had no one to talk to? All of this would be discovered later on when we were least expecting it.

Emmy was at her breaking point and wanted to go home. She still had one more round of plasmapheresis and possibly days of treatment after. We decided to try and create a little normalcy for all of us, so Randy brought in her siblings up to her room one night. For as long as we had been a family, we'd always celebrated Friday nights with pizza and a movie. We ate pizza and put a movie on. The kids sat with Emmy on her bed and we pretended it was all back to normal; even amid the hospital decor and beeping sounds of machines. Life would never be easy again, but we had to hold on to what we had at this very moment. Hospitals had become our second home, and medical jargon had become our second language.

Once Randy and the kids left, Emmy said she felt nauseous. At first, I thought the pizza had upset her stomach. But after she puked, I knew it was her brain. The dilated pupil and now puking? This unknown brain disease was winning, and Emmy was losing. The puking became so convulsive and nonstop that I begged the nurse to call the on-call neurologist. I knew that the only thing that would stop the inflammation was a large dose of steroids. I had seen it work the month before when her eyes uncrossed, and I knew it would work again.

After I begged and pleaded, the on-call neurologist actually came back to the hospital that night to check out Emmy before giving her the steroids. He listened to me explain how effective they had been the month before and how it was our only chance. Within an hour of starting the steroids, Emmy calmed down, stopped puking, and fell asleep. Steroids usually make kids agitated and sleepless, but this was not the case with Emmy. Steroids were what her brain needed, and she would be on them for years to come.

Veterans Day is day Americans remember the veterans who were lost in battle, killed or prisoners of war. But Veterans Day lost its meaning to us in 2014. It became a day that we will never forget.

The fifth and final round of plasmapheresis was started and going perfectly. Emmy was alert and seemed to recover with the help of the steroids the night before. After about twenty minutes she became sleepy, most likely from the Benadryl—or so we thought. She told us she wanted to take a nap, which was definitely different from the times before when she would just pass out. Her nap lasted about thirty minutes.

I remember the faint smell of antiseptics, the sound of beeping, and the whirling whoosh of the plasmapheresis machine as Emmy woke from her nap. Randy and I were standing at the foot of her bed watching her, like usual. As she opened her eyes and looked at us, terror ripped through our hearts, once again. Randy and I looked at each other, eyes instantly filling with tears, and I calmly walked out of the room to grab the nurse. What we saw when Emmy woke up was an overexaggerated smile like the joker, but only on the left side of her face. The right side of her face wasn't moving at all; it was paralyzed. This was what a person looked like after a stroke. Another stroke?

Randy and I were devastated. This proved that the night before was a sign she did have more inflammation growing in her brain. The neurologist sent her directly to get another MRI. The results and words barely made sense. Basal ganglia. Possible stroke. Blood product. Permanent damage. How had she had a stroke when the doctors had already told us this was an autoimmune disease? Satan seemed to be winning this fight. He'd successfully stolen her physical abilities and now was trying to steal her smile.

Randy stayed with me as long as he could that night. We were numb to the fact that Emmy could eventually die from this unknown brain disease. It felt like the wave of despair just kept pummeling us, at the expense of Emmy's life. Our other children had been at Melissa's house all day and it was getting late, so Randy finally left to pick them up. When they arrived home, everyone was unpacking when Everett snuck upstairs to his room. One minute later, Randy heard Everett saying, "Look, Daddy, Bellows is letting me carry him."

Bellows was our cat Emmy adopted in Hawaii. Hawaii was littered with stray cats, and many people would rescue them and adopt them out to families. We just happened to be at one of Ella's volleyball games when a family brought in a six-week old, orphaned baby kitty to search for a family to adopt him. Emmy saw that tiny, baby kitty and was instantly attached. She was only three years old, but her ability to convince us to adopt that kitty was astonishing. We were suckers for her adorable smile and a fuzzy baby kitty, so we caved. We named him Bellows after our favorite Hawaiian beach. It was our sanctuary. It was partly owned by the military, so we could go to areas that weren't overpopulated with visitors. Six weeks later, we quickly adopted another cat. He was about six months old and still a little feral, but we felt like animals did better in pairs. Randy named him Rex, "King of Mardi Gras."

As Everett walked down the stairs with Bellows in his arms, Randy instantly saw that Bellows was limp.

"Everett, go put him back down. I think Bellows is sick," Randy yelled.

Everett quickly laid him back down, and Ella, Eli and Randy ran up the stairs to look at Bellows. He was dead. Somehow during the day, Emmy's cat had suddenly died. When Emmy's brain was "stroking" out, her cat was dying. Instead of Emmy losing her life, Bellows lost his.

I didn't understand the rules of life and death. Were there a certain number of lives marked for death each day? Could it be a life for a life? Against everything I knew to be real as a Christian, I still believed that Bellows went to heaven for Emmy that day. I know it sounds unbelievable, like it came out of a fantasy story, but I can't explain it any other way. Nothing from that day makes sense. The ongoing damage to our little girl's brain didn't make sense. And where was God during all of this?

That night Randy, Ella, Eli, and Everett cried over the death of Emmy's cat. Randy and I secretly cried over the hemorrhage in Emmy's brain that stole her smile. We hadn't told the kids about Emmy, and we didn't let Emmy know, either. It was almost too much for any of us to bear. We were being pummeled over and over; the waves were relentless. We were all drowning with no life preserver in sight. Where was our God of mercy? Why wasn't He helping us?

Our wonderful neighbor, Al, took sweet Bellows and buried him in the forest by our house. We decided to not tell Emmy about Bellows until she got home. How would we tell a little girl who was losing more and more of herself as the days went on that her favorite cat had died?

For the remaining days left in the hospital, the team of doctors loaded Emmy up on Cytoxan and IVIG to keep her immune system from attacking any more brain tissue. They also put Emmy on a high dose of steroids, which would be taken daily for months to come. We decided against moving back onto the physical therapy floor. Home was where we wanted to be. The trauma was too much, and we just wanted to be together as a family, especially for Thanksgiving.

The day before Emmy was discharged, her primary neurologist, Dr. Toor, came by to check on her before he headed to his office. Emmy was still sleeping, so we quietly chatted about what we should be looking for at home and when to call when things just didn't seem right. Our voices caused Emmy to wake up, so I quickly told her Dr. Toor was there to see her.

As Emmy rolled over and saw Dr. Toor standing there, her eyes grew bright, and she grinned from ear to ear. Both sides of her face were working again! Dr. Toor was so excited to see the right side of her face moving that he quickly began doing a neurological check on her. He bent down and gave her a huge kiss on the forehead, which caused her to smile once more. Emmy was asked to give a smile again, and it was obvious her nonspontaneous muscle reactions were not working correctly. Her fake smile was very weak on the right side and you could see it in the way her lips moved. But when we made Emmy laugh, a real genuine smile formed, and her lips were even and strong. I called Randy and told him the good news. I felt like things were finally looking up.

7
CHAPTER

Hear my cry, O God; attend to my prayer. From the end of the earth I will cry to You, when my heart is overwhelmed; lead me to the rock that is higher than I.
—PSALM 61:1-2 (NKJV)

Researching medical documents is a difficult task for most people with a medical degree, let alone for those without a medical degree. Randy had taken a few medical classes in college which was probably why he joined the medical service corps. He seemed to understand medical jargon and had an easier time filtering through all of the medical research we were constantly reading. I, on the other hand, had to teach myself everything. Cross-referencing articles, looking up Latin words, cross-referencing articles again, and memorizing parts of the brain and body had become our full-time jobs.

We both understood that, even though Emmy was on steroids and the doctors kept reassuring us this would go away, she was not getting better. Emmy would have periods of incontinence, and then a week later, she would be fine. She would wake up one day and be unable to push her words out, and then the next day gain full use of her voice. All that we read in journals told us that, as the brain began to heal, her body should respond as well. Sadly, that was not reality.

What had once been a loud, boisterous home had now become a dark coffin of silence. Because of the constant headaches, the curtains were always drawn, and we all talked in whispers. Emmy had not slept soundly since July 15, waking every thirty to forty-five minutes. Crying excessively through the night became the norm, as well as through the day. No one could make a sound without Emmy crying. Keeping Emmy comfortable was our only goal.

The two older kids still homeschooled, but it wasn't the same. I was not mentally able to teach them, with all of my attention fixed on Emmy. Thankfully, Ella's homeschool tutor helped her with homework, and my cousin Sheri taught Eli through Zoom classes. Everett, our sweet little Everett, only four years old, was left to fend for himself. His natural personality was pure joy, and he would play, laugh, and sing all day long. Yet all day long, I would shout for him to be quiet, to sit down, and to go to his room. While being a good parent to Emmy, I was failing at parenting my other kids. This disease was proving to be more than unfair; it was hateful. Everyone was being tortured by it.

Randy continued his research on how a broken arm could trigger brain inflammation, and I began researching natural methods to help heal the brain. Back in November, while Emmy was still in the hospital, we had multiple family and friends doing research on their own. My friend Melissa sent me an article discussing how high levels of omegas had brought traumatic brain injury patients out of comas. That article helped guide me toward using vitamins, minerals, foods, plants, and even oxygen to naturally aid Emmy's body's ability to heal itself. I started Emmy on omega-3s within the month. Nothing else was working, so when I asked her doctor if it was OK, he said, "Why not?"

I spent way too much time trying to figure this out on my own. I should have been spending that time asking God what course of action He wanted me to take. I should have been waiting and praying for answers from God. I was so focused on finding answers that it became a full-time job. This was my first mistake. We were pouring money and energy into anything and everything we could think of to help Emmy, but none of them solved the problem. Thankfully, God is patient. He eventually got through to me—but when it was almost too late.

Christmas was very quiet that year and suddenly it was 2015. Emmy had not walked in six months, and she expressed daily how much she wanted to play outside with her friends again. My heart ached constantly for all that had been lost. But instead of losing hope, I signed Emmy up for speech, occupational, and physical therapies. Three times a week we drove fifteen minutes each way. I was determined to stay positive and believe that Emmy was healed. I surrounded Emmy in prayer and music that was uplifting and positive. There were specific songs Emmy begged to listen to.

"Play 'My Lighthouse,' please," Emmy would ask every single time we drove. Once that song by Rend Collective was over, it was "Good, Good Father" by Chris Tomlin. We would play those two songs over and over until we made it to therapy. Singing positive songs of life and healing became my obsession. Music had become the only thing left that could lift my spirits. Being reminded daily that God is good and that He loves us, even when we don't feel it, was what I needed to get out of bed each day. But each day was getting harder and harder to face. Even with therapy, Emmy was slowly losing what abilities she had left.

At this point, Emmy was still able to do some normal things but with great difficulty. Emmy could sit on the floor with her legs in a V position, but we still propped pillows around her to catch her spastic jolts. She could still squeeze tightly with her right and left hand but lacked fine motor skills. The left side of her body was still dystonic with a tight left arm, and her left leg stuck out straight. Emmy was able to roll around, sit up on her knees, and use a walker with my help. On really good days, she would play games and use her hands to play marbles.

Dr. Toor continued monthly MRIs. Every time Emmy would go back into the MRI, I would just sit with Randy on our "date" and pray that we would finally see just a hint of healing. It never came. Each time, the result was the same—stable. I eventually became thankful for the word *stable*. While it meant the active inflammation was still there, it also meant it wasn't getting worse.

No change in MRIs meant Randy and I had to keep searching for answers. We thought we were doing what every parent would do—search, search, and search until answers were found. The neurologist also did his part. He ordered a genetic panel to be completed on Emmy, which meant Randy and I needed to submit blood to test her genetic code against ours. We realized that now our research needed to include genetic diseases. We had four kids who were all born healthy. How could we have a genetic mutation and not know it? There was no history of any genetic brain disease in our family tree.

As the months progressed, instead of getting stronger and more playful from therapy, Emmy was becoming lethargic, and her body was much weaker. Headaches and nausea were returning, and suddenly on April 11, I found her lying on the couch in a silent seizure. She woke after eight minutes, but her neurologist made us bring her in for another MRI, even though one had been completed just two weeks earlier. Once again, stable. This time we were sent home with rescue meds for seizures and were told that she may become epileptic because of the amount of brain damage she had. This was one just more thing for me to continuously worry about.

Even with stable MRIs, the headaches, spasticity, and lack of sleep were getting worse. The active inflammation and brain damage were the culprits. *Is it going to be like this forever?* I was starting to feel trapped. I was trapped caring for a handicapped child, trapped in my home, trapped away from my other kids, trapped staring at a child who could possibly die with just one more "stroke" or whatever it was. I was trapped in a vicious cycle of hopeless despair.

Somehow, even with all that was lost, Emmy smiled and stayed positive. The only thing she asked for was to walk again. I still prayed daily that I would see Emmy walk, run, dance, and sing again. And I always prayed for a cure or a miraculous healing. Exhaustion was common, and my body ached from carrying Emmy all over the house. Our neighbors gave Emmy a power wheelchair, but her dexterity only allowed her to use it on good days. I would have used a manual wheelchair, but she was constantly wanting to be moved. It was harder transitioning her to and from the wheelchair than just picking her up and moving her.

Each day, every person I encountered said the same thing, "Missy, I don't know how you do it. Your entire life has been changed, and you do such a good job of taking care of Emmy. It was like you were meant to do this."

Somehow, I *was* doing this, whatever "this" was. My life *was* changed. But was I born to do *this*? To give up everything I enjoyed, my life, my whole world just to take care of one child? I had no understanding of space or time. I was consumed by all things Emmy. It wasn't like I purposely ignored my other kids, but there was one who needed me the most. If one of our children died, what would happen to our family as a whole? God had given me the desire to have four children, not three. I knew that was true.

It was when people came to visit our home that I was made to understand how awful it all really was. That look, the helpless, sorry look would be written all over their faces. There was no hiding what they were thinking. When the visit was over, each person would say the same thing once again, "You do this so well. It is like you were meant for this".

I was not meant for *this*. No one is meant for *this*.

Between the nausea, headaches, and multiple MRIs, Emmy's doctor decided to continue different immunotherapies to try to get the inflammation in her brain to subside. Emmy received chemotherapy once a month for a few months. When the MRI showed no change, the next therapy to try again was IVIG. IVIG is a common medicine for people with autoimmune diseases and used regularly for people with autoimmune encephalitis. Sadly, after two months of receiving the required dose, Emmy's MRI still looked unchanged.

The six months between November and May were grueling. Monthly trips to the hospital, multiple IVs, unchanged MRIs, weekly therapies, and even a seizure took what strength we had left.

When nothing seemed to be working, we stumbled upon a therapy that looked promising. Multiple articles lead us to hyperbaric oxygen therapy (HBOT). We had never heard of hyperbaric chambers healing diseases except for decompression sickness.

The metal chamber simulates the pressure of a deep-sea dive. As oxygen is pumped into the chamber, the pressure increases and helps creates new pathways in damaged areas of the body and brain so blood and oxygen can flow there. Oxygen is naturally increased by just pressurizing the tank, but when extra oxygen is added, healing can happen even quicker. The body already knows how to heal itself, but that added pressure and oxygen just gives it a little nudge.

The research revealed that wounds, broken bones, burned skin, and even brain inflammation were helped with oxygen therapy. I immediately went to online support groups and asked others if they had tried it. Many of the people who responded were parents of children born with cerebral palsy and had actually seen great results in increased memory, strength and relief of spasticity.

We had one problem. If Emmy's brain inflammation was caused by a genetic disorder called mitochondrial encephalomyopathy, some research showed that oxygen could actually amplify the disease. Mitochondria thrive with increased oxygen. But we were desperate, and we decided to sign her up.

We found a wellness clinic in Virginia Beach that had a fully functioning HBOT. As we were getting shown around the facility, Emmy's doctor called. The genetic testing had come back, and it was *not* genetic mitochondrial disease! That was great news, except the testing also showed that she had no genetic disorders at all. *So, what was causing her brain disease?* Her doctor did mention that a few abnormalities popped up, but they were said to be insignificant to her illness. It was common that every human being had a few genetic abnormalities.

Oxygen therapy seemed to be an answer to prayer, except for the fact that Emmy was going to have a hard time getting through the hour-long sessions. From the moment she woke up back in July, she had a constant itch on her neck. It was so bad that she never wore shirts at home. We had her checked for allergies, but her doctor believed it to be neurological, so nothing could be done. The only way Emmy would get the extra dose of oxygen was by wearing a silicone ring around her neck that attached to a plastic helmet. *How will I keep her still while something touched her neck for an hour?*

It was easy teaching her to clear her ears when they became plugged with the pressure changes, but after three sessions, I spent the entire hour trying to keep her occupied. She hated going into the tank, but by the grace of God, we made it through all forty sessions.

Despite many doctors dismissing oxygen therapy as a gimmick or a placebo effect, we knew it was working by the third dive. This was the main reason I made her keep going, even though she hated it. At first, we noticed she started sleeping through the night. After a few more sessions, tight muscle tone relaxed and she began using her right arm more. One day we actually found Emmy on the floor in her bedroom trying to put on her own socks! This was almost a miracle, considering she hadn't dressed herself since before she was sick. All of the signs were showing us her brain was improving and by September, her doctor requested another MRI. Amazingly, there was actually a spot of inflammation that looked to be healing!

That good news was followed by a sudden stop in the itch of her neck. Her doctor was so impressed by how well her body was responding to the oxygen, he began to decrease the prednisone she had been on since last November. For weeks, we were seeing improvements that finally allowed us to just breathe and stop worrying. Before the kids started school in August, my cousin Sheri came to visit, and we took all the kids to Busch Gardens. It felt like we were back on track to being "normal" again.

September 27, 2015, was our fifteenth wedding anniversary. Randy and I used to get away for one night alone on this special day, while family would come to town and watch our kids. Not on this anniversary. This was our second anniversary watching our daughter deteriorate before our eyes. Just when it seemed like things were finally looking up, it all abruptly crashed to the ground. Emmy woke that morning very spastic and rigid. Her body wouldn't stop moving, and she even broke out in hives during the night. We spent our anniversary in the ER watching the wavy lines on the EEG machine show us her brain activity. After a few days, we were sent home with no news as to why Emmy was getting worse again.

Oxygen therapy had ended at the beginning of September, and the only difference in routine was that the steroids were slowly being weaned. Another MRI was scheduled for October 5, and the results still looked the same. The next few days started to remind us of the previous year when Emmy's brain had been exploding with inflammation before our eyes. We were helpless then and helpless now. Suddenly, our entire lives were in free fall again.

A few weeks had passed with no answers. It was now Columbus Day and thankfully Randy was home from work to help me with a very miserable and spastic Emmy. By dinnertime, Emmy just couldn't control her hands anymore. She kept trying to roll up to the table in the power chair, but kept missing and became super irritated. I helped get her close to the table, but she began crying hysterically and pleaded for me to lay her on the floor in the living room. While I was sitting on the floor next to her, trying to feed her dinner, her entire body jerked, and she fell over. In an instant, her eyes shot to the left, and she starting seizing. This time, we thought we were prepared and gave her a dose of Diastat. The medicine didn't work. We had to dial 9-1-1.

PTSD—post-traumatic stress disorder. I'd only heard that word in relation to post-combat veterans. I was a veteran but never had PTSD from war. I had been through some stressful situations like being in Oklahoma during the Cat 5 tornado and living through Hurricane Katrina while stationed in Biloxi, Mississippi, but memories of those events never made me feel like I did when I heard an ambulance's sirens or stepped into a hospital emergency room. The ambulance ride took me right back to that horrible day in July. Nothing was stopping the seizure again. The medics looked concerned but tried hard to not let me see their worry. Once I started to cry, I couldn't stop. *God, why was this happening again? Can't you stop all of this, God? What did we do to deserve this? What did Emmy, our sweet Jesus loving child, do to deserve this?*

The hospital stay was only for a couple days. The neuro team decided to add another seizure medicine and then sent us home. Within a week, Emmy had another seizure. This time, after I gave her the home medicine, Diastat, she woke on her own. I called the on-call neurologist, and he urged me to still bring her in to be checked. Once again, nothing was found that had caused the seizure, and we were sent home. Confusion and hopelessness started to take over. I prayed this was not going to be the way we lived the rest of our lives.

Over the next couple weeks, Emmy became more lethargic and emotional. We also noticed that her eyes began to click. Somehow, we still managed to keep a positive attitude and just blame the symptoms on the new seizure medicine. It was October 31, 2015, and Emmy really wanted to go trick-or-treating. The costume she wore was one she had worn almost every day in Hawaii. She chose to be Super Girl.

As I woke up on November 1, terror had finally overtaken me. I found myself wanting to curl up in the fetal position. My mind was remembering the last November where Emmy lost her smile and had a stroke. I just couldn't go through another November like the last one. All I could do was pray—day and night. I prayed prayers that were simple, prayers that were written out and prayers that didn't even make sense.

While my initial prayers were long and drawn out, by the end of November, all I could do was pray simple, small prayers. "Dear God, please heal Emmy or find her a cure. Please make November better than it was last year. In Jesus name, amen."

I knew something bad was coming, but I didn't want to believe it. Crying and secretly screaming in my car became my ritual. It was the only way I could release my true emotions and not be heard.

I knew without a shadow of a doubt that God could still heal Emmy. I believed God had an answer to every single problem or disease or issue on this earth. "There is nothing new under the sun," said King Solomon (Ecclesiastes 1:9 NKJV). If doctors didn't have the answer, I knew God did.

8

CHAPTER

"Rabbi, who sinned, this man or his parents, that he was born blind?" Jesus answered, "Neither this man nor his parents sinned, but that the works of God should be revealed in him."

—JOHN 9:2–3 (NKJV)

If there was ever a time I needed bold, praying Christians, it was now. But some of my worst memories were when Christians would try to explain to me why all of this was happening to Emmy and our family. They spoke as if they knew God more than anyone else. These Christians read their Bible, went to church, did Bible studies, but then would try to regurgitate everything they'd learned into some horrible excuse for pain and suffering. Some Christians can be the worst confidants and friends when it comes to catastrophes. Why do Christians feel like they need to make excuses for God when bad things happen? It is the age-old atheist question, "If there was truly a God, why does He let children die?"

I was already struggling to understand why this pain and anguish weren't ending, but people were making it worse. I remember one day a Christian neighbor was over, and we were just talking and having coffee. It was just weeks after Emmy had been discharged back in November 2014. As we were talking, this friend began to question our Christianity. She wasn't so much questioning whether we were Christians but more whether Randy was the spiritual "head" of our home.

"What do you mean by that?" I asked.

"Well you know, is he the spiritual leader of your home? How the Bible talks about how men are the head of the house as Jesus is to the Church? Because no matter how much you are praying over your home and Emmy, if Randy isn't spiritually in charge, demons can continue to attack your family."

This friend proceeded to tell me a story of a baby who was being physically attacked by a demon, and no one could do anything about it because the father wasn't a Christian, even though the mother was. The baby eventually died, because I guess some priest saw the demons attacking the baby, and supposedly the father was the only one who could defeat it. It was the craziest thing I had ever heard.

Stunned and dumbfounded, I picked my jaw off the floor.

"Please, don't worry about us. Randy is a Christian. And while he is not as vocal in his prayers as I am, we both fervently pray over all of our children," I tried to say without showing the anger that was boiling inside of me.

I learned to choose wisely who I would have as my council. I needed praying, nonjudgmental people to help us spiritually, emotionally, and physically—not people who blamed this on our lack of prayer or faith.

Within the same month, another well-intentioned friend gave me a book called *When Life is Hard* by James MacDonald. This book was written by a Christian pastor who ended up getting cancer. I guess people who dedicate their lives to preaching and teaching about God have a hard time understanding how anything bad could happen to them.

This pastor wrote an entire book on how to work through pain and hard times with Bible verses, which did show me some valuable verses to read. But when he began to give specific reasons why pain and sickness occurred, I was dumbfounded. Just like others before him, he spoke as though it was punishment for our sin or lack of faith. He wrote that God is a father who teaches and corrects us when we do wrong, even causing sickness to occur, just to make sure we are really listening. And more cases than not, it was all our fault. We had sinned, or our children had sinned and put this on themselves. I believe that was the point I threw the book across the room and screamed.

God is a good father and has many other ways of teaching us lessons. We already struggle as humans with pain, sickness, and disease. Why would God send Jesus to *heal* people and then turn around and make people sick to get their attention? I do believe God knows and sees every single thing that happens on this earth, even the painful and deadly things we would never want to endure. I also believe God allows horrible things to happen, but I also believe He can intervene, create miracles, or help us work though whatever issues we are going through. No matter what happens, the truth is that God promises in Romans 8:28 (NKJV) to "work all things out together for good, for those who love Him and are called according to His purpose." God will take the horrible, broken, painful things and turn them into something beautiful. We may not see the beauty right away, but God does. And God's way is always good.

Was it our sin or Emmy's sin causing this disease? Neither. I never questioned God's goodness and mercy and I knew that whatever happened to us, God would be glorified.

I also found that, sometimes, God just needs us to be still and obey—not just obey the Ten Commandments, but actually listen to His voice and obey what He is telling us. I poured over verses in the Bible and found that, while God did send His Holy Spirit to help us, guide us and give us power over many things, He was ultimately in control. "Thy will be done" isn't just a saying for people who have given up and thrown in the towel. No. Allowing God to take every good and bad thing and make it into what He desires—that is what is truly hard. It's about giving up every ounce of control and giving God ultimate authority over what needs to be done—even if that means we end up with something we could have never imagined.

My prayers seemed to be echoing off my bedroom walls. I felt like something was keeping my prayers from reaching heaven. The rest of November was a living nightmare. Actually, it was nothing compared to the nightmare waiting for us around the corner. Emmy ended up being admitted to the hospital after we moved her MRI from the end of November to November 10. We did this because her eyes started clicking more and more, and she was rapidly losing muscle function. She resembled a rag doll. The MRI finally showed something. Oh, how I missed the word *stable*. Increased inflammation was the dreaded MRI diagnosis. But what else was there to do but give her high-dose steroids?

The doctors discharged us after the steroid infusion, but just three days later, we were back in the ER. Steroids usually calmed Emmy for a week or two, but every night after we left, she screamed and cried, while her body flailed wildly.

At the ER, the doctors decided to start with a spinal tap. After waking from the sedation, Emmy's body seemed to be moving in overdrive. Every part of her body was whirling, and every position she lay in made her worse. She was quickly admitted, and a repeat of the MRI was done in the morning.

That MRI showed something more than inflammation. This discovery would start a snowball effect of chaos.

The on-call neurologist pulled me to a computer monitor and showed me the images. "I think I know what's happening. There's an autoimmune disease that causes strokes. This image looks just like a stroke," she said while explaining the next steps. "I'm setting her up to get an angiogram this evening. We have to pull a doctor in from another hospital, since children don't usually need angiograms. Then we will be able to determine if this is really a stroke or a specific autoimmune disease that caused them."

I was speechless. Another *stroke*! What disease has no evidence in the blood or spinal fluid but can cause a stroke?

During this time, we insisted that it was time to send Emmy to a larger, more specialized hospital. The November prior, Randy had requested that we take Emmy to Boston Children's hospital, but the neurology team had insisted it was too early, when there were many more tests that could still be performed at CHKD. But now was the time. We were watching our daughter slowly die, and there was no more time to waste.

"We want Emmy to go to Boston. I know Dr. Toor said it wasn't needed in the past, but Emmy is going to die if something else can't be done," I said to the neurologist.

"Yes, I agree with you! I already spoke to the neurology team, and they also agreed it is time. Dr. Toor is afraid it will be hard on you and Emmy, but we have run out of options. Let's see what the angiogram says and then get her on a plane," she said with excitement in her voice.

I am so thankful this neurologist was a vocal, strong Latina woman. She knew the time had come for Emmy to get more specialized care from a hospital with unlimited resources. She wasn't going to take no for an answer from anyone.

Emmy went in for a full angiogram to determine if she'd really had a stroke. It was the morning of November 17, almost a year from her last stroke in her basal ganglia, and Randy and I were sick to our stomachs that our baby girl was undergoing another procedure. The doctors continually reassured us that angiograms were performed all the time and had very low risk and complications. *Oh, we've heard that line before.*

As we sat in the waiting room for hours, which felt more like days, we had a bad feeling something was not right. I just kept praying over and over that Emmy would survive all of this. The doctor finally called us back to the ICU five hours later and told us that everything had gone perfectly. Emmy showed zero signs of a stroke.

"If there wasn't a stroke, what caused this brain bleed?" I asked.

"We aren't sure yet, but tonight we will let Emmy rest and then go from there. If we wake her up, do you think she will be able to lay still for eight hours?" the ICU doctor asked me.

"No. She has been sitting on her knees a lot. And if she can't do that, we may need to leave her sedated," I said cautiously.

What a mistake that was. As I watched Emmy lay there, intubated, I couldn't take it any longer. I ran down the hallway and hid in the bathroom, crying whatever tears I had left. I wasn't sure I had enough strength left to take care of a damaged little girl, let alone myself and the rest of my family.

At 8:00 a.m., when the morning crew started their rounds, Emmy was extubated. It's hard to explain exactly what we saw, but our pastor, Randy, explained it the best. He came back to pray for Emmy, and when Emmy woke up, her entire body was moving and flailing. He said it looked as if she was sitting in "a pile of fire ants." Emmy was really wiggly before, but this was entirely different.

My friend Melissa and I were just standing over Emmy, trying to comfort her and holding her entire body still. Nothing we could do helped calm her. Finally, the neurologist came to see what was happening, and she gave her a dose of Haldol. I was confused because that was what was given for psychosis. We watched Emmy continue to squirm, which proved the medicine didn't work. Then the doctor tried a dose of Valium, which just made Emmy fall into a deep nap for twenty minutes. When Emmy woke up, she was still thrashing all over the bed. It was confusion and chaos. I was trying hard to keep it together. It was like a never-ending episode of the *Twilight Zone*. What was happening? Something from the angiogram had harmed her brain; I just knew it.

Later that day, I finally took a break and walked downstairs to the cafeteria. I was confused and hurt and scared as to what all of this meant. I was alone in the hallway when all of a sudden, I heard God say loudly to me, "Missy, you know these things only can come out by prayer and fasting."

Before I go on, I have to tell you about hearing the voice of God. Many people have never heard God speak or even know what to listen for. I never really cared one way or another about "hearing" God, because my whole life as a Christian I just always felt like God gave me a peace of mind when I had a hard decision to make. I never thought I needed Him to address me directly to know He existed. I just knew He helped me. Yes, it was my voice I heard as He Spoke, and I was the only one who heard it. But I knew it wasn't me talking to myself. This was different. I had actually heard God twice before, so I was certain this was God.

The first time I heard God tell me to do something specific was when we were in Minot, North Dakota, where Emmy was born. We had just received military orders stating that we were to be stationed at Hickam AFB, Hawaii. After getting over the sheer excitement of living in Hawaii, I realized I would have to find schools for the two older kids. We were not given much time before we moved, so base housing wasn't available for us. As I searched schools in the area, I quickly realized there were only a few highly rated elementary schools, and they were nowhere near where we were going to live. I just knew we had to get them into a good school in case our next move was to a state with top-ranked schools. As I researched and even tried to move money around in our budget to afford the overly priced private schools, I heard God tell me, "Homeschool the kids."

His voice had been just as clear then as it was in the hospital. How did I know it was God and not just common sense telling me to homeschool? Because at that point I thought homeschooling was the most pathetic form of education and did a great disservice to all children. Not only that, I'd actually vocalized my negative opinions to people who were currently homeschooling. I wasn't just adamantly against homeschooling, I ridiculed the parents who did it. I was like Saul before he was blinded and became

Paul. Yet, here was God telling me that homeschooling was my only option. Long story short, Randy said to try it for one year. That one year eventually became nine years. Talk about inserting foot into mouth.

The second time I heard God's voice was over the most ridiculous thing you can imagine—a car. For years, I had driven a GMC Yukon XL, which was my dream vehicle. I purchased it right before Emmy was born and had driven it over six years. At the beginning of 2014, I started getting a weird feeling that I was supposed to buy a minivan. Gross! A minivan of all vehicles. I was not going to ever let that happen. I nonchalantly told Randy about this strange feeling, and he nicely reminded me that I hated minivans. Every time I had the feeling I needed to buy a minivan, Randy would laugh and tell me, "I am not riding this car roller coaster with you anymore! You know you hate minivans!"

This dialogue went on for months, always ending with Randy laughing at me. Then early one morning in March 2014, God said, "Go buy a minivan." I woke up, told Randy I was going to buy a minivan, and left. Randy seriously thought I was joking, until I showed up with a Honda Odyssey that afternoon. Little did I know that a minivan would be the exact vehicle we needed to carry around a handicapped child and her wheelchair just a few months later.

But strangely, when I heard God tell me, "These things can only come out by prayer and fasting," I didn't want to hear it and I surely didn't want to believe it. I was angry that I would even think or hear about this specific verse from the Bible. Matthew 17:21 was the verse God was speaking to me and was about the apostles not being able to cast out a demon.

"No way, God. You know that Emmy is not filled with a demon. I refuse to believe all of this is from a demon!" I said in defiance instead of obedience.

There was no way Emmy was possessed or being attacked by some spirit making her body flail around. Of course, my mind would wander to those thoughts, but I knew that one cannot be filled with the Holy Spirit and the devil at the same time. If only I would have listened to the exact words God was saying to me, instead of drawing conclusions about what I thought I understood.

That night, Emmy was still visibly uncomfortable. Her breathing was incredibly fast, and her body was all over the place. Her cheeks became flush; it was like she was running a marathon. Finally, the neurologist came in and gave her a dose of Benadryl and Valium together and within ten minutes we saw Emmy calm down and finally fall asleep.

The next morning, her body started getting pretty wild again after waking, so another dose of Benadryl and Valium were given. It worked again! I thought we would finally see her calm down and get comfortable. Sadly, every four to six hours, extra doses would have to be given. Thankfully, her body calmed more and more each day.

Standing over Emmy, holding her body still, and watching her every move was exhausting. I finally let Randy take over, and I quickly left the room to catch my breath and gather my thoughts. God was waiting for me in the hallway.

"Missy, these things can only come out by prayer and fasting."

"No way, God. This isn't what is wrong with her; it's just her brain. Why do you keep saying this to me?" I questioned.

I can't believe I actually argued with God like this every time He would tell me to fast and pray. For some reason, my mind wanted to reject that verse because Emmy's body movements reminded me of what a person would look like if possessed. After days of hearing God say this, I knew I had to be making it all up. Whatever was really wrong with Emmy was a little more complicated than a simple "prayer and fasting" remedy, because she obviously wasn't filled with a demon.

That evening, the neurologist came and gave us the good news. Boston had agreed to take Emmy, as long as we were all right with waiting to start the tests the Monday after Thanksgiving.

"Of course! Just get us to Boston. We need to find Emmy a cure!" I said, relieved.

One step forward, seven steps back. On the nineteenth, the neurology team wanted to get one last set of MRIs for their records before we went to Boston. They wanted to do not only a brain MRI, but also a spinal MRI, to make sure the inflammation had not spread.

Upon waking up from the sedation, Emmy's body was in full-blown spasms again. This time, she was even worse than before. The left side of her body would tighten, and her whole body would flail for three minutes at a time. Her breathing was so rapid it sounded like she was hyperventilating. *Maybe God was right. She does look like she's possessed.*

How could this be possible? I had never been so helpless and hopeless before in my entire life.

Thankfully, the doctor started the Benadryl and Valium doses around the clock, which relieved the spasms partially. At night, clonidine was added to help her body rest, which also allowed her to fall asleep. Now we were playing the game of "what time is it" to see how soon she could get her next dose of medicine. I didn't even care that her brain had a disease; I just wanted to help her get rid of these cramps and spasms so she could relax.

Over the next few days, the oral Valium and Benadryl were barely helping, so the doctors had to start giving it through her IV. This seemed to help for a while but would quickly wear off. We were no longer worried her body was too erratic to fly to Boston, no we were fighting with insurance to approve the flight. It took five days for the hospital staff to realize that Emmy's insurance didn't need preapproval, and we could have flown out on the twentieth. What a mess! Confusion and frustration seemed to cloud every part of this journey. Something or someone was preventing Emmy from getting the cure and healing she needed to survive.

The day before Thanksgiving, Emmy and I were loaded on a small jet to finally get what we had been praying for over the past year and a half. I just knew God was going to answer our prayers. The new doctors were going to figure out why her body reacted negatively to the angiogram and figure out what was destroying her brain—or so I thought.

PART II
BOSTON

I would have lost heart, unless I had believed
That I would see the goodness of the Lord
In the land of the living.
—PSALM 27:13 (NKJV)

CHAPTER 9

*My tears have been my food day and night,
while they continually say to me,
"Where is your God?"*

—PSALM 42:3 (NKJV)

This was it. Emmy and I were finally on our way to Boston. I knew God would get us to the exact place where a cure would be found. The flight was over an hour, but she slept the entire way and didn't have body spasms once. I had been so worried that having her strapped down in a bed would cause her body to explode with movements. It was a total God thing she never spasmed, because once we were carted to her hospital room, the spasms and movements started up again.

Like we had been forewarned, the attending doctors were gone for the night. We were checked in by a "newbie" neurologist, and you could tell he was visibly upset at how uncomfortable Emmy was. Telling the doctor all that had happened from the moment she broke her arm until that day was like I was reading him the dictionary in Latin. All the dates and facts left him dumbfounded, but he needed to know all of it. Emmy's life depended on someone getting the facts right and finding a diagnosis.

The night shift nurse understood my urgency as I was telling the doctor he really needed to get the clonidine, Benadryl, and Valium ordered. She gave him a laptop and was able to get him to order the meds *stat*. Her body was moving a mile a minute, and she was starting to flush and sweat. Out of all her nighttime medicine, only clonidine seemed to calm her enough to fall asleep. I wish I would have just listened and obeyed God, because I had no idea the pain and horror that was coming. If only I would have prayed and fasted.

The room was still dark at 6:30 a.m., when we were woken up for an impromptu trip to the operating room. The nurse was so proud of herself because she had managed to get Emmy in for the first appointment of the day with sedation. Someone somewhere had decided that Emmy needed a PICC (peripherally inserted central catheter) line placed in her arm for all the blood tests they would be doing. While she was sedated, they were also going to get spinal fluid to send off for more testing.

I was so tired and confused as to where I even was, but I quickly realized we had not even talked to the attending doctor yet. This was too soon. *How will they understand what is happening to her body? And what if this procedure makes her worse?* I really wanted to talk to the attending neurologist and get them prepared to give Emmy medicine, but the nurse told me we had to go.

An hour later, Emmy was wheeled back to the hospital room, and immediately upon waking up, her body was more dystonic than before. The attending neurologist finally came to the room about an hour later. She was very welcoming and understanding, but she didn't talk much. This was the first real snapshot of Emmy this hospital had, and I could tell they were blaming what they were seeing physically, all on her brain disease. This was not Emmy's disease; this was what happened after procedures.

I think back about how every time I mentioned the full body spasms starting after her angiogram procedure and not one doctor or nurse actually "hearing" what I was saying. It was like my words were falling on deaf ears. The doctor just waited for me to finish talking, and then she recommended starting Emmy on a movement disorder medicine called Sinemet. I had not researched any movement disorder medicines, but if it could help Emmy, I was willing to try it. Maybe it would take away some of the misery Emmy was experiencing.

The next morning, just like clockwork, God told me what to do for Emmy. "Missy, these things can only come out by prayer and fasting."

Just like a stubborn, prideful child, I told Him He was wrong. Every single day for a month this occurred. I finally got to the point that I was so mad at God for telling me what to do instead of just healing Emmy, I started to block out His voice. I just wanted Emmy healed, and all He wanted me to do was pray and fast. *Who even fasts anymore?*

Randy joined me and Emmy in Boston two days after we arrived. He was so upset when he walked into the room and saw Emmy even more miserable than when we left. We both fed off each other's fears and seemed to fall into a deep hole of despair. How was this happening to our little girl? We should be happy to finally be in Boston, but we were scared about what was happening with Emmy's body.

It is hard to put the next week into words. How do you explain chaos and confusion when you are drowning in it? Emmy was still having spasms nonstop, with only a little rest at night from the clonidine. The doctors took away the new movement disorder medicine because her blood pressure started plummeting. On November 30, we met with a very large neurology team, including a movement disorder specialist. This team laid out all the tests, including a brain biopsy, that would have to be performed. They also recommended we try a common medicine for Parkinson's called Artane, known to help dystonia.

"Once we start the medicine, it will take weeks to get her to a therapeutic dose. Once her body calms down, then we know to stop increasing it," the movement neurologist explained to us.

They gave Emmy the first dose of medicine; three hours later, I saw her spasms strengthen. I was so focused on Emmy that it seemed I was the only one who noticed. Or maybe I was just so hyper-focused on her and only imagined them getting worse. Either way, I told the doctors, and they told me there was no way we would have seen any effects from one dose. Something was not right, but they convinced me to hold out for a few more weeks. This was the first time I realized I should have listened to my intuition and not backed down to the doctors. Nobody knows a child as well as a parent.

Day after day, Emmy's misery continued. Yet not one doctor listened to me when I said every time they sedated her it continued getting worse. Not one person heard me say her painful body movements started after the angiogram. They saw a damaged brain and assumed these spasms were the dystonia and chorea her chart said she was plagued with after the initial brain damage. Nothing made them take pause. They insisted on keeping with the timeline of tests, even though she was physically in pain. They had three weeks to do multiple tests, a brain biopsy, and possible treatment. At least that is what I believed they said. Three weeks. *I can make it three more weeks. I hope Emmy can make it three more weeks.*

A three-hour long MRI was set for December 1, and then a brain biopsy would follow days later. This MRI was so detailed a neurosurgeon could pinpoint where the brain tissue would be removed for testing by only looking at the images during surgery. Just as before, the spasms increased a hundredfold when she woke up from the MRI sedation. Emmy was in constant hyperventilation; her body was in a great deal of pain from muscles tightening and flailing. Because of the constant crying and screaming, eating was becoming difficult for her. And because of the spasms, she could no longer use a toilet.

"Emmy, can I ask the nurse to put a diaper on you? I know you don't need it, but it is just too hard holding you on the toilet while you are moving like this," I sadly asked her.

"Yes, it's OK," Emmy replied through her tears.

Clonidine was now given every eight hours, but it barely helped calm her muscles. They began trying higher doses of Valium and then added in gabapentin. Neither brought relief. Both made everything worse.

Emmy was originally put in a double room with a roommate. They quickly moved her to a double room but without a roommate because of her crying. A few days later, they moved her again to an even more "secluded" room at the end of the hallway. They were pushing her away from the hall that had the most traffic. Then it hit me; the doctors were avoiding us. *What kind of doctors can't even deal with the pain a child is going through? Isn't that their job?*

For some reason, Emmy was getting worse and worse, even though she had not been in sedation since December 1. I knew the medicine wasn't doing anything. The hyperventilation, flushing of her entire body, and sweating was now happening around the clock.

We began begging for something to just relieve her, even for a moment. Nurses on the neurology floor were trained to give sedatives—and a lot of them. They dealt with kids who would have seizures that needed high doses of benzodiazepines to stop them. At first, they would administer the Valium through her IV over the course of three minutes. When that did nothing, they began pushing it directly into her IV. That fast push would knock Emmy right out, but only for a few minutes. She would wake fifteen minutes later, screaming, crying, and flailing.

Randy and I were broken—physically and emotionally. Nothing we tried or said relieved her spasms or pain. Physical therapy brought in random things to distract Emmy, but nothing helped. At one point during the week, Emmy was in so much pain, she finally hit her breaking point. I was holding her in a weird position, trying to relieve the pain in her left side, when she cried out, *"Why is God doing this to me?"*

I remember that exact moment—that instant she cried those words out in her faint, sweet voice. Her cry to God broke me. The lump in my throat choked me and when I finally swallowed down my tears, I replied.

"Baby, God doesn't do this to little girls. God doesn't cause pain, the devil does. This is all Satan, and daddy and I are doing everything we can to stop it. I promise!"

That was the day I almost gave up on God. That was the day my faith wavered, and I truly questioned whether God cared about Emmy, let alone even existed. As we were wrestling Emmy's flailing body, Randy looked up at me after Emmy cried out those words and yelled, "Where is *your* God, Missy? You keep telling me God is good and takes care of His people, but it surely doesn't look like it to me."

"I don't know, Randy. I don't know why it feels like we are being punished," I cried back to him. I was beginning to believe the lies that God wasn't good, but as soon as those thoughts crept in, the truth pushed them out.

"This is not God; this is Satan. God heals and restores. He doesn't hurt and kill. God loves Emmy and would never do this to her," I said trying not to let Emmy see my tears.

I wasn't sure I believed my own words. Was God good? Was God even in Boston? I didn't feel him anywhere. I only knew He spoke to me every morning, telling me to pray and fast. I felt like we had been sent to a dry desert wasteland, when we were supposed to be going to Eden—the place of healing. We had no rescue plan, and we had no support system. God was obviously not hearing our cries because Emmy was getting worse by the minute. Maybe we *were* being punished; it felt like this was all happening on purpose.

As Randy was losing faith; I was lost in fear. We had no friends, no pastors, and no family. A chaplain came to my room one of the first days and asked me who she should pray to. *Who she should pray to?* Who else is there but God? I was so confused and alone. Randy and I were at each other's throats, angry and sick to our stomachs. We were both sad, weak, and starving, and it had only been a week and a half since we'd arrived in Boston.

None of that mattered to the "schedule" of tests that continued to be done. On December 8, Emmy was taken to have her brain biopsied. Every cell in my body was screaming for them to stop this; for someone to step in and help Emmy. My insides were quivering, and I knew she shouldn't go under sedation again, but the doctors still blamed everything her body was doing on her brain disease. They were rushing everything because they didn't believe us that this was not the disease. This was the angiogram and every sedation made it worse.

Emmy was in devastating distress. Somehow, she was still completely aware of what was happening, even with all the Valium she was on. She expressed her fear of the biopsy, so we told her they were just going to "peek" at her brain to see if they could find a reason for her illness. As we kissed her goodbye, the thought of them cutting open her skull crushed my heart. I couldn't stop kissing and hugging her sweaty little body. What if they caused her more disabilities by hitting an important area? How much more could her little body possibly endure?

Randy and I pretended to eat lunch at a cafeteria down the road. The place was filled with hundreds of people, but you could clearly tell who the parents of sick kids were. Heartbreak was hard to hide. I really didn't want to go back into the hospital, so we walked a little farther down the road and sat down at a coffee shop. As I was reading my Facebook messages, I burst into tears. A friend from Virginia had sent me a picture of Jesus. He was standing on water, reaching His hand to Peter, who was drowning in the water beneath him. That was me! This picture described my exact feelings, my exact fear of what was happening. *Why wouldn't Jesus just grab my hand? Was he going to let me drown?* And then the tears began to pour.

"What happened? Why are you crying? Please stop, Missy. We can't do this here. You are going to make me start crying, and then it will be a huge, ugly scene," Randy pleaded with me.

"Do you see this? This picture is me. I have felt like I have been drowning for eighteen months, and I know Jesus is there. But why won't He grab my hand? Or maybe it's my fault. Maybe I just don't know how to grab His hand. It's just all so hard," I said through the silent sobs.

That is exactly how we felt, day and night. We were drowning. Drowning in complete confusion. Drowning in sorrow. Drowning in medical jargon. Drowning in the pain of Emmy.

Just like we suspected, Emmy lived through the brain biopsy, but her brain couldn't handle the sedation. Within two days, Emmy was being pumped full of sedatives so strong it would knock out a three hundred-pound man. They didn't even touch her spasms.

That week, our pastor drove all the way from Virginia to pray over Emmy. It was perfect timing because of what was about to hit us. In all honesty, we probably needed a whole cavalry of pastors to pray over us. We had people on Facebook praying, and our families were supporting us as much as they could from afar. My mom and Randy's mom were taking turns watching our kids, while we tried to shield them from the obvious pain Emmy was going through.

The doctors added in morphine to help with the spasms, but just like the rest, it did nothing. At one point, she was on six additional medicines, but not one stopped her pain. She was getting Valium pushed through her IV every four hours, yet she would only find relief for ten minutes and then start spasming harder than before. Randy and I were taking turns leaning over her bed, holding her flailing arms and legs, trying to comfort her. We had to tag team, as it was like we were wrestling a bear. It was by far the sickest joke to ever be played on parents. Physically wrestling and holding down your own daughter, while she cried and hyperventilated. Would there ever be an end to this nightmare?

Where was Emmy's diagnosis? I knew we were here for a cure. I stood firm in that. I knew God had brought us here—but definitely not for this, not for this kind of torture and pain. The doctors seemed completely dumbfounded at the spasms and just kept throwing medicine at Emmy. At some point, I thought they would realize medicine wasn't the answer and would stop trying new pain medicines. But every time I mentioned the angiogram, no one gave me an answer. Then a glimmer of hope came when tests started coming in with actual results.

"Randy and Missy, we think we know what Emmy has. But to confirm these other tests are accurate, we need to get her genetically tested—" her neurologist started saying.

"She already had genetic testing done! The tests showed that there wasn't anything abnormal," I told him.

"Really? It isn't in her records. I will call the testing center. So, what I thought would take three months to get an answer will only take about three weeks. There are two other tests we did that partially confirm what we think is happening to Emmy's brain."

"What is it? Is there a cure? Like IVIG or steroids?" Randy asked.

"The cure is nothing like that. It is actually a pretty rough treatment plan. She will need a bone marrow transplant," he said softly.

"A bone marrow transplant? Aren't those done for people with leukemia? Is this a form of cancer? Does she have to do chemotherapy? How is she going to do any of that with her body spasming like it is?" I blasted him with question after question.

"No, it's not cancer. But it has a similar name. I'm going to tell you the name of this disease, but I don't want you to google it. Emmy's type of disease is not like what is commonly presented. Her disease is only in her brain and different than the common disease that originally starts in the body. The name is hemophagocytic lymphohistiocytosis or HLH," he said, like he had practiced saying it over and over in the mirror.

"Do you have any other patients with this? Why didn't her neurologist in Virginia know about this? Wouldn't he have known to look for this disease?" Randy asked.

"We just discovered another patient recently, which is why I believe Emmy has this specific disease. They both presented the same way, even both getting sick when they were six. Their MRIs are also very similar. Remember, we have to wait for the genetic results to confirm it," he said reassuringly.

"Can I talk to this family? How do I meet them and ask questions? This is so overwhelming. I can't believe a bone marrow transplant is the cure. You realize this is all new to us, even though we have been searching for answers for eighteen months?" I asked him.

"Yes, I will talk with the family and tell them you have some questions for them. Until then, do not google, and we will keep you updated."

A genetic disease with a name we couldn't pronounce. I had known God would find Emmy a cure—but one that was so invasive and life threatening? She would have to go through chemotherapy, which I was 100 percent against. Randy and I were left with so many questions, and Randy instantly did what the doctor told him not to. He googled HLH. And me? I remembered back to how many times I railed against using Western medicine chemotherapy for so-called healing. How could anyone believe poisoning our bodies was healing?

God has a most gracious way of humbling us, without openly mocking us before the world. When we think we know all the answers and try to figure it out all on our own, He gently reminds us that He alone is God and holds the answers. For two years, I had been teaching health and nutrition classes to women. I had given them resources to find natural alternatives to almost every illness under the sun. I even met a man in Virginia who was a pharmacist and told me that almost all medicine is created by replicating nature. Why use medicine if we can use the real thing?

My first thought when I heard the word chemotherapy was, *Over my dead body.* I had spent almost two years discovering what early American, European, and Asian holistic (pre-pharmaceutical) doctors used for things like ulcers, migraines, tumors, and even cancer. Why would anyone fill their body with literal poison if you could use a plant or herb and get the same results? Well, I never researched bone marrow transplants, and the only way you can get stem cells to "graft" into the marrow is by killing off the old cells and allowing room for the new ones. The only way to do that is with chemotherapy—poison. Plant cells are too "brilliant" and created by God to help our bodies, not kill them. There was no natural method or way to kill off bone marrow. What I'd deemed unworthy to be used for healing, God was using for good.

And now my mind kept repeating the verse from John 1:3 (NKJV), "And all things were made through Him, and without Him nothing was made that was made." If God made chemicals, He could use them to heal Emmy.

10
CHAPTER

For God is not a God of confusion but of peace.
—I CORINTHIANS 14:33 (NASB 2020)

I paced back and forth, trying to keep my sanity. I just kept whispering, "God is not a God of chaos, but of order. God is not a God of chaos, but of order. *God is not a God of chaos, but of order.* God would never do this!"

The situation we found ourselves in was spiraling out of control. We were in a full tailspin, and the only life jacket we had was missing. This was no longer a nightmare but a sick and twisted game that we couldn't escape from.

The doctors were still throwing different meds at Emmy, rather than finding out why her body was doing this after sedation. After trying numerous painkillers, hooking her up to a morphine drip, and increasing her Valium dose, they decided to Botox her muscles. We had no idea if this actually helped because the next day we were visited by the ICU pain management team. This group of doctors began discussing how concerned they were that one more dose of Valium or morphine could stop Emmy's breathing.

"What do you mean stop her breathing? What is going on? Why are you even here?" I asked.

"We have tried everything to ease Emmy's pain, but we are at a point that we feel she should be moved to the ICU so we can keep a closer eye on her. We need a nurse there in case these meds really do stop her breathing," one of the doctors said assuredly.

How did we get here? In just a few weeks, we had gone from being hopeful for a cure to being told Emmy could stop breathing and needed to go to the ICU. Confused and exhausted from wrestling Emmy twenty-four hours a day for over three weeks, I found their words were too much to handle. The floodgates broke open. Every hurt, pain, and fear began pouring from my eyes. It was unstoppable. The nurse tried to not cry, but tears were falling down her cheeks. The doctors were staring, not fully understanding what was happening. This was their first encounter with Emmy, yet I had no words to explain all that has happened and all I could do was cry. Randy quickly looked down at Emmy to hide his tears and then the doctors quickly walked away, leaving instructions for the nurse on what was next.

Words cannot fully describe the first three weeks at Boston Children's Hospital. It took only three weeks to rip the hope straight from our hearts and turn it into despair. Randy and I were like the extras in a horror film, who just hung out in the background and had no idea how to control the storyline. We saw the villain, but we were oblivious about what to do. We were all going to be caught and tortured, which was exactly how we felt.

There was no sleep. There were no breaks. Randy and I took turns wrestling Emmy twenty-four hours a day, while she flailed around on her bed, screaming, sweating, and crying. I can't imagine being in a worse situation, except maybe being forced to watch your child slowly tortured while you are tied up and gagged. But that was what was happening. We were witnessing our baby girl being tortured—not by some evil person but by her brain and the medicine she was given. The entire nightmare started over every day. This was not why we had come to Boston. *God, please help us.*

Emmy's muscles were no longer her own. She lost almost all control of every function that made her human. Her last words were, "Why is God doing this to me?" And her last meal was a cheeseburger that took two hours to eat. She had burned so many calories that her weight was dropping at an alarming rate, and she just kept pointing to the menu to order more food. Choking now became a concern, and she coughed after every sip of juice. The doctors and nurses had seen enough.

Being part of the medical staff, especially a nurse, means not only taking care of the patient but also the family. I have no idea what it was like for any of the staff watching the three of us in this nightmare, but they finally stepped in to try and help the situation. They decided this was too much for Randy and me to deal with day in and day out. On December 16, 2015, they made a command decision to admit Emmy to the ICU.

The ICU was big and overwhelming, unlike the ICU in Virginia. The team of nurses and doctors crowded around our screaming daughter, spotlights glaring down on us, making me feel completely helpless and exposed. And right then, it hit me. I was so embarrassed. I have no idea why, but I felt embarrassed that we were even here. I had spoken boldly, saying that God was going to heal Emmy. But things were only getting worse. How could I still say, "There is a God"? How could I get others to believe in God when we were going through so much misery? I felt betrayed.

Clothed in only a diaper, Emmy was dripping with sweat and screaming in pain. Randy and I were using what strength we had left to keep her arms and legs from hitting the sides of the bed. Questions were being asked about Emmy, stickers were being placed, and swabs were being used to test for bacteria. It was too much. All I could hear was the sound of crying, followed by the whopping sound that happens right before you pass out.

Stepping back from Emmy, preparing to fall down, I spotted a chair and ran to it. Somehow, I willed myself to stay awake. I was so weak that it took every breath to keep me from passing out in front of the entire ICU staff. My thoughts were floating and fleeting like a dream and somehow, I just knew I was going to wake from this nightmare. When I opened my eyes, it was all still there. The equipment, the staff, the lights and Randy leaning over Emmy while she cried.

The following twenty-four hours are still lost in memory. I can't remember the exact details of anything. I was barely coherent with the lack of sleep and overwhelming sense of dread that came with being in an ICU again. Crying while hyperventilating, mixed with constant beeping and alarm bells going off every time Emmy's heart rate exceeded 160, quickly followed by moments of eerie silence after a push of Valium—these were the sounds that echoed over and over throughout her room.

The nurses urged Randy and me to leave, to catch our breath, or to take a shower. But we couldn't. We physically couldn't leave her side. We knew something was wrong, so twisted that we couldn't take our eyes off her. She was fine—well at least not spasming—before the angiogram. Didn't that mean something? Didn't it matter that every time they gave her sedation, she got worse?

All I could see and feel was an unending nightmare. This was exactly like a reoccurring nightmare I often had. The one where I am running from a faceless, shadow figure down a dark alley and every time I try to open my mouth and scream, nothing but breath escapes. No one could hear my cries for help.

Pain is a horrible thing that penetrates even the toughest, most seasoned of doctors. I thought the staff was worried mostly for Emmy, but I found out they were more worried for me and Randy and how we were holding up. They had seen parents lose their minds while caring for a sick child, and they didn't want that to happen to us.

We were admitted to the ICU on a Wednesday, and by Friday they sat us down to tell us their plan to "rescue" Emmy.

"Emmy can't physically keep going like this. Her heart rate is too high, and she is in way too much pain, which medicine isn't even helping. We feel like the best course of action is to treat this like we do our patients who go into epileptic storms. We will sedate Emmy, allow her brain and body to sleep and then, hopefully, wake her up spasm-free," the attending said with question in his voice.

Randy and I couldn't speak. We stared at the doctor, shocked at what they were proposing, and began crying. After a few minutes, we came to realize that they were going to intubate her again. Why was this happening over and over? After blasting the doctor with a million questions, we realized we didn't know what else could be done. The anguish in Emmy's eyes and constant cries of pain were unbearable. Something had to be done, or—what I kept trying to say—something needed to be *undone*.

Randy and I never left Emmy's side. We watched the doctors push the propofol and ketamine into her IV to stop her breathing so the intubation tube could be placed, but something was wrong. We watched in horror as the sedatives would work for mere seconds and then she would wake from the dead. Twice that happened. The entire situation was new to us, but we knew this was not how it was supposed to go.

With the final additions of midazolam and dexmedetomidine, Emmy finally stopped breathing, and they placed the tube in her airway. If Emmy woke up with a tube stuck in her throat, I knew that was going to be the end of me. I had heard stories of people waking while intubated and losing their minds, thinking they were suffocating. The nurses and respiratory therapists finished up by making sure the vent was perfect and Emmy was in a comfortable position.

Parents were given one bed to sleep on in the ICU room. The small, shorter than normal bed was placed in an alcove surrounded by windows. We were on the sixth floor, and the winter wind would creep through the cracks and freeze the plastic mattress and anyone who was sleeping on it. I hated that bed. After Emmy was finally intubated, I fell onto the bed and broke out into a cold sweat. The whopping sound was all I could hear. I was stronger than this. I was not going to pass out now. But this was too much too handle. This was all wrong, so unbelievably wrong.

Our baby girl was not supposed to be here. Spasms were not part of the plan, and they were muddying the entire diagnosis and hospital stay. I began crying, uncontrollably again. There was nothing Randy or anyone could do to comfort me. This entire trip was wrong. We were wrong for wanting this. We prayed for a cure, not for a hospital to ignore signs that medicine was causing her tiny body to react like this. Should we have listened to her primary neurologist's advice and just stayed in Virginia? I passed out on that bed and woke the next morning utterly distraught and denying the fact that Emmy was inches away, being forced to breathe on a ventilator.

ICU parents were given an extra room to sleep, away from stress and noise, but more because the ICU room only had one bed. The sleep rooms were littered on either side of a long hallway, with three or four bathrooms to share. That is where Randy slept.

Early the next morning, Randy showed up to relieve me of my duties as "Emmy protector." He had finally taken a shower and urged me to do the same.

"I can't leave, Randy. I just don't think she is really asleep. What if she wakes up, and I'm not here. What if she thinks she's being choked? I just can't leave right now," I said as I stared directly at Emmy. We both sat down and just watched the heartrate monitor, proving she was really asleep.

After staring at Emmy all day, making sure she was really asleep, I snuck away and showered. Who would have thought that a communal shower, used by dozens of families, would feel like a spa? I went to the sleep room and fell to my knees and began to cry all over again. Would I ever run out of tears?

On Monday, the autoimmune neurologist woke us while we were napping in Emmy's room. There isn't much else to do after spending weeks wrestling with Emmy. He seemed more chipper than his usual stoic self and said he had "good news." His diagnosis was correct and was finally confirmed with Emmy's genetic results. As Randy and I sat up, we tried hard to understand what the doctor was saying.

"We received the genetic report back, and it confirmed Emmy does have Hemophagocytic Lymphohistiocytosis or HLH. We call it CNS-restricted HLH because it only affects the central nervous system, unlike the common HLH. HLH occurs when macrophages, lymphocytes and NK cells, part of our immune system, don't work properly. The overactive inflammation causes damage to the surrounding tissue. In Emmy's case, the immune cells attacked her brain tissue," he said, while obviously searching for signs we understood.

When we didn't ask any questions, he continued. "One mutation came from you, Randy, and the other one came from Missy. The good news is that multiple people with HLH have been given a second chance with a bone marrow transplant. This is the only known cure.

We will start by testing your other children to see if any of them are a bone marrow match. If one or all match, we will then test them for HLH. I doubt any of them also have HLH, but we need to make sure. If the test is negative, they can be used as a donor. Sibling donors who are a perfect match give the patient the best chance of not rejecting the bone marrow.

Because of this diagnosis, it will no longer fall under neurology. I am passing Emmy's primary care over to the bone marrow transplant team from Dana Farber. They are the experts on HLH. I will still be following Emmy regarding her brain health, though, and I'll attend all the team meetings."

Stunned. We just stared at the neurologist like he was speaking Greek. The weight of the diagnosis was gut wrenching. Randy and I were responsible for what has happened to Emmy. We had passed down a genetic disease to our daughter. Not only that, our other kids were at risk of having it, as well.

This was not the diagnosis I'd prayed for. This was not the cure I wanted for Emmy. I didn't look at this diagnosis as a relief but as a life sentence. What if the rest of our children had CNS-restricted HLH and it just hasn't "turned on" yet. *Could this really be happening? What if our other kids need a bone marrow transplant? What are the chances we both had the same genetic mutation?*

Ignoring the pleas from the doctor to not research anything, Randy and I instantly googled everything we could about HLH and bone marrow transplants. We discovered that there were many families who had multiple children born with HLH, which made us worry even more. Of course, their HLH was different, as it started in the main organs and only moved to the central nervous system and brain if the body was left untreated. This more common HLH disease was also very deadly and quick acting. Whether it was genetic (familial) or acquired by a sudden illness or vaccine reaction, the person could die within days if not given appropriate medicine and steroids. I didn't know if I should be thankful it was in Emmy's brain or not, since it didn't kill her right away. Except, the regular HLH didn't leave too many people disabled, if they survived. What an evil disease.

Genetics is a strange field of study. Statistics, numbers, sequencing and resulting diseases are almost too much for any human to comprehend. A meeting about our mutated genes was arranged so Randy and I could understand what had been discovered about our genetic mutation.

Stained, unkept, white lab coats and awkward social cues—those doctors fit the stereotype of people who loved science and numbers. Hopefully, they would also simplify the data and let us know the probability of our other three children having HLH.

The average human is known to have multiple genetic mutations, but when you have one healthy gene, nothing usually happens because the recessive gene isn't needed. There are a few instances of genetic mutations where only one mutated gene can cause a disease, like the well-known sickle cell anemia. In regards to Emmy's genes, Randy and I both have one healthy perforin gene and one mutated gene, yet we passed only the mutated genes to Emmy. It is unknown why this specific HLH doesn't occur earlier in infancy, but we were told most children are well past their toddler years when symptoms start occurring.

NK cells and T cells are the main source of perforin. When Emmy broke her arm, somehow the normal functioning perforin (or so we think) switched off and allowed the immune system to wreak havoc. With an overabundance of immune cells not being stopped, they began attacking her brain. We finally had a diagnosis, but nothing like we imagined.

Up until now, I had tried hard to push away the thought of Satan having his hand in all of this. I knew bad things can just happen, but with so many things going terribly wrong, it had to be done on purpose. Then, my thoughts were confirmed when the doctors explained our genetic mutations to us. The news was so ridiculous, it could have been part of a plot of a horrible B-rated horror film.

"We received your results and have identified the mutations on each of your PRF1 genes. One mutation has already been discovered and logged, but the other is new and not reported yet. The two mutation variants found are the 443 and 666," the doctor began before Randy and I instantly looked at one another.

"The 666 must be yours!" we both said, pointing to each other in unison.

The doctors just looked at both of us, wondering how to break the news.

"Missy, your genetic mutation is 666. And, Randy, yours is 443," the female doctor said, trying to keep a straight face as my facial expression said everything she needed to know.

"No way. This has to be joke? Right? Randy put you up to this!" I questioned while looking directly at Randy.

"No, the 666 mutation has already been discovered, and that is one of Emersyn's mutations. It is accurate," she said, returning to her stoic behavior.

"Ha, that totally makes sense," Randy smirked.

I was stunned, humiliated, and confused. I felt like this was another slap in my face as a Christian. I wasn't known as a "pompous, holier than thou" Christian, but I was very vocal about the goodness of God. The number *666* just made me tremble at the realization that this truly was a battle of good versus evil. Ephesians 6 was right. This fight was not against flesh and blood, but against something much worse, something unseen.

We left the meeting, and I just couldn't help wondering if this was some kind of sign or what it all meant. *Was I cursed? Is that why God isn't helping Emmy?* I was sick to my stomach as we entered Emmy's room.

The BMT doctor was waiting in Emmy's room ready to discuss the immediate protocols that had to be started so Emmy could get a bone marrow transplant. There were certain medicines that were used to slow the progression of this type of HLH. Chemotherapy and steroids would be given weekly, not into her vein, but into the spinal fluid to stop the inflammation at the source. Not only was Emmy going to be given chemotherapy to get a bone marrow transplant, but they wanted to also put it directly into her brain?

"No! You can't do this. It's all too soon. How can we put chemotherapy directly into Emmy's brain while her body is spasming? What if it makes her worse and we never get her back?" I questioned the doctor.

"I know this is all very sudden, but Emmy is not well. We have to act now, or she could get worse and the prognosis is not good. We have to control the inflammation before she receives the bone marrow transplant or it could fail," she said, urging me to understand.

But I didn't understand. These spasms were not caused from HLH; they were started during the angiogram. But try as I may, I could not get anyone to listen. My pleas for answers fell on deaf ears. The chaos of Emmy's spasms made everyone push for getting her the bone marrow transplant, even if she was physically unstable, and it could kill her.

Since she was already sedated, they decided to do her first spinal treatment on December 22. I cringed as they put the needle in her spine, removed some fluid, and then injected her with the mix of chemo and steroids. She made it through safely, but you could tell she was not fully sedated. Her heart rate jumped, and her eyes started to flutter. Randy and I could barely watch. *What does she think is happening every time she wakes up with a tube in her throat?*

I could physically feel my throat closing, making every breath a chore. My heart was tightening and the unknown of whether Emmy would still have spasms when she woke, haunted me day and night. *Please God, don't let this chemo damage Emmy's brain more than it already is.*

The next day, Randy and I were blindsided. Emmy's medical team referred our family to PACT (Pediatric Advanced Care Team). This small group of people just popped into Emmy's door, unannounced. No one forewarned us about these people or why we needed them. *Aren't palliative groups only assigned to kids who are dying?* They assured me and Randy that they just help with kids who have complex issues and are a voice for the families when issues arise.

The team consisted of an attending doctor, a nurse practitioner, and a few resident doctors. After discussing all that Emmy had been through and the fact no one was researching why Emmy woke up with spasms after the angiogram, they asked if they could do something just for me and Randy. They offered to pay for a hotel room for us, for one night, to take a break away from the hospital.

"That is really nice, but no thank you. I don't want to leave Emmy. This has become way bigger than we bargained for, and I feel if I leave, something even worse is going to happen," I instinctually answered.

"We totally understand. Please, just think about it. The offer will always be available. And if you have any questions about anything, we are here to support you and Emmy," the nurse said.

Randy and I never left Emmy's side. We ate on different schedules and alternated sleeping in the sleep room so one of us would always be with her. There was no way we would leave the hospital—until unexpected guests showed up one day. Melissa and a few other ladies from church drove all the way to Boston to be with us, comfort us, and pray for us. This was a sign that maybe we should leave for a night. We really were so overwhelmed that we barely slept, ate or thought of anyone other than Emmy. We called PACT and said we would take the room for one night— if Melissa agreed to stay in the room with Emmy.

Melissa quickly agreed to stay with Emmy, so we broke free from the strange comfort of the hospital that had quickly become our prison. The air was crisp, and the walk was long. We had visited Boston two years before, but now I saw a side of Boston I'd never wanted to see. The walk along Longwood Avenue was our first time seeing it up close but it would not be our last. PACT was supposed to book a room next to the hospital but accidentally booked us a room a mile down the road at a bed-and-breakfast. We tried to relax and enjoy our Chinese takeout, but the unspoken worries filled the room. The food didn't taste good, the antique bed was uncomfortable, Emmy was sleeping on a ventilator, and our other kids were hundreds of miles away. I should be home in Virginia with them, with Emmy, and sleeping in my own bed. This was all so twisted and wrong.

The moment the sun peaked through the lacey curtains, we packed our bags and left. Being away from Emmy for one night wasn't a break for us at all. It left us too much time to digest all that had happened over the last few weeks and filled our thoughts with even more worry. We walked in complete silence towards the hospital, both knowing what we were headed back to.

Halfway back, I had a sudden urge to run away. I didn't want to go back to that hospital room. The sounds of hyperventilation and screaming were ringing in my years, and I just knew she would wake up the same. I had never cowered away from anything before, but here I was, cowardly telling Randy I didn't want to go back to what was waiting for us.

"Can we just slow down? Maybe grab some breakfast first? I don't want to go back there, Randy. I can't sit by and just watch Emmy on a ventilator. How is this even happening?" I began questioning.

"I don't want to go back, either, but Emmy needs us. She needs you. We have to be strong for her and you even said God brought us here for a cure, so we are going to get it for her," Randy said as he made eye contact with me. He made sure I understood that I had to think about Emmy first.

Once breakfast was over, I heard God whisper in my ear like every day since Virginia, "Missy, you know these things only come out from prayer and fasting."

God, leave me alone, please. You have forsaken us and left Emmy to be tortured to death. Show me you care and let her wake up without spasms, please, I am begging you. I quickly pushed His voice away and silently walked into the rotating glass doors of the hospital.

Christmas was in one day, and the ICU team felt like it was time to wake up Emmy and hopefully give us all a little Christmas cheer. The sedation meds were barely weaned, yet Emmy popped right awake and was quickly extubated. An alarming amount of sedation meds were still pumping into her veins at a constant drip, drip, drip, so Emmy was in and out of sleep all day. She woke three times in a full body spasm, but each time, the spasm stopped about three minutes later. Christmas day was very similar, yet she smiled when I told her a joke. *Yes, thank you, God! She is going to be all right! Our prayers were answered.*

What no one thinks about when they are watching their loved one sedated and hooked up to a breathing tube is the amount of sedatives it takes to keep the person comfortable and sleeping. Once again, we were hit with the reality that she was only calm because of the benzodiazepines and pain medicine still running through her veins twenty-four hours a day.

Emmy was awake and semi-coherent on sedation that would cause a large person to be laid out cold. When the doctors started to wean the fentanyl, the spasms returned. They turned it off completely during the night and had to give her "rescue doses" of morphine, in hopes it would help the withdrawal. I just couldn't take it. Why they weaned it so quickly is beyond me and the spasms were back, just as bad as before. I looked at Randy, told him I couldn't take it, and went straight to the sleep room. It was actually his turn to sleep there, but I didn't care. The loss of control and sight of Emmy like this was dragging me down to a deep, dark place I knew I had to get away from.

That night, before going to bed, I opened my Bible and wept. The tears were from the depths of my soul. I had never known a sadness so heavy and so devastating in my life. The emotional pain had now become physical pain and I cried like it was me being tortured.

As I calmed down and finally looked at my Bible, I began reading. I knew the Word of God well, so I just started finding scriptures about having faith in God, asking and receiving, storming God's throne room, and healing by His stripes—all of it. I am not sure what time I fell asleep, but I woke up at 6:00 am and rushed to see if my prayers helped Emmy receive any healing at all. The Bible does say, "Ask and you shall receive," right?

To my dismay, we were back at square one—panting, sweating, spasms, wrestling. Randy and I were ready to quit when, out of the blue, Ella and my two siblings, Jonathan and Nicole, walked in. They'd traveled to Virginia from Montana to keep the kids occupied for Christmas but still wanted to come visit Emmy. My mother-in-law, Linda, stayed back home with Eli and Everett.

The day was filled with fake smiles and hushed voices. I could see the sadness on everyone's faces as they saw the sheer magnitude of what Emmy was going through. She was panting and sweating; her right arm flailing; and clothed in just a diaper, which was now much too large for her ever-shrinking body. Everyone took turns holding her right hand and speaking softly to keep her reassured that she was going to be all right.

Seeing familiar faces lifted our spirits for a while—until two days later, when the ICU team said Emmy just couldn't keep going like this. Her heart rate was way too high again; her breathing was too rapid. They wanted to sedate her one more time. They hoped a longer sedation would either ease the spasms or give the team time to figure out something else to do.

To us, that was about as ignorant as sedating her the first time. We saw her spasms increase with every push of medicine, then with every wean. It made no sense, but what did Randy and I know? We were just frightened parents watching our daughter's quality of life deteriorate every minute we stayed in this hospital.

Before they began, they sat us down and requested that we allow them to trach her. *Tracheostomy.* Cut her throat and place a permanent breathing tube in.

My voice went from calm to screaming in a matter of seconds. "Are you serious? She was eating a hamburger the day before she came into the ICU, and now you want to trach her? Why hasn't anyone figured out why she was totally fine before her angiogram in Virginia? Now, every time your hospital does a procedure she gets worse? You are supposed to be the best hospital in the United States. And not one person can answer our questions!"

"No way. Missy and I do not want her trached. You can try to calm her brain down again, but there is no way you are cutting her throat open," Randy retorted.

Once again, the doctors began pushing propofol and ketamine to put Emmy asleep. Just like before, Emmy would fall asleep for seconds then explode wide-awake screaming. The fellow and attending ICU doctors were utterly confused. How did a little fifty-pound body not respond to ketamine and propofol? After multiple pushes of medicine, so much I thought she was going to die, Emmy finally stopped breathing so they could insert the breathing tube. That night as I sat in my sleeping room, far away from the ICU, I fell to my knees once again.

11

CHAPTER

Does the Lord delight in burnt offerings and sacrifices as much as in obeying the Lord? To obey is better than sacrifice.
—1 SAMUEL 15:22 (NIV)

New Year's Eve broke our hearts. The rhythmic sounds of the ventilator, followed by beeping from the monitor was not a good way to start out 2016. The night nurse tried to lift our spirits and placed a tiny, black top hat on Emmy's head. It didn't help. It only made me angrier at how upside down our world had become.

Ella, Nicole and Jonathan had to get back to Virginia, so they headed out early New Year's Day. It was hard watching Ella leave, but I knew it was too much for her to handle emotionally. My heart was not only hurting for Emmy, but for my other children who were going through their own kind of pain and sadness.

After our family left, Randy and I were once again all alone with Emmy. Sitting and worrying came easy, so we decided we better keep busy. Researching HLH and what could cause body spasms was all we could think of doing. As we were busy reading medical journals, we received a Facetime call from our littlest, Everett. The call was utterly heartbreaking. Everett was talking to us like we were in the room playing with him. He walked us around the house and told us what he had been doing to keep busy. He even asked, "Wanna pway wif me?" When Randy and I told him that we needed to go, he started making up stories to keep us on the call longer. At that point, we knew one of us needed to go home. Everett was too young to be without both parents this long, especially when his best friend was sick in a hospital.

I woke up early on January 2 to see Randy off to the airport. When I said goodbye, I realized my voice was raspy. At first, I thought it was just a tickle in my throat, but as the hours went on, my throat began swelling. As Randy was flying back to Virginia, I was frantically taking medicine and throat lozenges to ease the pain. There was no way I wanted to be kicked out of Emmy's room because I was sick. But I had no other symptoms than a sore throat.

Throughout the week, my throat stayed swollen. It hurt to swallow or even talk. Medicine was useless, and I was afraid the nurses would notice and kick me out. Then I remembered a book I had read while researching Emmy's brain disease. This book on brain mapping talked about trauma and sickness and if past trauma is not dealt with, it will become fragmented and store within our bodies, in the actual cell memory. Some experience or trigger can wake the memories up, causing you to relive and experience the pain all over again. Some trauma is so bad that it can manifest in actual sickness, resulting in a disease.

It took me a while, but I remembered back to when Emmy was first intubated. I remembered how I instantly felt like I had something stuck in my throat, while constantly worrying about her waking up, feeling like she was being suffocated. It had to be an emotional trigger, so I quickly looked for something other than medicine to help release the deep-rooted emotional feelings associated with Emmy being intubated.

I had brought dozens of essential oils with me, along with all the normal things people pack for a trip. I quickly looked up each oil's purpose and found that Angelica, also known as the "oil of angels", was specifically for respiratory illness associated with past trauma. The directions said to rub a small amount on the throat and then inhale the oil deeply for a few minutes. Within six hours of using Angelica essential oil, the soreness in my throat subsided. Studying homeopathic remedies to help Emmy's condition, ended up helping me.

Each day was long and monotonous with Randy gone and Emmy just lying there, not screaming and flailing in pain. I just knew her spasms were medicine related, but no matter what I researched, I just couldn't find any correlation. I tried to push feelings of hopelessness aside and update Emmy's followers on Facebook, but who wants to read about never-ending pain and sadness?

About three days after being sedated, Emmy began waking up. She was waking up so often, the nurses began using almost twice the amount of sedatives she was already receiving. I was beside myself. The reaction her body was going to have after being woke up terrified me. How could Emmy survive getting so many sedatives and pain killers?

Then out of nowhere, a friend on Facebook told me to read about a little girl who was suffering from an explosive seizure disorder called FIRES (febrile infection-related epilepsy syndrome). Her seizures were so bad, that she had to be sedated with phenobarbital to get her brain to stop. I quickly asked the doctors if we could change Emmy's sedation to something else. After a brief discussion and telling me that phenobarbital is very hard to wean off of, I insisted. *Why keep a tube down her throat if she keeps waking up? Wasn't the whole point to keep her brain asleep to fix the spasms?* Thankfully, they agreed.

Days of isolation in the ICU caused my mind to start playing tricks on me. *Was the devil really doing all of this? Should I be praying over Emmy constantly, or calling a pastor to pray? Was Emmy really possessed? Missy, don't be crazy, you know better...*

After realizing I had to do something better with my time than worry and talk to myself, I quickly threw on my headsets and started listening to music to drown out the noise. Anything positive, anything relatable, anything that made me think of Jesus; that is what I listened to. And then I stumbled across a singer who wrote a song that seemed to written just for us. Darlene Zschech wrote a song called "In Jesus' Name." That entire song, even during the interlude when she prayed, became like a daily prayer for me.

Later that week as I was mindlessly scrolling through Facebook, I saw a post by a fellow Young Living distributor. She was leading a group study called *21 Days of Prayer and Fasting for Your Business*. I was not at all interested in praying for my part-time job with Young Living, but maybe this was a sign from God to just stop being hardheaded and do what He had been asking me to do all along. Pray and fast.

I found myself clicking the links to a pastor, who was teaching lessons on prayer and fasting, and writing down notes. This was it! I was going to pray and fast, even though I still didn't understand why God was asking this of me. My heart was still very troubled as to why God continuously referred to the verse in Luke, but my mind was made up. I was going to begin praying and fasting first thing in the morning.

The barbital drip was working, and Emmy wasn't waking every two hours. The neurologist on call decided it would be smart to put an EEG on her head for a few days to watch her brain activity and see if the dystonic spasms resembled seizures. Nicole, her primary nurse, assured me she would not leave Emmy's side and that I should take a break from the room and sleep in the sleep room.

I spent the night studying what to do during a fast. Religious fasts are not just about starving yourself; it has to go hand in hand with prayer. I looked up parts of the Bible where prayer and fasting were used and why it was so important. I re-watched the videos of the pastor explaining how to effectively line up prayers for the next twenty-one days, and I wrote them down in my journal. My head and heart were finally aligned to do what God had been asking of me for more than a month.

When I woke the next morning, I was prepared and ready to obey God. I spent the entire day in Emmy's room, sitting on the tiny, frozen bed, praying nonstop. I watched the snow fall and continued to either pray or listen to worship music.

"Missy, you've been in here all day. You should really take a break and go eat something," Nurse Nicole urged, not realizing I was fasting.

"Okay, if you don't mind just keeping an eye on Emmy. I hate when she wakes up and I am not here," I said as I walked towards the door.

When I entered the "prayer closet," as I nicknamed the sleep room, I kneeled beside the bed and began praying. No matter where I was on my prayer list, my prayers kept going back to my children.

"God, please take these spasms away. Emmy needs relief, now. I know you have all the answers, so please tell me or a doctor what to do. Also, please spare Ella, Eli, and Everett from this disease. Let Ella be the perfect match for the BMT, and please help us go home!"

Hours of praying, yet I never heard God. I wasn't sure what I was expecting, but I continued praying things I had wrote down the night before. Hunger struck me early on, but I fought the urge and continued praying. I lost most of my appetite and hadn't eaten much since after arriving to Boston and quickly lost weight. Even without an appetite, stress was exhausting, and I had to eat something to keep me from becoming weak and shaky.

My prayer list was long and started with praying for our government and leaders. I had many friends and family members who were sick and needed healing, as well. Along with all the children stuck in the hospital, I always prayed for Emmy. When my prayers felt scripted and I ran out of words, I would put on my headphones and just silently sing and praise God. Worship was about the only thing that came naturally to me. I was reminded of David in the book of Psalms to, "Enter into his gates with thanksgiving and into His courts with praise." I just wished I could have been more like David, completely confident that God would deliver us.

It had been twenty hours since I had eaten. Four hours left in the day, but it felt like a thousand hours as my body started shaking uncontrollably. There was nothing I could do to stop the feeling of passing out, so I told God how sorry I was for quitting early and ran downstairs to get dinner.

The next day I couldn't fast from food and still felt really weak. I did, however, begin praying and worshipping, just like the day before. I really thought God was going to just answer all my questions, but He didn't. I tried not to think of how far away God felt, so I just kept praying for anyone I could think of. I felt a strong desire to pray for my friend Dawn, who had been diagnosed with breast cancer the month before Emmy was diagnosed with brain inflammation. She had five children and needed all the prayers she could get. I prayed for family and friends and even Emmy's hospital team. Once again, I prayed all day, even though I was too weak to fast. Overcome with exhaustion, I fell asleep without going back to Emmy's room.

Early the next morning, I crept into Emmy's room, just in time to see the on-call ICU neurologist checking on her. Emmy had developed full-body twitches just days after starting the phenobarbital, but I was warned that it was a possible side-effect. As he finished up reading her chart and looking at her body movements, I asked him for the hundredth time, "How in the world could all of this start from an angiogram? I read they use dye during the procedure. Do you think she had an allergic reaction to the dye?"

"No. People do not react to iodine like that. It would have been a physical allergic reaction with hives. I just don't know, Missy. Have you called CHKD to find out what sedation they used because sometimes people can have an acute dystonic reaction to different types of sedation," he said nonchalantly, not realizing he had never uttered those three words to me before.

Acute dystonic reaction. What in the world was that? That was the missing key. I knew what dystonia was, but not an acute dystonic reaction. At that exact moment, God told me to look it up.

Some people think God only speaks exact words from the scriptures, but they are greatly mistaken. God is the creator of words and communication and is not limited to words of the Bible. God guided me through very detailed research, where I ended up finding a medical journal article on the NIH (National Institute of Health) website. I had searched before, but I never found anything close to what I had discovered.

The article I outlined had the exact bodily spasms Emmy had been having since her angiogram. Not only that, the article was written about the effects caused specifically by propofol. Propofol had been the medication used, not only to sedate Emmy for the angiogram, but every single procedure since then. The study showed that although patients had used it successfully in the past, a random occurrence can happen in the brain and cause acute dystonic reaction.

"This is it! Yes! Nicole, this is it!" I screamed to Emmy's nurse.

It had been the propofol ever since the beginning. The research clearly said to stop using the propofol immediately.

I begged for her to call the ICU fellow so I could show him what I'd found. He immediately came down and read the article.

"This explains why both times you tried to sedate her with propofol, she would wake right up. Her brain's signals were so confused; the sedation couldn't touch her!" I said, summarizing the entire article in case he wasn't reading fast enough "Look! The article also lists the medication to stop the spasms."

"Great find, Mom." (I hated that I'd lost my identity and was only referred to as "mom"). "I am going to discuss this with her team, but we also need to prepare to get her off phenobarbital. The movements she's recently started having while sedated are also acute dystonic reactions," he said in a calm and caring manner. "I will get back with you as soon as I can."

The doctor took the article and left. God did it! He gave me the answer. I was so full of energy, I could have run a marathon. Emmy was going to be alright.

But why did I need to pray and fast just to hear the voice of God? What did fasting change? I started to question, once again, why God had required me to do something so simple to get Emmy help. Why did my obedience matter?

"God, why did I need to fast and pray? Why did you wait to tell me the answer until after I'd fasted? This is just so wrong!" I screamed and cried to God.

"What does my Word say, Missy?" God quietly replied.

I searched scriptures and prayer books I had with me. I googled for explanations. After reading everything I could find, I realized they all said the same thing. Fasting doesn't change the plans of God; it opens and prepares our hearts for what God has for us. It prepares us for the answer we are about to receive or the battle that lies ahead. I realized, now, that not only did God need me to trust Him fully, but He needed me to stop relying on my own knowledge and strength. He was teaching me to trust Him in every circumstance, in every problem and in every unchartered territory He would send me in. All the white noise of HLH, genetic diseases, spasms, and medicine was distracting me from the one voice I should have been listening to all along—God's voice. I had no idea He was preparing me for an even tougher battle ahead.

Randy was still in Virginia, but I just knew this was the answer we'd been looking for. I talked with the ICU team and everyone seemed to look at me like I was "that parent"—the parent in denial of a deadly disease that was the cause of her daughter's pain. *Why aren't they listening to me? Didn't they read the published medical journal?* My mind was swimming with questions. They said they would discuss the article and figure out what to do. They claimed that propofol is the safest known sedation medicine, and none of them had ever witnessed a reaction like this before. I felt like they were dancing around the possibility that they'd missed something big in a patient's care. I started to get very defensive that they were going to ignore what I had found.

The next morning, I attended rounds ready for battle. As I walked out of Emmy's room, there was a new ICU attending starting that week. I hated changeover. Every two weeks, the attending doctors rotated out, and I would have to fill in the new one. I patiently waited for their daily medical recap on Emmy to finish, and then I inserted my voice into the narrative.

"Has anyone discussed what I found out about propofol? You all don't seem to care that it is the single reason she is in the ICU right now."

"Yes, we have read over everything," the new doctor stated very sternly.

"Well, are you going to do anything? Will you get her off the sedation and give her the medicine to stop the spasms? I just know this is it. I have been praying for this answer, and God answered me."

"We hear you. But we really need to look at everything and make a plan—" the doctor started to say.

"Do you understand that I am 100 percent certain that this is what happened to her? If you don't stop giving her propofol and take her off sedation, I swear I will run through this hospital naked till I get your attention!" I boldly stated.

"Well, Missy, that isn't necessary. But you are the parent. And no matter what we think, if you say she had a reaction to propofol, we have to put it on her allergy list. And as for the rest of you," she said to the residents, "make copies of that article and give it to the staff. See if you can find anything else related to propofol side effects."

God did it again. He put a doctor on her current team who finally listened. The last staff could have cared less. My heart was going to explode. Hope was returning. I just knew when they woke her up, the spasms would be gone. Then I received the second-best news of the day—Ella was a 10/10 donor match. Eli and Everett were only a 5/10 match, so the team would be sending Ella's DNA to Cincinnati to check if she had HLH. That news was going to be hard to wait for over the next three weeks.

Randy flew back to Boston, just in time for the next round of stress. About two weeks into the phenobarbital sedation, Emmy not only was having visual body twitches, her tongue became enlarged. The side effect of phenobarbital was called "pentobarb tongue" by the nurses. The tongue became swollen from the medication—so swollen it won't fit in her mouth. This was so disturbing to see on Emmy, especially when they had to move it out of the way to clean her mouth or adjust the breathing tube. A thin layer of moistened gauze was placed over her tongue so it wouldn't dry out. The entire scene was hard to look at.

January 10 was the day they started to wean Emmy off the phenobarbital. Not only was her tongue protruding out of her mouth, but her body was still twitching in a perfect rhythmic motion—arms and legs in unison. On the fourth day of weaning, she started to wake up. The dosages of the other sedation meds were still too high to let her breath on her own, so they gave her a muscle relaxer, also knows as a paralytic, so she wouldn't wake up and fight the breathing tube.

After the first week of this sedation, Randy and I began demanding that all the other medicine they started giving her back in November be weaned. The ICU team agreed but insisted that she remain on Artane, since it is specifically for dystonia. I told them I'd seen her get worse with the first dose, but they didn't believe me. We reluctantly agreed to keep her on it as long as all the other medications were stopped. We had learned to fight our battles one at a time, because we had a war to win. By the time Emmy was extubated 21 days later, she had been weaned off everything but Artane.

Three days before removing the paralytic, the doctors administered the medicine benztropine, which was recommended in the medical journal to stop the acute dystonic reaction. Even though she was on a paralytic, her entire body had still been pulsing. Within thirty minutes of the first dose, the pulsing body movements from the phenobarbital drip stopped. It was like someone had just turned a switch off in her brain. Everyone was ecstatic, so the medicine was given as directed for three more days.

The day before we all decided to wake Emmy up and extubate her, the nurse and I gave her a bath and French braided her hair. Emmy had not had a real bath since the day before her brain biopsy on December 7. I was so ready for her to wake up, dystonia free, so we could get a bone marrow transplant closer to home and be near our family. I quickly learned that no matter how positive I was, something was always waiting around the corner to crush it.

12
CHAPTER

Trust in the Lord with all your heart and lean not on your own understanding; in all your ways acknowledge Him, and He shall direct your paths.
—PROVERBS 3:5-6 (NKJV)

Another important day to sear a horrible memory of Emmy into by brain. January 19, Ella's fifteenth birthday, was the day the doctors decided to extubate Emmy. While the benztropine stopped the full-body twitches from the phenobarbital sedation, agonizingly she still woke up with full body dystonia. Randy was sitting on the windowsill bed, and I was in the bed holding Emmy, both of us utterly defeated. I knew I'd heard God, but maybe I was supposed to do more. Maybe I was supposed to fast longer, pray more prayers. But how? I was doing all I could do and barely keeping it together. Just as I was falling into thoughts of despair, the word Benadryl came to mind.

"Can you give her Benadryl? Can we just see if that will make a difference? That was listed as an alternate medicine to benztropine in the medical journal and it also helped before in Virginia," I begged the nurse.

"Hold on. I don't see why we can't. Let me just call the doctor and clear it," the nurse said as she picked up her phone.

A half dose of Benadryl of 12.5 mg was ordered, but Emmy was only half of a child weighing a mere thirty-five pounds or sixteen kilograms as listed on the emergency sheet above her bed. Her body was small and bony, but her left thigh and bicep had swollen with muscle from the spasms. She looked of death. It was so hard to see the feeding tube in her left nostril, the diaper sagging off her concave stomach, and her bony hips, knees and shoulders. And the tubes were everywhere. The tubes of IV fluid, IV nutrition, and all of the sedation meds were like a spiderweb of death. If I truly stopped and looked at her, I would have lost the last bit of sanity I was holding onto. A breakdown was inevitable; it was only a matter of time.

The nurse received the Benadryl and pushed it through one of Emmy's many tubes. *Please work. Please work. Please work.* I was praying so hard I could hardly hear any noise in the room. Three minutes later and everything was calm. Emmy's body went completely limp. At first, I began to panic, but then realized it was the Benadryl. The spasms stopped in three tiny minutes. All I could do was tell Emmy the most biblical words that I remembered: "It is finished. Baby, the spasms are gone. Jesus did it."

Emmy lay on that bed for four hours without so much as a spasm or muscle twitch. She was afraid of using her left arm, in fear of triggering a spasm, but it never did. She tried to smile, but every single muscle in her body was weak from months of spasming followed by twenty-one days of sedation. Randy and I smothered her, loving on her and telling her we were going to get her home.

Just like before, our high hopes crashed hard to the ground. At first, it was her right arm twitching. Then came the left arm followed by the rest of her body. The panting and hyperventilation heightened with every spasm. The Benadryl lasted only four hours, but we knew that when we saw the body spasms come back, it was because there was something else causing them. Was it the sedation still pumping through her veins or the Artane?

Later that night, the movement disorder neurologist entered Emmy's room. The room was dark and had an eerie feeling of hope lost. We were stuck in a moment of time, realizing the movements were not permanent, but also not sure how to permanently get rid of them. Fear was causing me to second-guess myself. I knew I heard God. He led me to that medical journal. I knew God wouldn't fail me, and there was no way my brain had made something like this up. Only God could reveal something that was unknown to any of us, including the doctors.

"Let's talk options," the movement disorder neurologist said.

Before he could say another word, I interrupted him, "Whatever medicine and sedatives she is still on, I want them weaned now. Something is still causing her brain to do this, and it isn't HLH. We have watched her body movements for eighteen months, and not until the propofol sedation for her angiogram did her body react this way. Medicine is not going to fix this. We need to get her off everything, but we need to keep giving her Benadryl. It is the only thing that has worked so far."

He stared at me for a moment and then began talking in a calm, condescending voice. "Benadryl isn't a long-term solution, but Artane is. It can help with the movements, especially if the phenobarbital is causing more dystonia. Benztropine, Artane and even some properties of Benadryl are all in the same medicine family. But Artane is specifically for dystonia and also listed as a medicine for acute dystonic reaction. We need to keep her on it to help her through what you think is an acute dystonic reaction," he said mockingly.

God was clearly telling me to not give her more meds. I picked my head up and looked him straight in the eyes and firmly said, "No! I know Artane made her worse just hours after she'd been given the first dose. She was fine before sedation and way better before you gave her Artane." I was not used to speaking like that to people who clearly were smarter than me. This was the point I realized I needed to find courage to fight for Emmy, because this doctor surely wasn't interested in what I had to say.

But then I heard Randy stand up and walk over to the hospital bed. "Missy, let's just do what the doctor says. If he thinks Artane will help, let's try. What else is there to do?"

"*No*! I know Artane made her worse. I don't care if he's a specialist; he hasn't seen Emmy day in and day out like I have. I won't do it," I cried. Randy's words cut me like a knife. Why was he agreeing with this doctor?

"OK, then if you think Benadryl is the cure, we will give Benadryl for one week to see if Emmy gets better. If not, then we go up on the Artane," the doctor conceded.

"Fine. But I still don't think Artane is the right medicine. Can't you research anything else?" I urged him through my tears.

"Sure, but just know we already tried Sinemet, and there aren't many more meds out there. And to be honest, the possibility of all these medicine reactions you say compounded one on top of another into a huge dystonic storm is not possible. I think you don't understand what's happening to her brain. First you say its sedation, Propofol and the rest; now you say its

Artane. We have never seen anything like this before. I'm really sorry, but I think you're wrong." And then he walked out of Emmy's room.

His words were the final knife to my heart. Was I really as ignorant as he was making me feel? Making up excuses for my child who has a brain disease that was probably causing all of this? Why had God told me anything at all? Did I just "want" to hear God so much, that I'd made all of this up?

Over the next few days, the spasms continued to get worse, so we opted to increase the dose of Benadryl to a full dose. I had to fight the new ICU doctor to even continue Benadryl because too much of an anticholinergic can cause horrible side effects. Artane and Benadryl are both in the anticholinergic family, and when the body is given too much without being able to build up tolerance, it causes a host of side effects like dehydration, the shakes, black stool, increased body temperature, cognitive delays, and more. The ICU doctor wanted to increase Artane over Benadryl, even though we had already discussed the plan with the movement disorder neurologist. Benadryl was going to be given for the next week and I wouldn't back down.

The tension between Randy and I was increasing. When I get my mind set on something, it overtakes everything I do. I was laser focused on stopping the spasms. I let Randy know every second of the day he was wrong to agree with the doctor and Artane was harming Emmy. He was so fed up with me that he refused to talk about anything regarding Emmy.

Marriage already comes with its hardships, but marriage during chaos and sickness is the test of a lifetime. Our marriage already survived while we both were active duty, which not many marriages do, but this was by far harder. I'd also read that couples with a special-needs child are 10 percent more likely to get divorced over the national average, which is at an all-time high of 50 percent. We learned from the first moment Emmy was brought home in a wheelchair that this disease was going to test the bedrock of our vows.

Randy had asked me repeatedly why God wasn't telling him the same information I was hearing. I had no idea why. I constantly prayed that God would reveal everything to him the same way He did to me, but He never did. God was working with Randy on other things, unknown to me and not so obvious to Randy at the time. We both would be used in this journey, but just in different ways. Hearing God speak was not because I was "holier" than Randy, but all my trust was always in God. No matter what the doctors could or couldn't do, I believed from the beginning God held the answers to what was wrong with Emmy. I clung to that fact day after day and focused my attention, prayers, and thoughts, purely knowing God held the answer. I also knew that, ultimately, God was in control, and nothing we or the doctors did could change that.

Finding the courage to use my voice was also a testament to this journey. Being bold in the knowledge of what God was telling me was one of the most difficult things I had ever done. To people who are not saved, I sounded crazy using God as a reason for what I was saying. "Oh, God spoke to you, did He?" was always the reply. How could people see life and death all around them and not put their trust in a higher power? Boston seemed so distant, almost unable to believe in faith and miracles. The quest for knowledge and information seemed to push out the need for faith. Knowledge overshadowed the supernatural.

At first, I was very confused and hurt as to why Randy didn't support me on the Artane issue. But knowing God was leading me to the answers, I just kept my eyes focused on Him and only Him. That disagreement eventually strengthened our marriage by teaching us to trust each other through thick and thin, even when we didn't understand the true intentions of the other person. We had to learn to trust one another, because there was so much more our family would have to endure.

A week passed by, and the spasms were still persistent. The Benadryl helped but not enough. As decided upon by the movement disorder neurologist, yet still against my will, Artane was increased the last week of January. I was heartbroken and betrayed. I knew I saw her body movements get worse with each dose they gave her. Randy said he couldn't see it, but I knew I did. My cries to stop the Artane and just continue with Benadryl fell on deaf ears.

A family meeting was scheduled a week later to discuss Emmy's bone marrow transplant, overall health, and whether Ella had HLH or not. I had almost forgotten about Ella's test and felt myself become nauseated as I walked in the family conference room. Emmy's BMT doctor started out by saying, "Hi," and began introducing everyone, but I instantly interrupted her by asking about Ella's test results.

"Well, Ella's test came back, and it says she is a carrier of HLH but does not have HLH. Mom, she has only your mutation, and because you have been healthy your whole life, we feel confident she can be the donor. Do you both want to use her as a donor?" she said and we both nodded yes. "We have used other siblings before with only one mutation, and the BMT was successful. If you decide not to, we have to find an outside donor. When the donor is not related or a 10/10 match, Emmy will have a bigger chance of getting graft-versus-host disease (GVHD). Her body could even reject the transplant, or parts of her body could be attacked by antibodies. The mildest could be a skin rash or stomach ulcers, or the disease ultimately could come back."

Randy and I just stared at each other and we both said, "Yes, use Ella!"

"We have another issue we need to talk about. When we did the echocardiogram last week, we found that 20 percent of Emmy's heart is not functioning properly."

"What do you mean? She had an echocardiogram in Virginia during the angiogram, and they said her heart was perfectly fine. What did this? Is it the medication she is on or the reaction to propofol?" I asked.

"We don't know. But we need to know if you plan on doing the bone marrow transplant here or if you want to be somewhere closer to home, like Duke University Hospital?" she asked.

Randy and I asked if we could discuss it, and the meeting concluded. Flying Emmy home in a medical airplane was going to be difficult, but the absence of family and friends was ultimately harder. We pondered and prayed for a day and decided that being alone here in Boston was way too hard, so we asked to go to Duke University.

The director of Duke's bone marrow transplant center called us, and we discussed Emmy's case. My biggest concern was having a neurologist present to help manage the body spasms. He was very enthusiastic and positive and stated that they had everything Emmy needed. We instantly told the ICU doctor to schedule our flight to Duke.

We had one more family meeting with the air transport team leader, ICU team, BMT doctor, and movement disorder neurologist to make sure everything was done correctly with Emmy's condition. The ICU team believed if Emmy was left awake while flying, it would put her at risk. They told the transport team that she needed to be sedated.

"No! I don't care if she's thrashing around for the two-hour flight, she can't be sedated again. We have to wean her off these meds. They are making her condition worse," I urged them.

"Patient safety and flight safety have to be our first priority, Missy. We can't keep her strapped in a bed like she is. You and Randy move her all day long. She will be miserable forced to stay in one position," the ICU chief told us.

Randy and I reluctantly agreed. We knew that if she had any huge episodes of dystonia while being strapped down, especially in the middle of the sky, it would quickly escalate.

"Remember, you cannot use propofol. The only reason why she is in the ICU is because of her reaction to it," I quickly added.

The air transport team leader said he understood, and then Randy and I left to call our kids about the good news.

It was a few days into February, and Emmy was not only spasming harder and more frequently, but her hyperventilation had also become worse. Before, she would hyperventilate only during a dystonic episode and would go back to normal when it was finished. The sweating, screaming, hyperventilation, and flushing were now worse than ever.

It was at this point, I realized we were surrounded by the kindest people on earth. I know God put these specific nurses in our room, at this exact moment. Most of them were in their twenties, and none of them had children, yet. I don't think they fully comprehended what they were getting into when they signed up to be on Emmy's medical team. Everything they learned in nursing school was put to the test with Emmy. They had to be on their "A" game with Emmy's exhausting yet fragile condition. Through the spasms, more than once, Emmy managed to yank out her feeding tube, break apart the sedation lines that led directly to her heart, and even defecate all over the bed. They worked fast, seamlessly and always knew what to do. Their quick thinking and understanding of every situation saved Emmy from so much more that could have negatively impacted her health.

These nurses wrote detailed notes in Emmy's hospital records, they had extended handovers so not one detail would be missed, and they maintained complete composure when I was an emotional wreck. All of them became emotionally attached to Emmy and were just as upset by her condition as we were. They grew to love Emmy, and I could see it by their actions. Many of them would send me on breaks, and I would return to them in bed with Emmy, just trying to comfort her and hold her little body still. They truly were a gift from God. Without them and all of the things they did for us, I am not sure we would have survived the ICU.

From January 26 to February 6, Emmy's dose of Artane had tripled from 3 mg three times a day to 9 mg three times a day. Every set of directions I read, this rapid increase was not protocol. During each increase, we still saw the painful body spasms, but the movements morphed into constant pulsing motions. It was very similar to what we had seen while she was sedated with phenobarbital. The IV sedation medicine was still being weaned, so it was hard keeping up with what was causing the worsened side effects. Was she withdrawing, reacting to Artane, or was her brain getting worse? Once again, confusion dominated coherent thinking.

Randy and I had begun fighting for the sleep room. The sound of Emmy hyperventilating was unbearable. This was the type of psychological warfare no parent should have to endure. We were borderline insane. We both needed that room, but we were too afraid to leave her alone, without one of us there to comfort her.

I don't know what Randy did while in the sleep room, but when I got there, I would just fall on my face bawling. In between the sobs, I just cried out to God. *Why is this still happening? Why isn't her pain over?* And do you know what He had the audacity to reply with? "Trust Me." Now I knew it was God talking. Trust and waiting for an answer were the farthest thoughts from my mind. I wanted to act, to do something *now* to end Emmy's suffering. I had no time to stop and trust anything or anyone.

Maybe I was holding back my trust, but who can blame me? I had done what He'd asked, even received an answer, yet Emmy was still in pain. I saw kids come into the ICU on the brink of death and walk out a week later. If God truly loved us, why was Emmy being tortured by medicine, her brain disease, drug withdrawal, or whatever else seemed to be part of her "care" plan.

"I know I told you to use me for your purpose, to help me submit to Your will and to help grow my faith, but this is not what I asked for. This unforgiving brain disease and now watching her body in constant spasms are not what I asked for. This is more than any human can bare. Are you even listening to me? Did you forget about us?" My bitterness and anger were obvious as I prayed that night to God.

During the day, I started wearing headphones almost nonstop to muffle Emmy's crying and unnerving hyperventilation sounds. I remember listening to "Oceans" by Hillsong United. It was strangely prophetic because, two months before Emmy ended up in the hospital, our family had presentation day at our weekly homeschool group. Every week, a family would get up and share something to the group, in hopes that getting up in front of crowds would help the kids become better public speakers. We had already done a family speech earlier that year, so I got up without my kids and played "Oceans" for everyone. I then talked about how I would listen to it while running or whenever I had a free moment. I explained that God calls us to scary, deep places, which will grow our faith, if we allow it and obey Him. The deeper we go, the more trust we need, and the more our faith will grow. I really had no idea at the time what that song truly meant, until now.

When it was my night for the sleep room, I would throw my headphones on and just silently worship and praise God for hours. I didn't know what else to do. Nobody prepared us on how to handle a child suffering so severely. I was following the advice of the song by Casting Crowns telling me to, "Praise Him in the Storm." That is what I was going to do until the storm was over, even though I had no idea when that was.

13

CHAPTER

In the day that I cried out, You answered me, and made me bold with strength in my soul.
—PSALM 138:3 (NASB 2020)

The month of February was a pivotal moment for me. I still hadn't truly found the courage to speak up. Fear kept me from saying when I believed and demanding changes be made. I had tried when I told the doctor Artane was making her worse, but he talked us into keeping Emmy on it. But not any longer. I was done living like this, in a hospital, watching Emmy get worse every day.

Emmy's spasms were still unimaginably incessant. The doctor insisted every day on increasing her dose of Artane, yet Randy and I strongly opposed increasing anything at this point. It was obvious that medicine was not the answer. Emmy's spasms were stronger and more painful. Her body was now pulsing. She was getting worse by the day. This had to end.

A call from North Carolina came up on my caller ID. I almost didn't answer it, but when I did, I heard the transplant doctor's voice from Duke University on the line.

"Missy, I am calling with some bad news. A certain doctor called us and stated that Emmy is just too sick to be moved for at least two more weeks. I understand that this disease is moving rapidly and they won't let her be moved. I am truly sorry."

"No! It isn't her disease. What's happening with her is a result of sedation or whatever she gets every time she has a procedure. Please, we want to be closer to home. Isn't there anything you can do?" I pleaded

"I'm sorry. The primary care team in Boston has to clear her to be transported, and they won't do it right now. If anything changes, please let me know."

Heartbreak after heartbreak. Why wasn't anything working in our favor? The world was still unraveling with no end in sight. Boston was no longer a place for hope, it was now our prison. The news affected everyone.

With my mind fixed on Emmy, I had not even thought about how our other kids were handling everything happening. I called my friend Melissa and she reluctantly told me everything. I knew she didn't want to burden me with any bad news, but my kids were suffering, and my mom was having a hard time adjusting to grandkids. I just slid down the wall onto the floor, in the middle of the hallway, and began crying uncontrollably. Melissa patiently waited for me to calm down and then prayed over me. I hit a breaking point. I was finally ready to quit, to throw in the towel. The ache I felt was too much to endure. *My God, my God, why have You forsaken us?* God was nowhere to be found. We were fighting too many battles on too many battlefronts, and we were doing it alone, with no backup cavalry in sight.

Compounding pain with more confusion, Emmy started spiking fevers daily. The nurses were sure it was anticholinergic side effects, from too much Artane and Benadryl. But who could really prove that with all of the other symptoms happening?

Another family meeting was held after talking to Duke, and we all decided to just move forward with the bone marrow transplant at Boston. It was not what I wanted. I wanted the spasms to be gone before anything was done to Emmy. I wanted to go home. I wanted to be with my other kids. But what I wanted had nothing to do with any of this. Whatever was happening was not being orchestrated by me, Randy or God. This felt chaotic and unplanned.

The bone marrow doctor then told us that Emmy would be scheduled to have tests done prior to doing her transplant, and many of these tests required her to be sedated.

"Again? Are you kidding me? Can't you do them while she's awake? Why do we have to keep doing this to her? Can't we wait a few months for the BMT? This isn't HLH causing all of these problems; it's literally the medicine, and you just want to keep giving her more," I cried.

"Missy, the last thing we want to do is make Emmy worse. I will schedule everything that needs sedation to be done all at once. We will immediately wake her up and try to keep her comfortable. But bone marrow transplants are hard on the body, and we need to make sure her body is healthy enough to withstand the chemo. We will also use these tests after her transplant to make sure it didn't harm her organs," the doctor said calmly.

If it wasn't for the bone marrow team from Dana Farber, I don't think we would have agreed to doing the bone marrow transplant. They eased most of our fears. I guess when you are used to seeing kids dying and then sending them even closer to death with poison, you learn to make everyone feel safe, heard, and important. Thankfully, everyone I met from Dana Farber did just that.

It was now the middle of February; confusion and chaos were the only constant. Emmy's body continued to increase in muscle tone on her left side from the sheer power of the spasms. But something else was happening, and we couldn't explain it. While her body had already started pulsing, now her mouth began moving in a rhythmic motion, along with her tongue. The sheer rhythm of the entire thing should have been a warning sign to the movement disorder neurologist, but he was barely around to check on her.

I thought back to a horror film I'd seen in high school. I rarely watched them, afraid to think that demons exist. But when I looked at Emmy, I saw that movie playing in front of me. Emmy's body was thrashing and contorting in ICU Room 30. Along with the constant hyperventilation, screaming, flushing, and sweating, Emmy's movements became far worse and indistinguishable from her original movements. Her body was stiff as a board in the hospital bed with her back arched, only her head and toes touching the bed. Her tongue was in constant movement, and her screams were turning into groans. She resembled the girl from *The Exorcist*. Exorcist. Possessed girl tortured by a demon.

I never uttered those words out loud, afraid it would come true or, worse yet, was true. My fear grew like a raging fire, and I became addicted to praying to hide my fears. I prayed everywhere I went. Bible verses I had memorized, simple prayers, and even repeating worship songs became my focus. I thought I could change the situation by my actions, by praying more. The fear convinced me that I was fighting the devil himself. Thoughts of evil things pervaded my mind. *What if she is being attacked by a spirit? How do I cast out a spirit? Am I losing my mind? Should I stay by her side praying all day and all night? What am I doing wrong, God? Do you even care about us? Are you punishing us for something? Are you listening to me?*

At this point, I think ICU psychosis had hit me hard. The nurses kept warning me how being stuck in a room, night and day, focused on one thing, can cause a person to lose their mind. But knowing what I knew about the forces of good and evil, seeing it all play out in front of me, I wasn't sure this was made up at all. First of all, there was the genetic mutation 666. Emmy's body looked like it was possessed. The one verse God repeated to me daily was also referring to a possessed boy. And all of this was happening in a Godless place, a deserted faithless place, with no Christian support system. Only God knew if this was spiritual or not, but it sure felt like we were living through a battle of good versus evil.

How quickly fear ripped the faith and boldness right out of my hands. If only I would have closed my mouth for five seconds and listened to what God was saying. But I was beyond that. I am not sure how people really stay calm and positive while they are looking at a small girl of only thirty pounds, screaming, hyperventilating, and arching in unimaginable ways.

Intubation was inevitable for these preliminary tests. Once again, it happened on another day that we should have been celebrating. Eli's twelfth birthday was shadowed by the fear that Emmy would not make it through another sedation.

The doctors promised me that they would accomplish all the tests in one day, but once again, they lied. One day turned into three days. Pulmonary test, echocardiogram, MRI, intrathecal chemo, eye and dental exam, and a diaphragm test—all were performed in those three days. Passing all the tests proved that she was now ready to be pumped full of poison and brought closer to the brink of death.

Emmy's brain was on fire, and the doctors continued to pour on the gas. I prayed every single day that Emmy wouldn't remember anything that happened in ICU Room 30. Randy and I were assured that she was on so many sedation meds that there would be no way she would ever remember. But we remember. We remember everything that happened the next few weeks like it was yesterday. I remember the nurses crying because nothing would help Emmy. I remember the doctors afraid to come in the room because they either had no answers or knew I would scream at them again. The fevers, hyperventilation, and spasms were out of control as soon as she woke from being sedated those three days. The nurse instantly recognized Emmy's breathing had changed, now sounding more labored, so she decided to intervene.

Those first hours sent us deeper into a world of chaos. Emmy seemed to lose even more of herself. I noticed she wasn't crying, as if her emotions had vanished. It was just hyperventilation and tongue movements while her body contorted. Her hand accidentally grabbed her NG tube from her nose and pulled it out again. This happened almost weekly, forcing her to be still while a new one was replaced. Her body quickly spiked a fever so high the nurses had to cover her in ice. The CPAP was used to control her breathing. All of this was in a matter of hours following extubation.

To make matters even more complicated, we had decided the day before to have my mom bring the kids up from Virginia. We didn't know that Emmy was going to be this bad. They stayed in the hotel next to the hospital. We wanted them to be close so one of us could walk to see them while the other watched over Emmy. We tried to prepare them for what Emmy was going through and fake our smiles, but they knew us too well. When they came into Emmy's room, my heart just broke. The look on their faces said it all. Their sister looked like she was dying. She was a shell of her former self. I tried to assure them that this was from medicine interacting with her brain, but that didn't seem to convince them. Emmy couldn't even interact with them. Eli and Emmy used to laugh and joke, but now she just looked past him while he tried hard to get her attention. I just wanted them to leave. The pain in their eyes was torture and too much to bear. Everything about Emmy was getting worse, and I just knew that, whatever it was, it had happened with the increase of Artane and the sedation.

Over the next week, I poured over medical articles on Artane. I tried alternate wording and different phrases during each search, but what Emmy was experiencing never showed up as a symptom. I was ready to give up, but then I received a text from my Aunt Teresa on love. "Love conquers all. Perfect love casts out fear." After reading and pouring over the verses she sent me, I realized that I was doing everything out of fear. What was I afraid of? Watching my baby girl die? But even death would be better than torture. Or was it the feeling of embarrassment that I spoke of God so boldly, yet God was still allowing all of this to happen. To tell you the absolute truth, it was both, but because my mind was so preoccupied with figuring this whole thing out on my own, I forgot the most important thing—love. I should have been working out of love for my daughter, but I wasn't. I was not her mom anymore, but a caretaker, a researcher, and someone to wrestle her body parts so she wouldn't fall out of the bed. I had forgotten I loved her, probably because, at that point, I saw her as the reason we were here. She was causing us to be separated as a family. She was the one who'd gotten HLH. This was all her fault.

Caretaker's guilt and blame had hit me hard. How could I ever think those mean, evil things? None of this was Emmy's fault, and I knew it. But the anger was pouring out at the seams. I hated it here. I hated the ICU, the doctors, the diagnosis, the evilness of the cure—all of it. I hated life. And that was when I knew I needed to leave that room for a few hours and find love again. Love was the only reason Jesus died for us, and if He could do that, I could repent and go back into that room and love Emmy the right way. We needed to find the reasons all of this was happening, not to help me leave the hospital but so I could love her through the pain and get our family back together.

The BMT team decided that March 4 or March 7 would be the starting day for chemo to prepare her for the bone marrow transplant. Chemo would last fourteen days, and then the bone marrow would be given on the day they call T-0 or day zero. At this point, I had to actually research how bone marrow is donated because I'd been so wrapped up in studying movement disorders I'd forgotten to research anything else. The process would involve drilling into Ella's lower back, the pelvis, sucking the marrow out and then taking what was harvested and removing the stem cells. Those cells would be put into an IV bag and given through Emmy's vein. Somehow, the stem cells just "know" how to find a way to Emmy's bone marrow and graft to create all new cells. The whole process was never what I would have imagined. All I knew was that the body and all of its parts were fearfully and wonderfully made (Psalm 139:14).

Benadryl, Ativan rescue doses, morphine, and whatever else they could give Emmy were being used around the clock. She was getting more meds than if they would have just left her sedated. Keeping track of the amount of medicine, the side effects, and how to keep Emmy comfortable was a never-ending job. But who else was going to do it if not for us and the nurses?

Many people were calling us and sending positive messages. Many of them would say that Randy and I were "heroes" for all we were going through and doing for Emmy. I would always be polite and say thank you. But what else were we supposed to do? Was there another option I wasn't aware of, because this life sucked the joy right out of my soul? I didn't feel a sense of accomplishment for all the hard work I was doing or had done for the past eighteen months. *No.* I felt robbed of life, of hope, and of all the laughter our family used to share. Now I understood why parents of special-needs kids never wanted praise. Receiving praise for a life you never asked for and definitely didn't want felt like cheating. "God only calls the strong!" That is not true. But our weakness is what led us to needing God. That was why we could do what we did. God was carrying us each step of the way.

The time had finally come for Randy to go to Virginia and bring Ella back to Boston. This was not what we wanted for Ella. We were assured people recovered quickly, but I was terrified of having another child put under sedation, let alone surgery. With the diagnosis of HLH, which now involved a bone marrow transplant, our family qualified to have a room at the Boston House, similar to the Ronald McDonald house. Before Randy left to get Ella, we moved some of our clothes to our new room and realized that this would be our new saving grace. On hard days, we could pretend like we were back home, eating homemade food prepared by volunteers. Randy and I needed to be able to look at four different walls to stay sane. Sanity was now our goal, but everything happening around us was insanity at the highest level.

The night before Randy left to go get Ella, I slept in the sleep room and prayed all night. I think I fell asleep for ten minutes before my alarm went off at 4:00 a.m. so Randy could leave and catch the earliest flight. The minute he walked out of the room, I instantly felt abandoned and isolated.

Once again, I was trapped with nowhere to go. The pressure caused me to start yelling at God, once again.

"God, this is it. If Emmy goes into a bone marrow transplant like this, she is going to die. Tell me what to do or just take her to heaven already. She is now yours to take care of. I give all of her to you! She is in so much pain, and it's not right if she is going to live like this forever. Fix this, please!"

And just like clockwork, after humbling myself in prayer and letting God have complete control over Emmy, even her life, God spoke directly to me—again. "Missy, go look up Artane."

"God, you know I have been researching Artane day and night, and nothing new is coming up. I can't find out why it's causing Emmy's body to react like this! I need proof to make these doctors understand what I can see."

"Just go look it up, Missy," God demanded.

So, I did. And guess what appeared? A new website, a new article, and totally different information on Artane appeared at the top of my search. This time, within the medical information and side effects section, there was this specific term that I had never seen before—neuroleptic malignant syndrome (NMS). Being pretty proficient at researching medical documents, I went to the website of the NIH (National Institute of Health) and pulled up the first journal article on NMS.

It explained that neuroleptic malignant syndrome was a life-threatening neurological disorder most often caused by an adverse reaction to neuroleptic or antipsychotic drugs. The symptoms it listed were all being experienced by Emmy—high fever, sweating, unstable blood pressure, stupor, muscular rigidity, and autonomic dysfunction. I read on, and it said that the syndrome could occur at any time, especially for those who were taking anti-parkinsonism drugs known as dopaminergics, but only if they were discontinued abruptly.

All of the side effects were the same, except I didn't understand why it said it only happened when dopaminergics were discontinued abruptly. Emmy's dose was being increased rapidly. I did a little more digging, and I found another article describing all the symptoms including different dystonic reactions—Opisthotonos (full arching of body when on the back), oromandibular dystonia (face, jaw, or tongue contractions), tachycardia (high heart rate), fevers, and altered mental states.

Even though I couldn't find any medical journals describing these side effects while increasing the dose, it was clear this medicine was causing the issues in Emmy's body. I knew that something was still causing harm to Emmy's brain, and now I had the evidence. The arching of her back; her tongue lagging in and out; the increased breathing; and her lost, empty eyes were hard to ignore, even for the most stubborn of doctors.

I remember the exact day she lost her ability to show emotion. The Artane was increased to 5 mg, three times a day. Two hours later, Emmy's eyes became stuck to the right, she stopped crying, and her eyes went empty—soulless. Oh, how I knew it then, but I'd allowed others to drown out my voice. I can't believe I let them overpower my God-given maternal instinct that always knows when something is not right with one of my children. That was the last time I cowered to others, even Harvard-trained doctors. This time I was ready for battle. My courage returned and I was ready to stand up for my baby girl.

14

CHAPTER

*Watch, stand fast in the faith, be brave, be strong.
Let all that you do be done with love.*
—1 CORINTHIANS 16:13-14 (NKJV)

My heart was pounding as I showed nurse Lauren the journal article. She instantly wrote everything down and then reminded me that Emmy was scheduled for a CT scan for her lungs that morning. Lauren was a fiery redhead nurse who was tough yet levelheaded. Somehow, she never got upset, even when I would yell at her for just doing her job. She cared so much for Emmy and always seemed to be the one working when tiny miracles would break through. Those tiny miracles kept us believing that Emmy was "still in there."

Before the CT scan, Lauren was fighting in my corner as I argued with the doctor about the procedure and not allowing Emmy to be intubated.

"There is no way we can keep Emmy still without sedating her. Look at her body. We are going to sedate her and then wake her right after we are done. She has to be intubated," the anesthesiologist said.

"No. Lauren and I believe that if you just give her ketamine, she won't need to be intubated. Intubation would just cause her to need too much sedation, especially while we are weaning her off of it. We have seen it work before. Please just try," I pleaded with her.

"I really agree. We used ketamine for one of the lumbar punctures, and her oxygen levels never fell, and she was still the whole time," Lauren chimed in.

The CT scan was quick, and Emmy was wheeled back just thirty minutes later.

"Good job advocating for Emmy, Mom. She only needed two doses of ketamine, and we were done. She was still the whole time and never needed to be intubated," the anesthesiologist said to me.

"Thank you! I think that is the first time I have heard those words from a doctor," I replied.

A few days later, I found myself sleepless. Medical words rolled over in my mind like a script. I had to get this right. The team had seen the article, but I had to convince the movement disorder doctor of what I found to get Emmy off Artane. He was coming in to meet with me first thing in the morning to discuss Botox and my information had to be foolproof.

We had decided to have him Botox Emmy while she was sedated for the placement of the central venous line (CVL) and peripherally inserted central catheter (PICC) line she needed for the chemo and bone marrow transplant. She had gone this long with only one PICC line, and it was almost unusable. The CVL was going to be hard for her to get used to, with two lines dangling from her chest and connected to IV lines, but it was a must for the amount of medicine and chemo she would be getting.

I had never felt the kind of rage I felt that next morning. Nor had I ever been so dismissed by another human being while I was pleading for my daughter's life. The movement disorder doctor woke me at 7:15 a.m. I must have just dozed off and barely slept because I felt light-headed and nauseous as he started talking to me. After he chatted away about how he was going to Botox the same muscles as before, I interrupted him.

"Did you even do an examination of her yet? Since you were here last, her movements have moved to the other side of her body, and she no longer even cries. Her body is constantly pulsing, and she pants like a dog. I believe this is all from Artane. and I can prove it," I started saying.

"What are you trying to say? Her dystonia has changed? How could that be? And how could Artane be doing any of this? If you were correct in saying the dystonia was caused from propofol, the Artane is the medicine given to treat it," he stated condescendingly.

"Look, here. I have an article that shows how Artane can cause a reaction called neuroleptic malignant syndrome and—"

"Missy, you are just grasping for straws," he interrupted. "Your daughter is sick and you just won't come to terms with the fact that she is going to have dystonia for the rest of her life. Neuroleptic malignant syndrome, seriously? I am not taking her off Artane because that is what happens when you stop Artane too quickly. I have to go. I will just Botox the same muscles, and we will meet up later," he said completely tone-deaf.

"I am her mom, and I want her taken off Artane now. You didn't even read the article—" I said to him, raising my voice with every syllable.

At that point, he just stood up and said sorry but he was needed somewhere else, and he left. He walked out on me while I was trying to explain everything I'd found. I was stunned.

Emmy was carted off moments later to surgery, and I was left alone in ICU Room 30, full of rage and anger. Who was going to listen to me? I cried out to God in a fiery rage, "If you want her off Artane, you figure this out yourself because I did my part, and I am done. This fight is too hard for me to do on my own!"

While Emmy was in surgery, the ICU neurologist fellow came in to discuss Emmy's daily needs and issues. I repeated what I had said to Emmy's movement disorder neurologist and showed her all the evidence. She agreed that her medicine should definitely be looked at and discussed with the team. Yes! *Thank you, God, for changing hearts and minds.*

The next morning, Emmy's BMT doctor was there for daily rounds. I quickly mentioned everything to her that I'd said to the movement disorder doctor and asked for Emmy to be taken off Artane right away.

"No way! We have a set protocol to stop weaning all meds weeks before the chemo starts so we can see her baseline," she said sternly.

"Well, if you read this article, you'll see that it's obvious that Emmy is experiencing neuroleptic malignant syndrome. That medicine is literally killing her, and she needs to be weaned immediately," I boldly stated.

"You didn't tell me she was having neuroleptic malignant syndrome! Why didn't anyone notify me that Emmy had this?" she said as she looked to the ICU neurology fellow. "You realize this is life-threatening, and she can't have a BMT in this condition?"

"I don't know why no one mentioned it to you. Mom just showed me this article, and Emmy is having so many of the symptoms. I am not sure it's really NMS, but we should try weaning just to see," the ICU neurologist said.

"I just don't know, Missy. I need to speak to neurology and look at what's happening. You know we don't like to touch anything before the BMT, which is why we won't be weaning any of her IV meds starting today. We have to have a clear baseline to see what is negatively affecting her. Please give me a few hours to think about this," the BMT doctor quietly said and left the room.

I knew that we had a family meeting the next morning, and God told me to do something I had never thought of. "Show them pictures and videos of Emmy before the angiogram."

Why had I not thought of that before? These people were doctors and needed pictures to explain everything. *How could they deny this is all from medicine after they see Emmy sitting up and drinking from a juice box right before the sedation in Virginia?*

Once again, I ignored my exhaustion and worked all night putting together a slideshow with photographic and video evidence. I included the first video of Emmy after the angiogram as proof. I was ready for this family meeting, and Randy would be there to back me up. Ella and Randy showed up early the next morning on March 2. Randy was overly exhausted because he'd decided to drive back to Boston so we would have a car to go back and forth to the Boston House. I filled him in on what I'd found, and he was finally relieved we had evidence to show. He now truly believed that all of it needed to be weaned, even the Artane.

Later that day, we all went to the family meeting. Ironically, the movement disorder neurologist wasn't even there. We still showed the ICU and BMT doctors the slideshow. They were utterly amazed and shocked at how well Emmy had been just before arriving in November. It was at this point that I told the entire team I no longer wanted the movement disorder doctor on Emmy's service. I explained how his behavior to me was the previous morning and I no longer trusted Emmy's care to him. Once I finished, one of the PACT doctors chimed in.

"I was told by another doctor that, when Emmy's team met with the flight evac team, back when we thought you all were going to Duke, something was said that just didn't sit well with me. When the type of sedation they would use to flight evac Emmy to Duke was mentioned, the flight evac medical team read that propofol was off limits due to an allergy. The movement doctor chimed in and said out loud, 'Just between us, propofol is safe to use. Mom doesn't truly know that it's an allergy. It is obvious HLH is causing her dystonia, not the sedation.' I just can't keep that to myself after you said mentioned his behavior," he said looking around the room.

I cannot believe he said that! I want him off Emmy's team now! I reported him to Patient and Family Rights once before, and I am going to again," I said with my voice starting to quiver.

"Missy, you should have come to us before going to Patient and Family Rights. We could have done something sooner. I am so sorry you had to go through that," the lead BMT doctor said as she rubbed my arm.

I quickly added, "Is there any way you can find me an older neurologist to oversee Emmy's medicine? Someone who was trained before every doctor was specialized in just one area? One like her doctor in Virginia who was an autoimmune, epilepsy, and movement disorder neurologist?"

The team instantly knew of a doctor and said they would send him up after his rounds. I was pacing back and forth, waiting to tell this new neurologist everything I had found. I just prayed he was willing to listen and had the compassion as Dr. Toor did, back in Virginia.

He showed up after his rounds were over but was instantly on the defensive. He began by questioning my motives for wanting to take Emmy off this movement disorder medicine. He wasn't at the family meeting, so I just figured he needed to be caught up. I explained everything I'd found, and stunningly, he cut me off mid-sentence, just like the other doctor.

"You can't just demand we take your daughter off a medicine that is potentially saving her from dystonic episodes. We put her on that medicine because we felt it was the best thing for her," he boldly stated.

"I am telling you right now, these spasms were caused by propofol. Somehow Artane made them worse. And yes, I know, it is a medicine usually given for acute dystonic reactions, but this time it is making the patient worse—making my daughter worse. I cannot let you keep her on this medicine. It is unethical for you to knowingly harm a child, and that is exactly what this medicine is doing. Her MRIs have not gotten worse, yet she has. The team already said it is fine. Now you need to approve it and wean Artane now, or I will report you, too!" I said, holding back the floodgate of tears swelling in my eyes.

Emmy's nurse, Nicole, gently tugged at me and told me to go for a walk to cool off. I walked straight to my sleep room and cried out, once again, to God. "Why are you making this so hard, God? I have had to physically fight the entire staff to get Emmy the healing I know exists, but doesn't Your Word say that *You* will fight the battles for us? How are You even helping when I am doing all the physical fighting? God, I don't know how, but You have to change that doctor's heart. We need this bone marrow transplant, but not while she is in so much pain. We need Emmy calm."

I gathered myself and washed my face. I marched back up to the room to go back into battle, and I was stopped dead in my tracks.

The doctor was waiting for me and was smiling. "Once you left, I went straight to Emmy's MRIs, and you are right. Her brain hasn't gotten worse at all, but the dystonia has. So, I am willing to do one wean and see what happens to her movements. We will wean one dose down to 5 mg, and if she shows improvement, we will wean another dose every third day until she is off."

"Thank you! And I wanted to show you how she really was before the angiogram, so you can understand how this all started," I said as I opened up the slideshow. I pushed play and watched the doctor's reaction.

"This was in Virginia before the angiogram? And this was right after? Oh, and this is how she continued to get worse after all the other sedations? Wow, it really was the sedation," he said in shock.

The next morning, the first dose of Artane was weaned. I sat and stared at her for hours. And just as the first time she took Artane, and every dose after that one, within three hours I saw a change in her body. Only, this time, it was an improvement! Emmy's tongue stopped lagging in and out of her mouth. We all were so excited and couldn't wait for the next wean.

The second small wean was three days later. Just like clockwork, three hours later, her lost, empty eyes broke free from the distant stare, and she began to cry. Oh, how the floodgates opened up. Emmy cried so hard for hours upon hours. My heart was broken that she had been trapped inside her own mind, unable to communicate, to show her emotions, or to tell us how she felt for over a month. I couldn't stop smiling and crying. God did it again, just like He said He would.

The next wean would come again just three days before the first day of chemotherapy. The pulsing in her body suddenly stopped, like someone turned off the power to her muscles. There was no denying that Artane was making her body worse. I was so thankful the positive effects were so quick that no one could deny it.

When the transplant doctor said that they didn't mess with any medicine before the transplant, that meant everything, including the sedation meds. Emmy was no longer experiencing withdrawal and her body was calmer than it had been since we arrived at Boston Children's Hospital in November. I am so thankful they agreed to wean Artane before, because Emmy could now show us what she was thinking. Her words were still gone, but her eyes were back to telling us all we needed to know. We still noticed that her face would twitch after each dose of Artane, but the proof was evident that this was all caused by medicine and not HLH.

Final preparations were made for both Emmy and Ella to begin the bone marrow transplant protocol. Blood was taken from both and analyzed one last time. The hope was that Ella had antibodies to dormant viruses Emmy had, just in case they reared their ugly heads while she became immunocompromised. It can be devastating for an immunocompromised patient to get sick from a virus hiding in their own bodies. Adenovirus, cytomegalovirus (CMV) and BK antibodies were present in Ella's blood work, and everything seemed to be lining up perfectly—or so we thought.

CHAPTER 15

For the Word of God is living and powerful, and sharper than any two-edged sword, piercing even to the division of soul and spirit, and of joints and marrow, and is a discerner of the thoughts and intents of the heart.

—HEBREWS 4:12 (NKJV)

Nobody should ever be forced to take poison, but until God reveals another way to transplant a new immune system into humans without needing to kill the original immune system, chemotherapy is all we have. The chemotherapy protocol for CNS-restricted HLH was a lower dose than normally used for bone marrow transplant patients with actual cancer. They weren't killing a growth or cancer in Emmy but, rather, killing the stem cells (including red blood cells), so the new ones could implant and grow.

T-14 (transplant day minus 14) was finally here. This countdown was the way they kept track of which day Emmy was on throughout the entire transplant. T-0 is how they identified transplant day. Each day after that would be counted as T+. These numbers were important as certain medicines needed to be given and also gave us a countdown as she was infused with different types of chemotherapy.

Emmy was given chemotherapy for three days straight with no negative effects. I pleaded with them to wean Artane one more time since she was doing so well. They agreed, and each of the three daily doses were weaned by 1 mg, over the course of nine days.

A whole week of chemo went by, and Emmy was calm and alert, so different than the entire time since we'd arrived in Boston. Physical therapy brought in a chair for her to sit in, and her arms and legs just hung limp off the sides. We spent hours trying to get her to lift her legs and arms, but her strength had been ripped from her muscles. I was afraid she would never move normally again. Emmy's body responded like it was paralyzed.

I was so hopeful we wouldn't see any side effects from the chemo, but on the eighth day, Emmy started getting terrible fevers and became increasingly irritated. We could tell she was fighting it, though. Emmy would smile and try to move, but only if she thought her body wouldn't react in a spasm. She even started communicating through hand movements. The nurse would ask if she had pain, and she would point to her head and then her stomach, alerting us she had a headache and felt nauseated. Later, I even understood a series of hand gestures that meant she wanted to use the toilet instead of using the diaper. The nurse quickly brought in a bedside commode, and we managed to gather up the dozen or so IV lines and put her on. She seemed so relieved to use the toilet. The small improvements helped us all stay positive, but as our luck proved, the calmness and improvements quickly faded.

The fevers and then strange physical reactions to the last doses of chemo were taking a toll on us. Randy, Ella, and I just watched in pain. We had known chemotherapy was horrible, but watching it firsthand was different. I truly thought God would spare her any adverse reactions, but that was wishful thinking.

The chemo ravaged Emmy's brain. The spasms came back, and her breathing once again quickened. Her skin began flushing with a red rash. To the touch, her skin felt like she was on fire. She would show me she felt dirty and begged to be bathed. The stress and anxiety to keep her comfortable and taken care of were building up inside me, and I just needed to get away from that hospital, just for a day. I had lived in that hospital without going back to Virginia for 118 days. That was longer than any military deployment I'd ever been on. It was longer than anything stressful I had ever experienced. I looked at Randy and told him I needed to spend a day away with Ella before she donated her marrow to Emmy. I needed to be reminded that I had other healthy children, and I was more than a caretaker of a sick child.

The famous Newbury Street was our first destination. Ella loved looking up popular attractions, so I just drove where she told me to go. We peeked into Tiffany's windows, and we chatted about senseless things. Shake Shack was first on our agenda, and I ordered a mushroom burger, which mistakenly was only mushrooms without meat but tasted wonderful. I kept all conversation upbeat and light, as I knew Ella was nervous about the upcoming surgery, even though she wouldn't say so. She was very skilled at hiding her feelings, but moms know their children.

It didn't matter how much I had sacrificed over the previous years or all that I'd witnessed happening to Emmy, guilt was constantly knocking on the door. I was aching with guilt over spending a few happy hours with our healthy daughter, while the other one was being poisoned with chemo. I felt guilt for experiencing a little joy, while Randy sat and watched Emmy suffer. This life of pain was more than anyone could have imagined. This life of constant torture was very close to what I believed hell was like—if it weren't for the freezing cold Massachusetts weather.

I sat and watched the snow fall from the 6th floor window and silently prayed as the last days of chemotherapy became increasingly dark and daunting. But just like the first rays of light break through after the darkness of night, the goodness of God shone brightly. Emmy made it to the cure that we had hoped and prayed for. Then it dawned on me, transplant day, or T-0, was on Friday, March 25, 2016. Transplant day was on Good Friday. I saw signs everywhere that God was still in control. Life was just within our reach; we just had to make it through this day.

Randy and I both took Ella first thing in the morning to pre-op and prayed that this procedure would be quick, error free and painless. Randy stayed with Ella, and I returned to be with Emmy. The process of taking the bone marrow and then processing it would be a few hours after it was removed from Ella. The surgery only lasted an hour and went perfectly. Ella was given a room on the transplant floor to recover for a day or two.

Throughout the day, the ICU nurses were being updated by the transplant team as to which stage the stem cells were in. We were in a very strange predicament being in the ICU, since transplants are usually done on the transplant floor. Over the course of the previous two weeks, we'd met multiple transplant nurses because they were the ones who had to administer the chemo. Precautions had to be made, since each dose was poisonous, and the ICU nurses were not specifically trained to handle chemo. Every scenario we found ourselves in at this hospital was not according to procedure. I felt like all eyes were on us, all the time.

I later joined Randy in Ella's recovery room, and we sat with her until she woke up. The doctor said the team had harvested more than enough marrow, and Ella would feel better in a couple of weeks. Her lower back would be tender from the two spots they'd drilled into. Ella became my superhero overnight. She modeled complete selflessness. From the moment that Emmy would need a bone marrow transplant, Ella had said she hoped she was the match. She didn't want to see her baby brothers go through the surgery, and she was willing to do it all herself. Imagine being sixteen and giving part of yourself to save another. My heart was exploding knowing I had been given such amazing children.

Randy and I spent the day walking between rooms, torn between two daughters. As we were walking from Emmy's room to Ella's room, we were met with a huge surprise. Randy's dad, Leslie, and his stepmom, Cheryl, were standing right there waiting for us.

"What are you guys doing here? I thought you hated flying, Dad? Did you drive?" Randy asked his dad in complete confusion.

"Oh, we flew here. We knew we needed to be here on this big day," Leslie answered.

"This means so much to us. Thank you!" I said as I hugged each one.

Having family with us gave a comfort we hadn't felt in a long time. We had done so much of this alone, without family, that we had learned to rely only on each other. But now we had parents to lean on, to watch Emmy as we went to comfort Ella. It was exactly what we needed. Every need was still being met, even when we didn't know we needed it.

The healing we had been praying for was finally here. It wasn't the healing I was expecting, but it was what we were given. Back in Virginia, we had begun losing hope after reading numerous medical journals that stated most undiagnosed inflammatory brain diseases have no cure. It was a miracle, in itself, that this was a rare brain disease, yet still came with a cure. But the journey, the fight, and the medicine effects were not part of the plan. This was still proving to be so wrong. Nevertheless, I still believed God had brought us here for a cure. He had a plan.

It was now the evening of Good Friday, and Emmy's body was on the verge of death. The chemo had done its job. Emmy had no immune system, no red blood cells and no platelets. She was given platelets and red blood cells the day before because no one can survive without those. She was still weak, but her body continued to spasm. As we talked about the cure, it seemed like she didn't understood the importance of the day. Ella was wheeled up to the room so she could watch her cells be given to her baby sister. When entered, the nurses surprised her with signs and balloons. It wasn't just a celebration for Emmy; it was a celebration of what Ella had selflessly done.

The infusion was started early in the evening and lasted about five hours. The whole thing was very boring, watching blood enter Emmy's IV, but I just kept praying that it was supernaturally the blood of Jesus healing Emmy. Once it was over, I was emotionally and physically drained. We had spent months hoping and praying for this day. We physically had to move heaven and earth to get here. I ended up spending the night in Ella's room, while Randy stayed with Emmy, helping her survive the aftereffects of the transplant.

Early the next morning, Randy called and asked if I would come to the room so he could finally go to sleep.

"Is Emmy all right? She didn't sleep at all? What happened?" I bombed Randy with questions.

"Right after you left, Emmy started reacting to the transplant and began puking, screaming, and crying uncontrollably. She spiked a fever and was a mess the rest of the night. I have to get some sleep or I am going to lose it." His voice sounded very frustrated and angry.

I grabbed a coffee and ran to the room. Emmy had only slept an hour but was back to screaming, hyperventilating, and throwing her body all over the bed. We were back to square one. I'd thought we were finally out of the valley, but actually we were still stuck in the lowest trenches.

Randy, Ella, and his parents left two days later on Easter Sunday. Ella had missed a lot of schoolwork and needed to get back. I was all alone again. Terror squeezed my chest as I thought about how I was going to do this by myself.

During the next week, I witnessed my first ICU death. A teenage boy, who suffered traumatic brain injury, was placed just three rooms down from Emmy. I saw him for days, unresponsive, with his parents in constant prayer. The doctors would come by throughout the day and try everything to wake him up. One day, I heard screaming and walked to the hallway to see the doctor screaming, clapping, and shaking the boy. Nothing could wake him. I am not sure how many days he was in a coma, but I remember the day it all ended.

Nurses watch each other's patients so they can take lunch breaks. Emmy's nurse had this boy's vital pulled up on Emmy's monitor, helping another nurse keep an eye on him as she went to eat. Suddenly, his heart just stopped. Code red was announced over the speaker, and every available nurse went running to his room. Usually, the nurse shuts off the monitor, but this was too unexpected, too hectic, and she just ran out of the room. I witnessed him die and be revived multiple times as I stared at his vitals on Emmy's monitor.

As I stared at Emmy sleeping and then back to the monitor, I fell to my knees in prayer. I sat and cried out for God to save that boy—to not let him be taken from his parents. And then as quickly as he was revived, he was gone again.

Minutes later, Emmy's nurse returned, eyes red and puffy. She quickly realized she left his vitals on the monitor and apologized over and over, saying that I should have never had to witness that. Desolation and depression continued to grow deep into my soul as Emmy's body quickly deteriorated from the side-effects of chemo and the transplant.

It only took six days after the transplant for Emmy to start showing devastating side effects from the chemotherapy. Mucous membranes are sensitive to chemotherapy and can cause ulcers to form. The stomach, nose, throat, and any other area can be affected. Emmy's first sign of mucositis was that her drool became pink and her respirations became increasingly fast and labored. The first intervention was done by placing a nasal canula with a small amount of oxygen into her nose. That was quickly changed out for a BiPAP, when her oxygen levels continued to drop. On the eighth day, they went one step higher and changed her to a CPAP, which gives constant, high-pressure airflow. Bloody spit would just fly out of her mouth as the CPAP constantly blew air into her lungs.

A woman's hair is her crowning glory. St. Paul declared those words, and they never made sense to me until I saw Emmy's hair falling out in chunks. One touch, one movement of her head on the pillow and her head just let them drop. I pushed back tears as I tried to hide the collateral damage from her. Emmy was the odd man out in our family when it came to hair. Our other kids wore my thick brown hair, minus the curls, while Emmy's thin blondish hair didn't even come in until she was three. She worked so hard to grow her hair out. All she wanted was princess hair like her big sister, but it only ever made it to her shoulders.

One morning, I woke up and rolled over to see two nurses sitting next to Emmy. I didn't know what was going on, but they assured me Emmy was fine and told me to go back to sleep. As I slept, they worked diligently brushing all of the clumps of hair out before I could see it. Emmy lost almost all of her hair that morning, and her nurse saved me from seeing the worst of it. The little things nurses do can actually save a mother from suffering more pain than needed.

Later that day, the Child Life specialist came and buzzed the rest of her hair off to match the bald patches, which made a world of difference. I'd never understood why women shaved off their hair before losing it, but now I completely understood.

Morphine was going around the clock to make Emmy feel more comfortable, but her breathing was becoming more and more labored. While I was sitting eating lunch, ten days after her transplant, the ICU doctor called and told me to get back to the room as soon as possible.

"Missy, we're going to have to intervene. We've been monitoring Emmy's oxygen levels, but when we started monitoring her carbon dioxide levels, we found it way too high. Her oxygen has been dropping to thirty, and she needs to be intubated now. Can you be here in five minutes?" he quickly asked me.

As I ran back to the ICU, I tried to not let fear get the best of me. *How are they ever going to sedate her? She is still getting sedation meds around the clock. They haven't been weaned for weeks.* Two steps forward, a hundred steps back. The same routine kept happening over and over. My feet followed the worn path from Dana Farber to Children's ICU, while I prayed silently the whole way.

I learned to never leave the room while a procedure was happening. I felt like I had to watch every intubation, every medicine dose, every needle poke, or I would miss something that would keep us here longer. I didn't trust anyone at this point. The ICU attending allowed the fellow to do the intubation. It was a teaching hospital, after all.

Propofol was not used, and the fentanyl did the job. Emmy was asleep, but her throat was so swollen that a camera was needed to help guide the doctor to place the tube in the correct place. On the third try, I heard the loudest *pop*. I had never heard that sound, but the doctor confirmed the tube was in the correct place. No one said a word, so I just guessed that sound was normal.

Randy and our boys walked in four hours later. Randy had decided to drive them up from Virginia. They needed to see their sister as much as she needed to see them. But as soon as they walked in the room, the boys looked at their sister with confusion and pain. We quickly decided to spare them the pain and take them to town. The nurse assured us, as usual, she wouldn't take her eyes off Emmy. That night we all went to a movie and slept at the Boston House together. As we returned the next morning, we were alarmed to see Emmy wide awake with the tube still in her throat. Her nurse said the doctors didn't want to over-sedate her, so if she woke up and didn't fight the tube, they would keep her meds steady.

My throat closed instantly. I couldn't believe she was awake with the tube in her throat. I just knew she felt like she was suffocating. I saw the terror in her little eyes as she completely relaxed and submitted to a machine, forcing air in and out of her lungs. Emmy was living my worst nightmare—the recurring dream where I was being chased and, when I opened my mouth, nothing came out. *Please, God, save her from this torture and heal the mucositis quickly.*

Fifteen hundred—that was the magical number we were told to listen for; it was what Emmy's absolute neutrophil count (ANC) needed to be to prove she was engrafted with Ella's stem cells. ANC is a type of white blood cell that is the first to form after the bone marrow has transplanted. That day came on day fifteen, just one day before they decided to extubate Emmy.

As expected, Emmy began withdrawing instantly from the extra sedation meds they had to give her. And while she stayed strong the whole time, she needed a lot of medicine to keep her comfortable. The spasms were returning, and the same old pattern began to repeat. The boys were so comforting and gentle with Emmy. I could tell her body relaxed when they were near her. But they couldn't stay forever. Randy and the boys needed to get home to prepare our house to sell.

It was hard to imagine any life outside of the hospital, but so many things were happening that I had no part in. The Air Force found a job for Randy at Hanscom AFB, Massachusetts, so our family could be together again. When Randy told them there was no way Emmy would be leaving Boston any time soon, they went to work looking for positions near Boston. The Air Force, especially the medical service corps, took great steps in taking care of our family. Randy and I had sacrificed a combined total of twenty-nine years for our country, and now they were showing us their appreciation by moving mountains to get our family back together. How many businesses would do something like that? I was finally understanding why God had led us both to the Air Force.

I wasn't alone for long—once Randy and the boys left. Back in December, when my brother and sister were visiting, I asked a huge demanding question of my sister. "Would you come live with us for a year to help us out?"

Nicole owned her own small business as a massage therapist. She was active in her church and was always on the go. I didn't really think she would do it, but we needed someone strong and reliable. After going home, she said she prayed about it and felt like she needed to help us out. I was giddy when she showed up on April 11.

The presence of my sister was probably the only thing that kept me sane. I would have never been able to face what was coming alone. Over the next days, Emmy's bone marrow cells continued to multiply, but her body began having serious tremors, nothing like we had seen before. We were warned the chemo could do something to her brain, but we didn't know what to expect. At first, her right arm started twitching and jumping. A day later, the twitch turned into what looked like a windmill motion. Emmy's right arm was now swinging in circles, and she couldn't stop it. The nurse, Nicole, and I would take turns holding it down. A few days later, her left arm began twitching, like she was freezing. I had a horrible feeling the chemo had damaged her brain even more. What were we going to do now?

Cells were continuing to grow inside Emmy, but the last to show up were the platelets. Those would take months to start growing. Without platelets, Emmy began bruising all over her body every time we touched her. Grabbing her arms, flipping her uncomfortable body side to side, and adjusting her legs left horrible dark bruises. If not for her natural beauty, her naked head and bruised body would have resembled Gollum from *Lord of the Rings*.

Weaning Artane was always part of my daily questioning. The BMT doctor finally allowed the nurses to begin weaning Artane around day fourteen post-transplant, which was now almost down to the smallest dose. When Emmy's cells also began maturing into red blood cells, blood transfusions were finally stopped. Up until now, she'd been getting either platelet transfusions or red blood cell transfusions daily. Thirty days post-transplant, the tremors in her arms finally stopped. Emmy was medically more stable than ever, even though her body was left limp and seemingly paralyzed.

Emmy was unable to move her skinny, weak legs, even to do a small adjustment. Her arms just hung limp again. I was so afraid the right one was now paralyzed from the unbelievable flailing it had done for weeks. I would watch as she moved her left arm but only a few inches. I wasn't sure if it was also weak or if she was afraid of spasms. I couldn't get a clear answer out of her because she was still unable to speak. Thankfully, I was still able to read her thoughts, and Nicole began understanding her eye gaze movements to help keep her comfortable.

Morning rounds came day after day. The daily reminder of how many days we had lived in the ICU was infuriating. Then came the daily reading of Emmy's cell count, viral test results, updates on breathing, and her inputs and outputs; it was all so monotonous. Finally, after being in the ICU for 132 days, the decision to restart her weaning process began. Dexmedetomidine was initially decided upon because all studies showed there was no withdrawal associated with it. I wondered if they studied it after a child had been receiving it twenty-four hours a day for 129 days straight.

You could also sense the ICU was trying to get Emmy off the IV meds and stable enough to be placed on the transplant floor. Not only was the ICU a hub for germs, it was no place to keep an immunocompromised child. Whoever led the morning rounds would smirk while saying the number of days we were in ICU room 30.

"Patient, Emmy Bosch, day 147, day 156, day 170," each doctor would loudly say. But no matter what they did, how slowly they would wean each medicine, or how hard they tried to get her body to accept formula through the feeding tube, Emmy was not leaving that ICU any time soon.

16
CHAPTER

*Please, run now to meet her, and say to her, "Is it well
with you? Is it well with your husband?
Is it well with the child?" And she answered, "It is well."*
—2 KINGS 4:26 (NKJV)

Once I stopped trying so hard to figure out Emmy's issues all on my own, listening to God became the easy part. There was no denying God's voice or ignoring him any longer. When He spoke, my insides shuttered. I knew God was leading us this whole time, but instead of the instant miracles we desired, He was still fulfilling his promise in Psalm 23. He was leading us, more like dragging us, through the Valley of the Shadow of Death. We didn't want to go through this anymore, but we had no choice.

At the end of April, just weeks after Ella's stem cells started showing growth in Emmy's bone marrow, they began to die. The doctors scrambled and administered every test they could think of. Viruses are common in all of us, but a healthy immune system keeps them in check. Emmy was lacking her immune system, and Ella's donor cells weren't mature enough to kill whatever viruses were starting to grow. Preventative testing was done weekly for these viruses, but something must have popped up in between the tests.

The virus tests came back, and Emmy's viral numbers were exploding. The team started an infusion of antivirals, but the numbers continued to increase. Within days of testing positive for adenovirus, Emmy then tested positive for CMV (cytomegalovirus). Emmy was now fighting two viruses at once.

Around this time, God introduced me to a very special family. Back when we'd first heard about HLH, we had asked to meet the only other family who had went through CNS-restricted HLH. I'd never heard anything back, so I thought nothing more about it. Then our paths crossed at the perfect moment, at the exact place I never thought I would meet them.

On a day like every other, I walked up to the ICU doors and grabbed the phone to request to enter. The front desk answered, "Who are you here to see?"

"Hi, it's mom. I am here to see Emmy, room 30."

As I hung up the phone, a woman grabbed my arm and said, "Does your daughter have HLH? I am the mom of the other little girl with HLH. Dr. Gorman said you allowed us to know your names, but didn't he tell you ours?"

"Hi! My name is Missy. I told the doctor we wanted to talk with you but never heard anything back," I said.

"My name is Beth, and I emailed you months ago. I can't believe you didn't receive it. Did you just tell the ICU your daughter's name is Emmy? That is our daughter's name as well!" she said, completely surprised.

"Yes. Her real name is Emersyn, but she goes by Emmy!"

"Emmy's real name is Emily, but she also goes by that nickname. I can't believe we are the only two families who have a child with CNS-restricted HLH. We are truly alone on a very special island. I can't find any other children like ours," she said.

As our conversation continued for what seemed like hours, we discovered that the timeline for our daughters' illnesses were eerily the same. Emily, who also had a sibling with an E name, was a spunky, fun, energetic girl just like our Emmy. At the age of six, Emily came down with a cold or flu. A month passed after she recovered from her cold, but her mom noticed her weaving and tripping as she walked. She also saw she was having trouble standing up straight. Her doctors were much more responsive than ours had been to her symptoms and instantly did an MRI.

The MRI showed inflammation all over her brain but mostly in her cerebellum. For four years, the neurology doctor at Boston Children's gave her every type of anti-inflammatory medicine, including chemotherapy and multiple sclerosis medication, but nothing worked. She endured a brain biopsy, spinal fluid tests, and blood testing, yet no disease could be found. Eventually, a very harsh medicine was prescribed, which could possibly leave Emily infertile. Emily's family wanted a second opinion, so they went to Johns Hopkins.

Once again, an entire medical team was stumped. They had no additional tests or medical journals or information that Boston Children's hadn't already tried or read, so the family went back to Boston feeling defeated. Emily took the medication, which seemed to halt the progression of inflammation for a while, but within a year, the active inflammation returned. This time, the family demanded the doctor send them to the National Institute of Health (NIH) near Washington, DC. The NIH is where all the "cold cases" of the medical community are sent, studied and hopefully diagnosed.

What seemed like horrible timing and a drawn-out process for them was very much perfect timing for them and us. If they would have gone to the NIH just a year earlier, they would never have had a neurologist who remembered Emily from when she was completing her schooling at Boston Children's. That doctor wouldn't have been to a specific symposium where she learned of a child with a similar type of HLH. And without that symposium, she wouldn't have known to do genetic testing on Emily, looking specifically on the perforin gene.

Genetic testing was accomplished at the NIH, and six months later, Emily was going in for a bone marrow transplant at Boston Children's, exactly three months before our Emmy arrived. During this current visit, Emily just happened to be admitted into the ICU at the same time as us, because she had developed fluid around her heart, one of the many side-effects of bone marrow transplants. There are so many adverse reactions to chemotherapy and bone marrow transplants, which I could now ask a mom who had been through it all.

Having a person like Beth to answer all my questions was a huge blessing. We also relied on each other to vent our frustrations about doctors, mistakes, the loss of function our daughters were experiencing, and how our once perfect worlds had been turned upside down.

The next day, Beth asked me to meet her for lunch at Dana Farber

Hospital cafeteria. I asked my sister if she would stay with Emmy, and of course she said yes. Nicole and I both lived in the hospital, but it was her day to relax in the sleep room or wander off into Boston. I knew how much I loved those hours alone, so I didn't like taking them away from her. But Nicole understood she was there to help me and Emmy and was always willing to make this stay easier on me.

During lunch, Beth and I continued analyzing our daughters' disease. We unloaded our family histories, our sadness and disappointments and ultimately the stress all of it had caused. I mentioned the Air Force was moving our family to Boston so we could all be together. At that precise moment, just weeks before Randy and the kids would be in Boston, she told me they had a rental apartment just blocks from the hospital, we could use, free of charge. Beth said they thought the entire bone marrow process was going to be much longer than it was, so they had signed a one-year lease on an apartment on Boylston Ave. Once Emily was released, they would no longer need it. God was working out so many tiny details that had been weighing heavily on my heart. He showed me that there was no need to sweat the small stuff.

I cannot fully explain the mysteries of God or how He operates. All I know is that He is good. He is just. He is full of mercy. All these things I understand, but when people say, "His timing is always perfect," I am conflicted because I still wish he would have intervened sooner. But for every miracle we have experienced, God's timing was right on time. If it was up to our timing, Emmy would have been in Boston when no disease had been diagnosed yet. It was all working out according to His plan, His timing.

Emmy's ANC count was still plummeting, not only from the viruses, but also from the medicine that killed the viruses. The viruses weren't being affected, so they tried one last option. Viruses can't be attacked the same way bacteria can, so there aren't many options. The change in medicine finally gave Emmy's ANC a chance to slowly rise again. It seemed that all was well—until Emmy's breathing become more labored and extremely loud.

The team quickly signed Emmy up to have another echocardiogram. The results were exactly what Emily had been admitted into the ICU for, fluid was building up around Emmy's heart. Because of her labored breathing and high heart rate, Emmy was quickly placed on BiPAP. Emmy's oxygen level was high, but she seemed to be struggling to get air. They quickly changed it to a CPAP. The stress of keeping Emmy comfortable with a huge face mask was now another task added to our daily list of "must dos".

The next morning, a cardiologist came and took Emmy to surgery to remove the fluid. Emmy returned shortly after, and the cardiologist said they had pulled 190 ml of fluid off her heart. Emmy's breathing instantly slowed, but it remained labored. They decided to keep her on the CPAP to see if she just needed more time to start breathing easier.

Swollen face and body are usually the marks of a child who is going through chemo or has been on steroids. Emmy never really had those side effects from steroids, but now she was swelling before our eyes. Emmy's organs were having a tough time releasing all the fluid, and her veins were weak and leaky from the poisons that were pumped through them. When her breathing and heart rate starting to decline again, an X-ray showed fluid now filling around her left lung. The small hole the surgical team had made when draining her heart was allowing fluid to leak down into her lung. On top of that, the adenovirus and CMV were still showing that they were more powerful than the medicine.

Hope was hard to hold on to. Every step forward was quickly met with negative blunt force, pushing us back to the start. Emmy could not catch a break. At the time, I had no idea how deadly adenovirus was to transplant patients. Just doors down from Emmy, another transplant patient was dying because adenovirus had worked its way into his lungs. Never once did the doctors or nurses reveal to us that Emmy was within inches of death if the virus was not stopped.

We were now deep into May, and an emergency family meeting was called to discuss options regarding the adenovirus, CMV, and newly discovered BK virus making Emmy so sick. The doctors already knew Emmy had the latent BK virus before the transplant, which is why they had made sure Ella had the antibodies. But with Ella's cells being stunted and Emmy not creating any white blood cells, the BK virus had reared its ugly head. The bone marrow doctor felt it was time to request special T-cells that are designed to specifically attack all three viruses.

If they continued using antivirals, Emmy was on track to lose the entire bone marrow graft. But the doctors also couldn't stop using them, because they felt they were possibly helping stop the viruses from being worse. Thankfully, Randy was back in Boston with all of our kids, settled into the apartment on Boylston Street. I'm not sure I could have made any coherent decisions without him. We agreed that anything and everything should be done to kill the viruses. The latest chimerism test (test analyzing the donor cells versus the original cells) was showing that Emmy's cells were growing back and taking over Ella's donor cells.

"These are the times that try men's souls." I know Thomas Paine penned those words going up against tyranny and fighting for life, liberty, and the pursuit of happiness, but I felt those words echo in our hearts. Watching every single thing go wrong, all at once, was more than any soul could handle. The only thing I had left to cling to was knowing God had sent Emmy to Boston at this exact moment to be cured. It was what dragged me out of bed every morning, ready to fight, every day we were there.

It was discovered that Emmy's bloated body and belly were not just a result of fluid buildup. At the first sign of tortured cries before an explosive bout of diarrhea, the nurses knew she was now fighting something new. After losing all the good bacteria in her gut from the antibiotics, a bad bacterium had taken over. *Clostridium difficile*, commonly known as *C. diff*, was causing Emmy's stomach to swell and inflict more pain in her belly. I had no choice but to spend hours sitting in Emmy's bed comforting her, knowing I would be covered and have to sanitize my clothes. The bouts were quick and without warning, so I often would end up with it all over me. This "new normal" was disgusting and painful, but I would do anything to help Emmy just get to the next point of her healing, whatever that looked like.

It was obvious Emmy wasn't going to catch a break anytime soon. If it wasn't painful spasms, it was painful diarrhea. Her stomach had been in pain from the first day they had tried to feed her liquid nutrition through a feeding tube. Her stomach rejected each formula they tried and she was still not getting any good nutrition. Emmy was now twenty pounds lighter than she had been when we arrived. Her bald head looked so much bigger than her pale, frail body. It was so hard looking at her and not seeing a child who was on the verge of death.

A nutritionist was called early on and tried every type of formula they could—regular, low lactose, and even elemental. Every single formula made Emmy throw up or scream in pain. The nutritionist would stop everything and start over by putting Emmy on IV nutrition, hoping her stomach would settle down. When it came to try the tube feedings again, screaming would start within the first hour. As Emmy would curl in pain and begin puking, it was obvious she was going to starve to death if something else wasn't done. IV nutrition was not a long-term solution, but it was all she could handle.

Too much was happening all at once. While Emmy continued fighting for her life, we now had to find a house to live in. We only had the apartment until July, as the lease was running out and apartments on Boylston were too expensive for us to rent. The cost for doggy daycare was also getting outrageous. Randy and the kids had dropped our two boxers, Gumbeaux and Nola, off at a doggy day care when they'd first arrived. Beth graciously took in our two cats, Rex and Kevin, so we wouldn't have to pay extra for them. Beth was such a blessing through all of this.

The lack of personal space was also becoming an issue in the apartment and made us all want a house even more. The one-room, trendy apartment was only a few hundred square feet. There was one small table and three air mattresses lined up in the living room. It resembled a large tent for weekend campers. Our lives had been upended, and it was taking a toll on all of us. We needed a place to call our own. We needed stability.

As we expected, the homes near Boston were very old and very expensive. We couldn't live in base housing because we had too many pets. We also couldn't rent a house with four animals, so we had to find a house to purchase. Thankfully, a couple had just purchased our home in Virginia, which made purchasing in Massachusetts much easier. My sister did all the legwork by going to the surrounding cities and looking at every available home. Nicole and I had started searching before Randy and the kids had arrived so we had an idea what was out there and what we could afford. House after house, city after city, we found each one totally unfit for a child who was immunocompromised and in a wheelchair. Our search area became bigger and bigger, farther and farther from Hanscom AFB and Boston Children's Hospital, but nothing seemed available to fit our very specific needs.

The week before Randy and the kids arrived, Nicole found a house available about forty-five minutes from the Air Force base. She went to the first open house and returned with great news. It had enough bedrooms for a family of six, was in immaculate condition, and had a huge yard for our dogs. The only downside was the small town of Pepperell, Massachusetts, was an hour and half drive from the hospital—longer during Boston traffic.

I went a week later to do a walk-through and instantly knew this was the house. Of all the houses we'd looked at, this was the only viable option. The long drive would be another sacrifice we were just going to have to make.

Randy, the kids, and I drove out the next week to see if we should put an offer on the house. The hour and a half drive seemed like we were going on a road trip, but being in traffic was something we would eventually get used to. The whole family loved it. The woods in the back yard, the theater room, and an attic loft for the two boys to share seemed to be exactly what we'd prayed for. We all left the house filled with excitement, hopeful for the future.

This quaint little farm town would become the most beautiful backdrop during our years in Massachusetts. It was in the country, and houses were spread apart on nice large lots. The four-level colonial with a finished attic and basement, topped off with a theater room—in immaculate condition, was another answered prayer. It was within our military housing allowance budget and had just enough room for our family of six, plus Aunt Coley.

As we were enjoying our drive back to the hospital, I was talking with the satellite company representative to move our service from Virginia to Massachusetts and noticed a small car speeding around the highway traffic in the breakdown lane. Randy and I both took notice and looked ahead to see where the car was headed. Then we saw it. A motorcycle was broken down in that exact lane, and the car was heading full speed toward him. I couldn't speak. The driver of the car either didn't see the motorcycle or had lost control, as the car never slowed down. Right as it was about to hit the man on the motorcycle, I screamed out loud, "*No!*" All we saw was the car disappear behind the traffic and a motorcycle fly straight into the air.

My heart stopped. I screamed and then inhaled deeply. I slammed my body back into the seat and started hyperventilating. The kids, who had never seen me afraid or overreact to anything, stared at me wide-eyed. I forgot I was on the phone and started yelling, "Oh no, that man just got killed by a driver. Randy, did you see it? I just know he was killed—"

Randy quickly interrupted me and grabbed my arm. "Missy, stop. The man was fine. He ran up the embankment and was clear of the motorcycle and car. He's alive!"

The customer service agent was silent and then started asking what had happened. I'd forgotten he was even on the phone. I quickly hung up and sat stunned, forcing myself to breathe.

The sheer thought of death in such a traumatic way left me sick. It was right then I realized how much trauma and anxiety were affecting me. I was not OK, and I fully realized I may never be the same. The scene was on repeat in my head, like a skipped record. I barely moved from Emmy's bedside the rest of the evening. Every single thing that had happened to Emmy had not only scarred me but had also changed the way I saw the world and now reacted to it.

What was originally supposed to be a two-week trip to Boston Children's Hospital had become a three-year (at least) military assignment for our entire family. My heart was heavy. I was done seeing my child suffer. I started to feel suffocated and trapped, and hope was nowhere to be found. My very breath became my prayers. My words just felt empty; tears were all I had left for God. What was the finish line going to look like? A child permanently hooked up to a feeding tube and in need of constant airflow to breathe? What if she had spasms for the rest of her life and we had to put her in a home?

As I sat silently in my dark sleep room, I heard the words spill out of my mouth again before I knew what I was saying. "God, this has to end. Please just take her to heaven where there is no more pain. She can't live like this. I don't want her to live like this, and you know I will spend the rest of my life trying to make her life better, forsaking all others. I want to enjoy my kids and husband again. I want Emmy to live without pain. God, just do something now."

17
CHAPTER

I can do all things through Christ who strengthens me.
—PHILIPPIANS 4:13 (NKJV)

Emmy's mutated HLH cells were winning and killing off the new cells. Ella's cells now only inhabited 45 percent of Emmy's immune system. Not only that, we were expecting to get the results of our sons' genetic tests, revealing if they also had CNS-restricted HLH. Stress was at an all-time high.

Right before everyone moved to Massachusetts, Randy and I had gone forward with having the boy's perforin genes tested, against the doctor's wishes. They said it was better to wait and deal with one child at a time, especially when the other kids were healthy. Randy didn't want to wait. Everett was having horrible stomach pains and constipation. While I knew it was because he lived on mac and cheese, never eating any fruits or vegetables, Randy was worried that Everett could possibly have the other form of HLH that attacked the organs. His mind ran wild thinking about the boys having HLH, and he couldn't let it go. I tried hard to convince him that God had already shown us the boys didn't have HLH.

Sometimes, God doesn't tell you exactly what's going on. Sometimes, we have to just be still so we can see the signs and evidence of what's happening beneath the surface, beneath the unknown. I knew without a shadow of a doubt our other kids did not have HLH, specifically right after Ella was tested. God quickly reminded me of all the signs that proved they didn't have CNS-restricted HLH.

Right after Ella's HLH test was sent to the HLH clinic at Cincinnati Children's Hospital, God reminded me of all the things that would have turned on the HLH if she or her brothers had it. Ella was born six and a half weeks prematurely. Her little four-pound body had her immune system disrupted with vaccines and later with constant earaches and the flu. All the research we had found during our quest for answers showed that vaccines are one of the top instigators for autoimmune genetic mutations. Plus, most genetic HLH cases were evident by six years old, and she was now sixteen.

Eli was now thirteen and well over the six-year-old threshold. He was also born prematurely and fully vaccinated. The year we left Hawaii and visited Montana, Eli had a swing set collapse on him at my aunt's house. His head was badly cut, but he refused stitches. A week later, an infection set in, but it never "turned on" HLH. I was confident his test would be negative for CNS-restricted HLH.

Everett, still younger than six, seemed to be the one Randy was most concerned with. I tried hard to set his mind at ease, but nothing worked. Then God reminded me He already told us Everett would never be sick with HLH.

Back when we all lived in Virginia, four-year-old Everett fell off his bed and broke his arm. It was a little over a year after Emmy broke her arm and was admitted into the hospital with a seizure.

"*Mommy!*" Everett's scream, similar Emmy's scream when she broke her arm, echoed throughout the house.

"What happened, Ev?" I said scooping him up.

"I slipped off my ladder and hurt my arm! I'm fine. I don't need to go to the doctor. Please, don't take me to the doctor," he said, crying hysterically.

As I forced a smile and told him we just had to make sure his arm wasn't broken, I fought back every emotion I was feeling. All I wanted to do was scream, cry, and curl up in the fetal position. *Why is this happening again, God? Please, spare Everett from getting sick.*

After calling Melissa to watch Emmy, I ran Everett to the nearest ER. My stomach was in knots as I dialed Randy at work. Everett was listening so I kept the conversation as cheerful as possible.

"Hey, babe. Ev and I are on the way to the ER. He fell off his bunk bed and hurt his arm. I think it's just a sprain. He only cried a tad, but he doesn't want to go to the doctor. Can you give him some words of encouragement?" I said.

"Missy, are you serious? I don't think I can take this … Yes, put him on the phone. Hey, buddy! You got this. All they are going to do is take a picture of your arm. Nothing is going to hurt, OK?"

"OK, Daddy," Everett said in the most pitiful voice.

I didn't tell anyone. There was no way I wanted to give any power to the thoughts running through my mind. I was sick, almost to the point of needing to run to the ER bathroom. I had never worked so hard to keep smiling and making jokes. The X-ray showed his little arm had a buckle fracture in his left arm, opposite of where Emmy had one. As we drove home with his little arm wrapped in a temporary cast, panic began to set in. *How will we handle two kids with brain diseases at the same time?*

But God was quietly waiting for me on the front steps of our house. He was waiting for me in the form of a simple bouquet of flowers. Only Melissa and Randy knew we were at the ER, and they didn't send them. I quickly opened the card and saw that they were from a friend I hadn't talked to in months. The card read, "Missy, God woke me up this morning and told me to send you flowers. I hope this helps. Still praying for you and Emmy. Gigi."

God couldn't have been more obvious. He knew before it even happened. He was there, keeping my focus on Emmy and not worrying about the other kids getting an undiagnosed brain disease. God would use people like Gigi for the next few years to keep my mind steady on him. When fear and doubt would creep in, He was there. When I thought there was no other way, He made a way. People in the form of angels were surrounding our family every step of the way.

As we were told the results of the boys' genetic tests, the words finally brought us the peace we needed to move on.

"Both boys, Eli and Everett, are only carriers of HLH. Dad, they inherited your mutation on the perforin gene, but not mom's. Now that we know Emmy's three siblings are only carriers, we can put all our focus on Emmy. The other three kids will just need to have their spouses' blood tested before they decided to have children," Emmy's BMT doctor said with a smile on her face.

"Oh, thank God!" Randy said with a huge sigh of relief.

I was so thankful for God showing me the obvious signs about our boys, but the truth is that the other distractions were what we really needed in the moment. The monotony of withdrawal and all its effects on Emmy's body was taking its toll on everyone. I hated medicine. Sedation medication, pain medication, illicit drugs—they all became the same to me. After watching withdrawal over and over and over, I became fierce in telling my other kids, if they ever tried drugs and put us through this willingly, I would lock them up for life. There is no difference between addiction to hospital drugs and addiction to street drugs.

The dexmedetomidine and midazolam were at a constant wean but now on alternate days because the withdrawal was too painful for Emmy to sustain. Some days were filled with endless spasms, sneezing, body jerks, and nausea. Other days, Emmy would sleep like she was in hibernation. Once we thought she had a three-second seizure, but we couldn't tell. One minute her body was flailing, and then she just froze. Three seconds later, she began flailing again. We had to take her medication wean day by day. Slow and steady seemed like it would turn this stay into a life sentence, which made me fear we would never leave.

On calm days, the nurses would try "sprinting" Emmy off the CPAP. A nasal canula replaced the CPAP, and we would all stare at the monitor to see if her oxygen decreased. Her breathing was slow, but the loudness didn't make any sense. The nurses would also try adding in tube feeds, since the CPAP seemed to cause her belly to fill with air, and everyone was afraid of aspiration. The airflow didn't seem to be the problem. As soon as Emmy would get up to a teeny, tiny amount of 10-ml an hour, it came right back up. Her body was still rejecting liquid food.

Malnourishment, viruses, medicine-induced spasms, and a lacking immune system were all working together to steal Emmy's beauty. Bones protruding, head way larger than her body, and hips barely big enough to keep her diaper on, were all we could see. Thankfully, daily blood tests showed us that her organs were holding strong, and they adjusted her IV nutrition to fit her vitamin needs.

The pain in her stomach and the rejecting of any oral feeds and medication became too much for her to bear. A GI doctor was finally called in to perform an endoscopy and colonoscopy while also taking a few biopsies to see if she had graft-versus-host disease (GVHD). Once again, she was sedated and would have to be weaned off that extra medication. This vicious cycle was almost a horrible joke at this point. There was no way we were every going to leave this hospital—ever.

While Emmy's ANC constantly teetered above and below 500, Emmy was still getting red blood cell and platelet transfusions. A large dose of platelets were given before the biopsy to keep her from bleeding out, but they didn't do enough. Two days after the endoscopy/colonoscopy, Emmy starting passing blood clots the size of softballs.

The first time it happened, the nurse and I both gasped in horror. We couldn't physically witness anything else go wrong. We sat with tears in our eyes as Emmy would scream, throw up her legs, growl, and then pass a clot. What was the purpose of that procedure? It just made her worse. *God, just do something, anything, but this has to stop. Don't let her survive all of this just to be tortured the rest of her life. That is not a life worth living.*

I left the hospital for one day to spend time alone with Ella, Eli, and Everett. I noticed the kids were at each other's throats and were fighting. I felt like they were just as upset as Randy and me and had no other way of expressing how they felt. I knew they were resentful, so I decided to say something.

"You guys, I am really sorry I haven't been there for you. I love you so much. Please don't be mad at me for only paying attention to Emmy."

"Mom, I'm not mad at you. I love you. I just know that it's more important being with Emmy than us," Everett said in his tiny five-year-old voice.

"No, you are not less important than Emmy, and we are going to get her home so we can be a family again; I promise," I said as I flung my head around to hide the tears.

When deep calls to deep, the fear of drowning becomes inevitable. Not only was the guilt of being a horrible mother weighing on me, Randy and I were also arguing about anything and everything. I had no idea what was happening around me, but my life was no longer my own. I didn't want this life, and here I was stuck with it. I just knew all those years of being a rebellious teenager were going to catch up with me. Was I being punished?

Every day was a reflection of the last. From morning till night, it was all the same. No matter if I prayed or didn't, skipped meals to cuddle

Emmy or just sat and cried, nothing changed the outcome of the day. The hours and days blended into one another. The room only changed once or twice when the nurse would rearrange the equipment so Emmy could look out the window. The staff knew me by name. I knew which doctors would listen to me and then the ones who didn't care about solving the mystery of Emmy. I knew personal details about Emmy's nurses, and quickly realized who Emmy's favorites were; I would dread when they weren't on shift. I hated having new nurses, but I tried to be nice when they did everything wrong. This life was the most stressful, monotonous life anyone could have. We saw no end in sight, but God gently reminded me truths in His Word. He was ministering to me every wakeful minute, keeping me sane, if I listened.

Living in ICU Room 30, which had only a toilet and sink but no shower, made me realize what was truly important in life. One day I finally understood the true meaning of what the Apostle Paul meant when he stated, "I can do all things through Christ who strengthens me" (Philippians 4:13 NKJV). We Christians use this phrase for various things, not fully grasping the true meaning of what Paul was saying. I remember quoting this before a difficult test or a competition or even a run that seemed too hard to finish. But when you read the entire passage, it cuts to the heart of the matter.

"I am not saying this because I am in need, for I have learned to be content in whatever circumstance. I know what it is to be in need, and I know what it is to have plenty. I have learned the secret of being content in any and every situation, whether well fed or hungry, whether living in plenty or in want. I can do all things through Him who gives me strength" (Philippians 4:11–13 NIV).

As I was walking to my sleep room, trudging up the same back stairwell for my daily exercise, that verse came to mind and warmth washed over me. I had lived in that hospital well over two hundred days, eaten the same food, walked the same halls, and worn the same four outfits; but I was suddenly, blissfully at peace. The presence of God washed over me and I suddenly stopped and started crying—right there in the stairwell. It wasn't that I had accepted Emmy's diagnosis or was content being in a hospital; I realized that God truly was the only one who took care of my every need. No matter the outcome, God was there preparing me for what was next.

18
CHAPTER

Casting all your care upon Him for He cares for you. Be sober, be vigilant; because your adversary the devil walks about like a roaring lion, seeking whom he may devour.
—1 PETER 5:7-9 (NKJV)

It was almost two years since July 15, 2014, when Emmy had a seizure at the pool. In those two years, Satan had stolen Emmy's livelihood. The echoes of Emmy's giggles, the sound of classical music followed by Emmy dancing like a swan and the random thuds we heard as Emmy practiced gymnastics were gone. But while we still had Emmy with us, we yearned to see the old Emmy. It was the strangest feeling to look at Emmy and miss her all at the same time.

God was so merciful, though. He gave us a peak at the true Emmy. The extraordinary gifts she was born with. God showed us Emmy's capabilities—before the disease ravaged her brain. Some parents don't ever get to know their child's true potential and that's OK, because as parents we love our children with unconditional love. I have listened to the pain in other parent's voices and read the heartbreaking stories of their children being born with cerebral palsy or another debilitating disease. They can only daydream and imagine what gift their child truly had hiding behind the diagnosis. It makes me so thankful that we did get a glimpse of Emmy's true potential, even though the disease took away a part of our child that felt like we lost her for good.

Yet, no matter what Emmy lost, Satan was hungry for more. I felt like Job when God allowed Satan to attack everything Job had—his family and his fortune, yet not his life. *Was I Job or was Emmy?* Here we were, day after day, praying for a miracle, just a glimpse of hope, yet nothing changed. Emmy's team was curious as to what was happening inside her brain, so they scheduled another MRI. The results of the MRI almost broke our will to keep fighting.

"We don't know when it occurred, but there is another active lesion on Emmy's brain. It looks similar to a stroke, like before, so now we watch and wait. We feel confident the donor's cells will hold any HLH at bay. We just don't know if this occurred during or after the BMT," the neurologist explained.

"Did Emmy go through all of this for nothing? I thought the chemotherapy and bone marrow transplant would help. How do we know if HLH is still there?" I asked with tears in my eyes.

"I will send off a sample of spinal fluid to check the neopterin, but I still am hoping the bone marrow transplant won't allow anything else to happen," the neurologist said as he shook our hands and walked out the door.

Was HLH still in Emmy's brain? Did we just put Ella and Emmy through all of this, to end up right back with HLH still attacking what was left of Emmy's brain and mind? God, what is this pain proving? What lessons are we missing in this struggle? I felt emptied and hollow. I wasn't sure I could keep up the façade of positiveness and hope.

After weeks of nurses telling the doctors to just look into Emmy's throat, the ICU doctor decided to use a camera and figure out why it looked like Emmy was straining to breath. The ICU is a place of quick action and busybodies always looking for answers, so I wondered why it had taken almost four months for them to finally look. The result was alarming; Satan stole the last thing Emmy had left—her voice.

The left vocal cord was paralyzed, stuck in a closed position. I knew exactly when it had happened. It was the week after her BMT when she was struggling to breathe as a result of chemotherapy-induced mucositis. The loud pop from the intubation tube was actually the sound of the left vocal fold being broken. There was no fix or cure. Emmy's voice would never be the same and oxygen may be a lifelong need.

The probability of botched procedures and side effects from medicine were evident, nothing ended up as planned with Emmy. If there was a warning of a rare side effect, it always happened to Emmy. Randy and I just expected anything and everything bad to happen. How do you even stay positive, when your hope is shot down after every prayer? I knew if God didn't intervene soon, my sanity would soon be gone.

It was once again time for ICU attendings to change over. The nurses kept telling me that a specific doctor was finally taking over Emmy's team. "He is exactly what Emmy needs," they would say over and over. We had already met this doctor once before when he'd caught wind of Emmy's dystonic episodes. He was trained in a specific neuroscience specialty and had a strong grasp on the brain and exactly how it relates to the body and organs. He was a doctor I would like to call an "old-school doctor"—one who learned how to treat the whole person.

The first time we met him, he had walked into Emmy's room, watched her spasm in pain, and was able to give her a diagnosis in minutes. "What I see is that she has two to three types of dystonic reactions happening. One looks permanent, from the brain damage, but one or two are from medicine. We need to watch her for a few days on video and see if there is a correlation between medicine and movements."

Of course, that was before I fired her movement disorder doctor and at the time he didn't see the "need" to use a video monitor to watch her. No one else in the ICU pushed the issue, either. The sedation and Artane may have been stopped earlier, saving her from months of needless misery, but I try not to think of the what-ifs too much. There are so many times I wish I could go back and change what happened, to scream out what I knew needed to happen, but it wouldn't have helped what was happening at that exact moment. It sure did change how Randy and I reacted to everything after that, though.

Attending morning rounds had become the one thing I never missed. I would always attend or watch from the back, even if I was half-asleep. This time, I wanted to hear what this specific doctor, who recommended having Emmy watched on video, had to say about everything that had happened to Emmy.

The primary resident mumbled through the blood tests, inputs, outputs and the result of the latest echocardiogram. Emmy's heart was still not fully functioning, even though there was no medical reason for it. But this doctor understood the whole body and quickly explained what he believed to be happening. I couldn't believe I still had enough heart left to be crushed even more. *How can a heart break over and over and not leave the person dead?*

"I am glad to see Emmy off Artane and not fully dystonic like she was before. But her heart is still not functioning like it was in Virginia. The results of the test show a mild case of stress cardiomyopathy."

"What is that?" I asked him. "I haven't heard that diagnosis before."

"Stress cardiomyopathy is the name given when nothing can explain the weakness in the heart. Another name for it is 'broken heart syndrome.' All that she has been through has taken a toll on her. This happens a lot in older couples when the love of their life passes away. Their heart is literally broken," he said gently.

A tortured body, a brain that was scarred, and a life we loved now lost, but to know Emmy suffered from sadness so deeply it was damaging her heart was more than I could bear. "Why is God doing this to me?" Those were the last words she uttered before the spasms overcame her entirely and was admitted to the ICU. *Was she truly heartbroken? Did she think her daddy and I had failed her? That God had failed her?* The emotional weight of this diagnosis was too much, and I felt the last bit of strength leave me.

The strength I once had to power though any situation finally became obvious that it was gone. Independence Day was being celebrated all over the U.S., but I was stuck in a hospital room, watching the monitor lights flicker every time Emmy's heartrate became too rapid. Randy and the kids were watching the fireworks at Fenway Park from the rooftop of the Boylston apartment rental. The medicine wean was still causing Emmy to go through withdrawal, continuing the cycle of dystonic episodes. When not sleeping, her body was stiff as a board from her head to her toes.

Time was no longer a thing. Daylight beaming through the windows was the only way my mind understood the time of day. During the night, I had no recollection of what had gone on. I woke in a moment's notice, but I rarely remembered how many times I would get up with Emmy. Morning rounds was the only time I heard the date. It just didn't matter anymore. I was sleep deprived, depressed, hopeless and nothing really mattered. Living in a hospital seemed like it would be how I spent the rest of my life.

During the night, after the fireworks died off, I continued my ritual of waking upon first cry, repositioning her body and then laying back down, hoping I would sleep longer than 15 minutes. Over and over I did this. How many times, I never knew. But then it happened. As she cried, I followed the same steps as before. I repositioned her, rolled her to her other side, bent her knees, and bent her ankles to the neutral position. But as I tried to relieve the pressure in her left ankle, a sudden *pop* echoed in the room. Emmy screamed in pain, and I felt myself instantly go weak and light-headed. *Did I just break her ankle?* I stumbled to the nurse's station, opened the door, told Jordan what happened, and then everything went black.

"Missy. Missy, wake up. Are you OK?" the ICU fellow was saying as she shook my arm.

After the fogginess lifted, I realized what happened and began asking about Emmy's ankle. "Is her foot broken. Oh, no! I was pushing her ankle, and it popped. You need to do an X-ray. I just know it's broken!"

"Missy, we are looking at Emmy's ankle and it's not broken. She is fine, but have you ever passed out before?" the fellow asked.

"Yes, I have before. Sometimes I pass out when I get sick or see blood. Oh no, I really think I broke Emmy's ankle. Please do an X-ray now!" I replied.

"We will. But I need to know if you have ever urinated on yourself while passing out? That usually only happens when someone suffers a concussion, but Jordan said she caught you before you hit your head."

I was mortified. That is why I was shivering and so cold. I was lying in urine with the entire night staff looking at me. "No, I have never peed on myself. How embarrassing. Can I go change, please," I said as I tried to sit up off the floor.

"Wait a second. Take it slow, and let me help you. When you finish changing, we are going to send you next door to Brigham Woman's to get checked out. Something could be wrong, and we just want to make sure you're fine," she said as she shut the bathroom door behind me.

How did this happen? I had somehow humiliated myself while passed out, and now everyone in the ICU would know. Like they needed anything else to think I was crazy. *Could this entire stay get any worse?*

The next thing I knew, I was being carted on a hospital gurney through the hospital tunnels that connected Boston Children's Hospital to Brigham Women's Hospital. The worst part was that I had to call Randy and tell him what had happened. I covered my face in a blanket. Not only did I still think I had broken Emmy's ankle, Randy had to walk to the hospital from Boylston St., in the middle of the night. Was he going to hate me for breaking Emmy's ankle? She was already in so much pain and I just added to it. By morning, the entire ICU staff would be secretly laughing at me, and I just knew my husband was going to divorce me.

After being hooked up to an EKG, the doctor at Brigham Woman's told me that I had a condition called vasovagal syncope. Certain triggers cause the heart rate and blood flow to drop suddenly, causing loss of oxygen and blood flow to the brain. My entire life I had fainted at very inopportune times, mostly when I was sick. The first time I remember fainting was when I was just five years old. I was sleeping in the back seat of the car and became car sick on a mountain pass in Montana. We had stopped at a rest stop, and all I remembered was my mom picking me up off the floor of the bathroom stall. This would happen to me so many more times as I grew up, but none where I would make such a fool of myself. At least I now had a name for why I was prone to passing out.

When I returned to Emmy's room, the X-ray showed nothing broken, so they thought it was probably just a sprain. We have no idea why it popped because we spent hours a day stretching her ankles and wrists. Either I was too rough, or I pushed it the wrong way. No matter what happened, I knew the stress was too much for me to handle. I was sleep-deprived, stressed to the max, and fighting the dark feelings trying to overtake me.

The nurses encouraged me to wear earplugs or headphones while I slept in the room and that they would do everything to make Emmy comfortable. They reminded me that was what they were paid to do, so I reluctantly agreed. The foamy earplugs did just the trick. I was finally sleeping three straight hours when it was my night with Emmy. My mind was on a timer, so I still woke just to peek over at her. I worried that she would feel scared when I didn't get up with her, but she never showed it. Emmy loved the nurses, and I needed to fully trust them to do what they were trained to do and proved to me over and over again.

As the sedation medicines were slowly weaned, Emmy's ANC numbers began climbing above the sacred number of 500. After days of being above 500, Emmy started growing red blood cells and platelets, stopping the need for transfusions. With this period of stability in knowing the bone marrow transplant was holding, Emmy's mental health was now weighing on everyone's mind. Emmy was still only communicating by eye movements and barely uttered a sound.

On July 16, Emmy's nurse, Lilliana, had finally convinced the BMT team to allow her to take Emmy to the courtyard and get some fresh air and a change of scenery. Randy and Aunt Coley helped Lilliana wheel the entire hospital bed, laden with oxygen and IV poles, to the Pouty Garden. Still garbed in only a peach diaper and blankets, Emmy went on her first field trip since she was admitted in November. The entire experience only lasted five minutes, but it gave everyone a glimmer of hope. She'd had no fresh air and no direct sunlight on her face for 235 days. Everyone cheered for her as they rolled her back into ICU Room 30.

During the next week, Emmy was finally weaned off of the first of many sedation medications, midazolam. She remained on dexmedetomidine, but had Ativan added to her daily meds to aid the withdrawal of midazolam, but this was the first step in getting off the ICU floor.

Then, when least expecting it, they were gone. After months of fighting the deadly trio of viruses, the most recent blood test showed zero signs of any virus activity. Zero. Once Emmy's ANC remained steady over 500 for one week, the viruses just died. I had never seen doctors so relieved. They no longer needed to go through the very difficult process of ordering special T-cells. I later overheard nurses talking about how happy they were because not many immunocompromised people live long with adenovirus, coupled with BK and CMV. Sometimes, I was often angry if the nurses and doctors withheld important information from me, but I am so glad they never let me know that death was just around the corner if these viruses were not stopped.

The viruses were long gone, but pain still haunted Emmy every time she used the bathroom. Even the colonoscopy couldn't identify what was wrong, because the samples taken showed healthy tissue and no signs of GVHD. Knowing this, the nurses started Emmy back on tube feeds, always persistent to leave it going, even if she puked. Their hard work paid off and by the end of July, Emmy was getting all of her nutrition from formula. One more thing we were able to mark off the list holding Emmy in the ICU.

These small accomplishments caused the doctors to want to push Emmy out of the ICU faster than she was moving.

"We are happy at how far Emmy has come, but we can't move Emmy anywhere while she's still on CPAP and getting dexmedetomidine. It is classified as a strong sedation and rules are rules. She definitely can't go home until she has a permanent feeding tube placed, because it is her only way of nutrition and pulling it out would be detrimental. So, the questions remain: how do we get Emmy off CPAP and a permanent solution for nutrition?" the ICU chief asked rhetorically, quickly answering his own question. "Once the dex is weaned, we think if she has a GJ tube placed and then also a tracheostomy, she can move to the BMT floor…" he began saying before I cut him off.

"How many times do we have to tell you that Emmy will not be given a tracheostomy? You will have to find a different solution because we will not have you place a tube in her throat, just so you can get her off the ICU floor. No way!" I said, gritting my teeth, trying to hold back the tears that were burning my eyes.

"Okay, so let's take this one step at a time. What about placing a more permanent GJ feeding tube? Emmy pulls the one in her nose out weekly and every time the nurse has to replace it, it is painful and uncomfortable. Once the GJ tube is surgically placed in her stomach, it is very simple to remove if she starts eating solid foods. The tube is simply pulled out, and the incision closes and heals on its own," he quickly added. "So many people have GJ tubes placed in their abdomen and have no issues, whatsoever," he confidently finished.

After Randy and I discussed the GJ tube, we finally conceded. "Okay, a GJ tube is fine. But there is no way we are allowing you to trach her," Randy firmly stated.

After a date was scheduled to place the GJ tube, we requested Botox to be done at the same time. Neither of the current neurologists covering Emmy did Botox, so we were referred to a physiatrist. I was done with movement disorder neurologists, and this new doctor was just what we needed. This time, Emmy's calves, thighs, and left arm were Botoxed, but he also added alcohol blocks for her inner thighs. Alcohol blocks numb the nerves and last longer, where Botox only decreases muscle tightness for a few months. Emmy's legs had been crossing so hard during spasms that her hips looked dislocated sometimes. Thankfully, they were still combining procedures to keep Emmy from being sedated too often.

At some point, the margin of error had to pass over Emmy. I was praying and pleading the protection of Jesus over her hourly, but nothing went right. Just days after the GJ tube had been placed, we noticed that it kept sliding out of her stomach. After inspecting it, the nurse found that the inside balloon had popped. GJ tubes are kept in place by a small balloon that is on the inside of the stomach, attached to the tube. A plug is on the outside, so it doesn't pull into the stomach and the balloon is filled with fluid so it doesn't get pushed out of the stomach. She told me the balloons never pop, especially just days after being placed.

"This is so unheard of. I have never seen this happen, ever," the nurse said to me while she put tape around the GJ tube to hold it into place.

"If you only knew how much this doesn't surprise me. If something can go wrong, it always does with Emmy," I said shaking my head.

As soon as a doctor was available to replace the GJ tube, Emmy was scheduled and given extra Ativan and clonidine to keep her calm. The entire procedure was five minutes and Emmy barely knew what was happening. Regret was haunting me. *Was this another sign that we made the wrong decision for Emmy?*

I began worrying non-stop that Emmy wouldn't get off of the CPAP. The thought of leaving this hospital with not only a new feeding tube, but also a trach in her throat was making me physically ill. How could she come to this hospital eating, breathing and talking and leave breathing through a hole in her throat? Only God could fix this one. I knew without a shadow of a doubt she didn't need to have a tracheostomy tube placed, so I went to my knees again and prayed specifically for God to intervene.

Morning rounds never presented any new ideas to help the CPAP issue, so I hoped the weekly meeting would bring new ideas. Weekly meetings were always on Wednesdays. It was the one time everyone would discuss issues, get on the same page with Emmy's care and decide what to do next. Representatives from the PACT, ICU, BMT, and neurology teams would be sitting at a long table, ready to hear our concerns. We assumed this week would be no different. You can imagine our surprise as we walked in and saw new faces mixed with the old. Specialists had been called and meetings were held on what to do with Emmy's dependence on the CPAP. So far, the staff believed the CPAP was keeping her alive and couldn't be removed. Emmy could move to the BMT floor with it, but could never go home. Emmy's regular doctors saw no other options than to replace it with a tracheostomy tube, but then someone quickly spoke up. A new female doctor, one I had never seen before, was there giving options.

"What we need to do is a sleep study. We first have to figure out if it is Emersyn's brain causing her to strain while breathing? Or is it that she has been on constant airflow so long she just needs to get used to using her diaphragm again?"

"Yes, that sounds like a great idea. Let's do a sleep study and watch what her brain is doing on an EEG while she sleeps with no extra oxygen. I will set it up and get it planned for tomorrow night," the ICU doctor chimed in.

The next night was quite entertaining. Watching two nurses fight over Emmy's wellbeing was a scene to behold. Emmy's regular nurses had all become watchdogs for her. I witnessed nurses go toe to toe with doctors and even write letters to the ICU director, just to help get Emmy the care she needed. So, when the sleep study nurse came in and said they would be doing the entire study without oxygen, Emmy's nurse came unglued. The argument lasted so long that they had to bring the ICU doctor in to lay out the clear plan. Emmy's nurse was worried that it would be detrimental if she desaturated below 90 percent oxygen, so they agreed to only intervene if her oxygen level fell that low. Emmy's nurse watched the monitor like a hawk.

All night long. Emmy went without any oxygen and never desaturated below 90 percent, actually hovering around 98 percent the entire night. This simple sleep study proved Emmy didn't need oxygen, and we would never have to hear about Emmy getting a tracheostomy tube again. The CPAP was quickly replaced with a BiPAP to start strengthening her diagram. And over the next week, Emmy was weaned completely off air. I'm not sure who that doctor was that attended Emmy's family meeting and requested the sleep study, but I'm pretty sure she was an angel. We never saw her at another meeting again.

Like a master plan had already been planned out, once the extra oxygen was stopped, the last drips of dexmedetomidine that flowed into Emmy's vein was shut off. God worked it all out, according to His perfect timing.

Then, another miracle presented itself. When Emmy had the GJ tube placed, she had been given a dose of steroids. For a week, Emmy had stopped cramping and screaming from pain in her bottom. The doctors and I realized that when Emmy got that dose of steroids, it helped her colon. Sadly, steroids can reduce ANC count and can harm the transplant, so they decided to try a local cream steroid. The reaction was not as strong as IV steroids, but it helped reduce enough pain for Emmy to not fear using the bathroom.

The list of items that needed to be checked off to leave the ICU floor was finally accomplished. It all happened so quickly; I was awestruck. Word quickly spread and the BMT nurses began preparing a room for Emmy. The only problem was that there are a limited number of rooms and many kids had priority over Emmy. She already had a room, so post-transplant and chemo kids took precedence if they came in through the ER. We patently waited for a room, preparing our hearts for a change in scenery and medical care.

Nine months. We lived in the ICU for nine straight months. I still couldn't believe we were finally going to break out of ICU Room 30. Each ICU staff member came by to tell Emmy how happy they were and to wish us well. Everyone seemed to be so relieved to finally get Emmy off the ICU floor. The joy was not because they would have another room open up for another child, but because Emmy was leaving alive, despite the initial diagnosis.

19
CHAPTER

My God, my God, why have You forsaken me?
—MATTHEW 27:46 (NIV)

Two days before Emmy's tenth birthday on August 26, the ICU threw a huge going-away party. They all lined the hallways, clapped, cheered, and blew bubbles as she was rolled to the BMT floor. I missed the entire thing. For days, they kept saying a room was opening, and then it never did. I had stayed four nights in Emmy's room, waiting for the move, but I couldn't go another night without sleep. The night before, I went to our new home to sleep, but early the next morning, the room opened up and Emmy left the ICU. Aunt Coley was there when they moved Emmy, and thankfully, recorded the whole parade.

The day was complete as Emmy arrived on the floor with kids who looked just like her. Emmy was no longer the only bald kid, and the nurses seemed to understand the magnitude of a child suffering more than regular nurses. These nurses knew what it was like to care for kids, months at a time, with their precious lives hanging in a perfect balance of poison and antibiotics. Emmy instantly loved the nurses. I instantly loved the cleanliness and mindful sanitation of everything. This floor was shut off to regular visitors, and no one who was sick could enter.

The BMT team was amazing. They brought in therapists and swallow experts to get Emmy back to being off tube feeds and using her hands again. Emmy was ready to get real food in her belly, but they didn't know whether or not her vocal cord issue would cause her to choke. Emmy started with foods like Jell-O and juice thickened and fortified with protein. Her stomach still ached with tube feeds, even though the formula was broken down to the most elemental of food. Everyone was so wonderful in trying to get Emmy healthy and on the road to recovery.

While many of the families were always coming and going, I met a family who had been fighting for years to help their son. Like many children, he was born with a genetic mutation and had received two BMTs by the time he was two. Here was a mom who'd lived in the hospital longer than me, yet she smiled and had learned to take each day as it came. I learned a lot from all the parents we met, but I also became aware of the toll sickness takes on families. Many families were in the process of divorce or would soon be.

I remember telling Randy that nothing could ruin our marriage. Why would people get mad at each other just because their child was sick? We would soon find out that answer as time went on. Stress and frustration were already building under the surface of our family, and the crack was widening.

Emmy was only on the BMT floor for four weeks before they felt she was stable enough to go to in-patient rehab. Emmy and I didn't want to go to rehab. I was done living in hospitals, separated from my family, but the amount of Ativan Emmy was taking on a daily basis was definitely out of the "safe range" to deal with at home.

Three hundred and six days—that was how many days we'd been at Boston Children's Hospital. It was now September 26, the day before our seventeenth wedding anniversary, and we couldn't even understand the emotions we were feeling. We knew Emmy should have never been in the hospital that long, but now we had a child who had survived every type of medical torture, misdiagnosis, virus and rare genetic disease.

Franciscans Rehab facility and others like it, don't have the nurse-to-patient coverage like an ICU or BMT floor, but we kept saying this was actually a good thing. Emmy was well enough to not be monitored so closely, but that meant we had to watch her more, without any breaks. Aunt Coley and I still took turns, but it was so much work. Soon, we would be home, and Emmy would start to feel like a normal kid again. Of course, our normal would be nothing like it had been before the day she broke her arm, but anything was better than living in a hospital.

Franciscans was an older rehabilitation facility that also had long-term care. I met some of the most beautiful women and their children during our one-month stay. One mother had a son who was experiencing dystonic crisis; his doctor reduced his movement disorder medicine in half instead of weaning it slowly and sent his body into non-stop spasms. Elizabeth was a single mama fighting insurance companies and hospitals for approval to get him deep brain stimulation (DBS). Each time the basal ganglia fails to filter out a movement or spasm, the DBS reacts against it, stopping erratic movements. At one point, we had also been so desperate in the ICU, we asked if DBS would work for Emmy's constant spasms. Doctors said it wouldn't work on Emmy because most of her basal ganglia was gone. I'm glad they said no, because we would have done anything to get her body calm. But Emmy might have hated us because with DBS comes a small box that is implanted into the chest, which she would have hated.

Franciscans was a great transition for Emmy. The nurse practitioner who oversaw Emmy's care quickly reduced the number of calories per milliliter in her formula, and the puking finally subsided. Emmy's formula was the most basic formula, but it was very condensed so she would get the most nutrients in the least amount of fluid. Essentially, it just needed to be watered down. What a simple fix that was overlooked before.

The speech therapist started working on feeding Emmy daily with small corn puffs to see if her ability to swallow was still there. I prayed every day Emmy's ability to eat would return because her body was rejecting the GJ tube in her stomach. A granuloma, which had to be burned off with silver nitrate, continually grew around the hole. The nurse would burn off the growth and it would reappear the next week. The promises that the GJ tube would be painless and unnoticeable by Emmy were obviously broken.

Even though Franciscans checked Emmy's blood daily, Dana Farber wanted Emmy to come during our third week for a check-up and more in-depth blood work. It was our first outing, so they called a wheelchair accessible taxi. Emmy was rolled and latched into the back of the van, which was hot and stinky. I could see Emmy becoming very sick, with every turn and stop at traffic jams. I started to become worried that we'd bought a house much too far from Children's, and I was not ready to deal with a puking kid every ride.

Dana Farber Cancer Institute has a pediatric clinic called Jimmy Fund. It's a fun place for kids to hang out while they're getting chemo or weekly checkups. The nurse called Emmy back while I was making a craft for Emmy. If it weren't for the craft stations, Emmy would have never wanted to go, but crafting is Emmy's love language.

Blood work revealed Emmy's cell numbers were still stable and not dropping any longer. The stable numbers prompted the BMT doctor to schedule the removal of Emmy's CVL tubes from her chest. This was a huge milestone, because it meant they were confident no more treatments would be needed. It truly felt like this nightmare was coming to an end. Instead of weekly visits to Jimmy Fund, Emmy was cleared to come twice a month.

Insurance was never an issue with us. Tricare took care of every need, every therapy, and every procedure, every time. During our stay in the ICU, Emmy was also signed up for MassHealth. It was Medicaid for Massachusetts, and they always covered people with disabilities of every kind. Emmy's condition and lasting disabilities were so complex, her monthly payment was waived, giving us a way to make sure co-pays and yearly caps from Tricare were covered. But something was wrong with our insurance while at Franciscans. The social worker came to me and told me the bad news.

"Missy, for some reason, Tricare won't cover Emmy's stay here. And while Emmy has MassHealth, we can't get it approved from them either. I have never seen this happen. Do you think you feel confident taking Emmy home next week? We can't afford to have her staying here, for free."

"Yes, of course. But if our insurance doesn't cover this stay, does this mean we have to pay? We were told we had to come here," I said, caught by surprise. This stay had to be around five hundred dollars a day, at least.

"*No!* We will cover the cost of your stay. But that's why we can't keep Emmy longer than a month. She has made great progress while here, started accepting feeds and even weaned off some of the Ativan. I am confident she will do great at home," the social worker said with a smile.

Randy came with our minivan prepared to take Emmy home. Even though Emmy was ten years old, she still needed to use a car seat. A year of being bedridden made Emmy weak, especially her back and neck. I sat next to her, while Randy drove us home. It felt like we transported back in time, ten years to when we first brought newborn Emmy home from the hospital in Minot, ND.

It was a stressful drive home, and Randy constantly checked us in the review mirror, making sure Emmy was OK. Within ten minutes, Emmy became carsick. Besides holding a puke bucket in front of her, I had to constantly maneuver her body so she was comfortable sitting upright in the car seat. Pain was in every inch of her body, especially her back. The pain forced her to lay forward, on her lap, like she had back in Virginia.

The reaction on Emmy's face as we pulled into the driveway of our new home was incredible. She had been without a home for almost a year, and we made sure she felt like we'd brought Virginia up to Massachusetts. It must have been a shock for her to leave one home, never to return. I had gotten over the feeling of loss, but I wasn't sure Emmy ever would.

November 25, 2015, to October 27, 2016, felt more like a decade than a year living in hospitals. It was actually longer, counting the stay in Virginia. But God. He answered my simple prayers. Emmy was cured and back home with her family. Our family was reunited, all under the same roof. The kids surrounded Emmy with cheers and hugs, as we showed her the house. Joy began to fill our hearts again, ready for a new future.

Halloween marked the start of that new future when the CVL tubes were removed from Emmy's chest. It was a perfect way to celebrate October 31. The staff kept Emmy overnight to monitor her after the sedation, which allowed Emmy to be pushed around the BMT floor by nurses to go trick-or-treating.

Once back home, our nursing skills were soon put to the test. I was now acting as doctor, nurse and clinician, as I dealt with symptoms of withdrawal and every other issue that came up. Emmy was taking 1.5 mg of Ativan every four hours, which would keep any adult in a state of grogginess. I quickly moved it from every four hours to every six hours, which she handled pretty well. Teeth grinding, left arm spasms, and minor withdrawal symptoms were present—but nothing like we'd witnessed in the hospital. The full-body dystonic spasms had ended before we went to the BMT floor, and I was so sure we would never see them again. But then, why did I have an ache in my heart as if this pain and trauma was far from over?

December was upon us, and we saw Emmy grow and heal the way we had been praying for over the past years. She slowly transitioned back to underwear during the day, which was a huge priority for her. Emmy may have been physically disabled, but she was fully aware of how things were supposed to be. She knew she wasn't supposed to be in diapers and she worked hard to retrain her muscles. She also began working her atrophied body muscles by allowing us to stand her up a few times a day. I just knew that the simple prayer I prayed nonstop was coming true. "Father God, I believe that I will see Emmy sing, dance, play, and jump again. She will be fully restored. In Jesus's name, Amen."

Then, within just weeks of being home, Emmy began to eat solid foods. It was obvious that she didn't need to be tube fed by her desire to eat everything in sight. Being starved for so long caused her appetite to be insatiable. Emmy's weight gain proved to the doctors she no longer needed the GJ tube, and at the next visit, they gladly removed it. Since its original placement, the tube irritated Emmy's skin and a granuloma was always present. The pain from the granuloma and then burning it off was just too much for Emmy to handle. Emmy's CVL was gone along with the GJ tube, and we truly felt like it could only get better from here.

When I thought things couldn't get any better, we found that God had answered our prayers to be placed next to good neighbors. We learned early on in our military career to always pray for good neighbors. We moved too often to be stuck next to neighbors who didn't like kids. At first glance, I thought we bought a house too isolated from others, but we soon came to see the woods between our house and the neighbor wasn't very thick. Dan, Rebecca, Kate, and Grace soon became our best friends. Not only were they wonderful people, Rebecca specialized in special needs and their girls were around the same ages as Emmy and Everett.

Rebecca and I bonded almost instantly and could talk to each other like sisters. I finally found someone who I could tell all my dark, sad feeling to, without fear of judgment. It was hard discussing my feelings of hopelessness and despair to Randy. He obviously could relate to me, but how could he help me out of my pain, when he was drowning in his own?

The week before Christmas in our new home, we had very special visitors show up unexpectedly. Rebecca knew Santa and Mrs. Claus and asked if they would visit our family. Without really knowing us that well, Rebecca went out of her way to help make our Christmas truly special.

Our kids were so surprised. That Christmas was everything I hoped for. Emmy and the kids were finally able to breathe a sigh of relief and enjoy the season. The Bosch family was all under one roof again, celebrating the birth of Jesus without the fear of sickness.

Amid the return to normal and added stressors of handling all of Emmy's medical needs, Randy and I truly felt like we needed to get away for just one night to reconnect. We felt the vice grip of fear slowly loosening its hold just enough for us to leave Emmy for a few hours. Aunt Coley wouldn't be living with us forever, and who knew when we would get this chance again.

It was a new year, and 2017 was finally going to be a year of renewal and restoration. Randy and I spent New Year's Day at the famous Omni Parker House, home of the original Boston cream pie. We relaxed and reconnected over a quiet dinner at Ruth's Chris Steak House. Reconnecting in times of stress and chaos was what held our marriage together—that, along with a lot of grace and forgiveness. I was realizing how easy it would be to just throw in the towel and not work on the marriage God had ordained.

As life around me seemed to be going back to normal, I soon realized that my mind was stuck in a place of shock and not advancing with the world around me. I never understood trauma and PTSD until that exact moment in time. As the actual trauma of our hospital stay was fading, I found that areas of my brain had turned off to protect itself. I was unable to perform many tasks that came naturally to me as a homeschooling mom. I envisioned my brain like a pie cut into pieces. Each slice related to aspects of my life, but many pieces seemed to be gone. As I spent almost a year with Emmy, living through every minute of trauma with her, the parts that remained were the ones that allowed me to focus solely on Emmy's health and care.

I would try to do normal tasks or even talk about certain things, but I would become completely overwhelmed and just freeze. Whatever parts that had turned off in my brain were making my everyday life impossible. I was unable to do the dishes or clean if someone was not physically sitting with Emmy. Cooking was unheard of without help from Ella or Aunt Coley. Multitasking, which I felt was my greatest strength, was now physically impossible. I found myself yelling at everyone to just,

"Help out." Yet I couldn't help out either. I was a physical and emotional mess, and nothing I did helped those areas in my brain turn back on. Thankfully, my family gave me more grace than I probably deserved and quickly picked up my slack. But whatever progress I was slowly making abruptly stopped in February.

Sleepless nights had never ended since Emmy became sick in 2014. I was exhausted, never getting more than thirty minutes of sleep at once, and felt like a zombie. Most nights, I would sleep through Emmy's cries and Randy would have to wake me up. He was working full time and the constant cries of Emmy made his days hard to get through.

One morning, Randy heard Emmy cry and carried her to our bed before he left to work. Within fifteen minutes of his car pulling out of the driveway, I woke to Emmy seizing next to me in bed. Besides the sudden shock of seeing Emmy seizing, I was confused on how she got there. I yelled for Ella, whose bedroom was just down the hall. The sudden shock caused my ears to start ringing, my body to freeze up and cold sweat to run from my forehead. I was going to pass out.

I reached for my phone and dialed 9-1-1, forcing myself to stay awake. As I told the dispatcher what was happening, I stared at Emmy next to me, helpless to stop her seizure. When Ella finally showed up, I could see she was also shocked from the sudden screams that woke her up. I asked her to get me a cold washcloth and as soon as she stepped in front of the linen closet, I heard her collapse onto the floor. The dispatcher heard me yelling at Ella to see if she was okay, and asked if another ambulance needed to be sent. After hearing Ella say she was fine, I told her no and that Ella was fine.

A few moments passed and Ella walked into the bedroom holding a wet washcloth, then suddenly collapsed again. The entire scenario would have been hilarious if it wasn't for Emmy seizing next to me. Ella inherited more than my genetic mutation; she also inherited my vasovagal syncope. Ella stood up just in time to open the door for the paramedics. They came upstairs and saw me lying next to Emmy in a cold sweat. They tried to call me an ambulance, but I explained that I just needed a few moments and it would pass. They scooped Emmy up and carried her to the ambulance, where I met them two minutes later. As soon as Ella felt better, she quickly packed our hospital bags and brought them out to the ambulance.

As soon as I felt the fog lift, I frantically called Randy. He was still in the car, so he quickly turned around to meet us at Boston Children's. I tried to force myself into believing the seizure was just from weaning Ativan, but I couldn't. I was too careful with each wean and only decreased it at a fraction of what was recommended. The team of doctors decided to do an MRI, which came back stable. Nothing new was visible. But fear was getting the best of me.

I should have known something wasn't right, by what I did next. The first thing I did when Emmy was discharged was call a local business who performed hyperbaric oxygen therapy. The only time I searched for outside help, for alternate sources of healing, was when Emmy's brain wasn't healing naturally.

The drive to the oxygen therapy business was just as bad as the drive to the hospital. Emmy clearly told me she didn't want to get into the oxygen chamber, but my fear forced her to go. It was like Emmy knew it wouldn't work. After three rounds, Emmy was still very spastic and showed no improvements, unlike the results we saw in Virginia. In my heart I knew her brain still had inflammation, but I wanted to stay positive so we continued going. After ten rounds, I decided to call neurology and tell them I didn't like how Emmy's body was reacting to the seizure. Neurology ordered blood work, spinal fluid tests, and another MRI, but all came back normal. According to science, Emmy was still disease free. Blaming the seizure and increased body movements on drug withdrawal was hard, but I forced my mind to believe.

Why I never learned from my past is so beyond me. I knew that when anger and depression became unbearable, it was because Emmy was sick. My behavior had become directly related to her health, even if I didn't fully understand it. Days were getting worse; the nights were still sleepless. I found myself secretly placing all of my misery on Emmy and her disease. But the nights were the worst.

I hated nights. I dreaded them. The sound of Emmy's breathing and cries sent shock waves up my spine. Rage would fill every inch of my body. I couldn't even look at Emmy without wishing her dead. I knew those thoughts weren't of God, but if this was our new normal, I didn't want it. I was raging like a trapped animal.

On one of the really bad days, I found myself driving aimlessly, screaming out to God. This form of prayer was very common when I found myself alone. God reminded me that help was always present, but I had quit using it. Being angry was so much easier than submitting, but I began reading certain Bible verses that I had forgotten about after bringing Emmy home. I began studying Ephesians 6 again until it occurred to me the real purpose of the armor of God. The armor is 90% defensive and only 10% offensive. I was using it to attack, when I should have been using it to stand strong and rely on God's power. For years, I had been trying to fight this battle with all my physical and emotional might, but it was not enough. Reading the Word and praying were the only things that kept my anger at bay.

Emmy made it to the twentieth dive and still showed no signs of improvement. She started randomly wetting her pants and began crying all night long, with no periods of sleep. On April 21, we were driving to HBOT to start dive twenty-one when God told me, "No more dives." I instantly looked at Emmy and cheerfully told her we wouldn't do any more dives after today. This assurance to stop forcing Emmy to do HBOT and stop trying to heal Emmy myself was what I needed to hear.

But God was telling me something different that day. God was telling me to not take Emmy in the dive chamber ever again, including that day. He knew her brain wasn't going to be able to handle it. As the tank began to pressurize, I noticed Emmy's eyes blinking strangely. I began asking her what was wrong when all of a sudden, her eyes began blinking uncontrollably. As I turned her to fully face me, she went into a full-blown seizure. We had only been pressurizing for three minutes, so the technician was able to quickly depressurize and open the door.

I carried Emmy out of the large, metal tank and realized I didn't have her seizure medicine. I quickly called 9-1-1 and the ambulance was there within five minutes. The paramedics treated her with two doses of medicine, but neither stopped the seizure. Oh, how my heart knew what was coming, so I begged them to just drive all the way to Children's. The paramedics were scared the medicine didn't work, so they took us to the nearest hospital. Emmy ended up being taken to an adult hospital, with only one pediatrician on call.

As soon as I met with the pediatrician, I regurgitated Emmy's entire medical history in a matter of minutes. From the look on the doctor's face, he was not equipped or trained for an "Emmy". After trying as many meds as he felt safe in trying to stop the seizure, he became nervous that she would stop breathing. I reminded him that she was still at 100 percent oxygen and to just send us to Children's for further care.

Fear clouds even the best of doctor's judgement and my words were ignored. Protocols were put into motion and Emmy was quickly intubated as they contacted Children's transport team to come get her.

Randy quickly left work to meet us. The minute we saw each other, feelings of anxiety and fear poured out of our eyes. This felt like Déjà vu, except it did happen before on July 15, 2014. Once the ambulance arrived for Emmy, I froze with fear and told Randy he had to ride with her. I wasn't ready to do this again. Each moment from the last three years flooded my memory. All I had to do was think of the ICU and my ears began ringing. My knees became weak and I knew I was either going to pass out or puke if I stepped foot in that ambulance.

"Missy, I can't go in the ambulance. I wasn't there when Emmy seized and I can't answer specific questions. I don't even know how much of each medicine she is taking. They need someone who knows everything about Emmy's care," Randy said in defiance to my request.

"Are you serious, Randy? It is your job as a dad to know his daughter's medicine. Why do I have to be the responsible one?" I quietly yelled at him.

"Are you serious, right now? How dare you make me feel bad that I don't know the exact doses of medication. Thanks for calling me a bad father, Missy," he loudly whispered to me before walking back to Emmy's bedside.

I angrily turned and walked directly to the ambulance, marched up the steps, sat down and buckled up. I was so mad that he didn't understand the torment this caused me. That small argument would be the beginning of a period of resentment between the both of us. But taking care of a sick kid can do that. But arguing about this would have to wait; Emmy was admitted back into the hospital. Not only were we back at Children's, we were sent directly to the ICU. I was thankful the doctors on call knew Emmy, because they instantly extubated her and began weaning the sedation. The neurology team immediately hooked her up to an EEG and increased her daily dose of Keppra. The EEG looked stable, so they opted to not do another MRI so soon after the last one.

For two days, Emmy recovered in the ICU. Nurses and doctors came by to see Emmy and were so excited to see her doing so well, as opposed to her first stay. I quickly perked up because, yes, she was not in dystonic distress and attached to a dozen tubes and wires. Maybe this stay was just to remind us that Emmy may be in and out of hospitals the rest of her life, but she was better than she used to be.

After we made it back home, there was an evening all the kids were in bed and we were alone, at last. That heated discussion finally caught up to us, and our words just spiraled out of control. Randy and I had our first real fight in over 16 years that included words like divorce and leaving. Every word, every offense, every sacrifice made, and everything we thought wasn't worthy of mentioning before came out as daggers straight to the heart. Even the small things we laughed at that seemed so miniscule before, but were cause for others to get divorced. Medicine, bed-wetting, no sleep, lack of faith, responsibilities, who should wake up in the middle of the night, who should carry Emmy, and on and on—all were fought about that night. And disrespect. That was a big one that weighed heavy on Randy's heart. Disrespected in front of the medical staff for not knowing Emmy's medicine. Making him feel like a failure of a dad. I knew he didn't know Emmy's meds that day, because I was always weaning something. I was the only one who truly knew the amount of medicine she was on. But I was sick and tired of being the one who gave up everything to care for Emmy, who had to ride in ambulances, who had to witness every IV stick, every intubation and every procedure done in the hospital. We both had hit our limit and it poured from our mouths like we were enemies. After all was said and done, we both secretly knew that this entire fight and the harsh words were just a reaction to the realization the disease was back.

Day after day and nothing changed. May was just another month of Emmy begging God for healing. She prayed nightly to walk again and to be like other kids. All I prayed for was sleep. Who cared about walking and being normal when I had gone days without sleep? I was losing my mind being woken up six times a night to adjust her, cover her up, or give her a drink. All I wanted in life was sleep, nothing more. I had begun convincing myself that, even though she had two seizures and never slept, she was healed. I mean, hadn't God led us here, to Boston, for healing?

Lack of sleep, growing anger, and the feeling of being trapped caused me to snap. I had to get away, or who knows what would happen.

I had earned a weekend retreat with Young Living the year before, which I had already pushed off while we were living in the hospital. But the retreat was offered again in June, and this time I wasn't going to miss it. This was my chance to get away from everything and ignore reality, even for just a couple of days. After I begged Randy—telling him I was going to end up in an insane asylum if I didn't leave—he reluctantly agreed. Two days before my trip, the glaring signs we willfully ignored, became even more obvious.

"Mom, wake up, wake up! Emmy is having another seizure. Don't you hear her on the baby monitor? Hurry, Mom, help Emmy!" Ella cried to me as I jumped out of bed and ran to Emmy's room.

"Grab her medicine, Ella. How long has she been seizing?" I frantically said, trying to hold back my tears.

"I don't know. I just heard funny noises and ran to her room," Ella said in a worried voice.

This time I was prepared and had the medicine next to Emmy's bed. Five minutes passed after the first dose and nothing happened. We patiently waited ten minutes and administered the second dose. Emmy snapped out of the seizure but was extremely lethargic, so I called her neurologist. He recommended that we bring her to the ER because a double dose of Diastat could affect her breathing and blood pressure.

Randy was already at work, so I drove Emmy myself. The ER staff monitored her for a few hours until she fully woke up and then discharged us to go home. I kept telling myself she was just fine. This is all normal for a person with brain damage. I fought back each thought of going through another bone marrow transplant and living in the ICU again. I refused to believe that HLH was back. God said she was healed, so she was healed. No matter what anyone said, I was leaving town.

I left for Montana to visit my family and friends before heading to Salt Lake City. I had completely forgotten what it was like to ignore reality and enjoy myself. *Is this what normal life is like? To actually be able to travel and visit people again?* I yearned so deeply for our old life it ached in my heart. I missed the freedom, the traveling, and the fun. We used to travel somewhere, anywhere, every month just because we loved being together experiencing places as a family. Now, we never traveled as a family and were trapped in either a hospital or our home. I envied every single person I saw that had healthy kids. The entire trip left me envious and angrier than before.

After I arrived home four days later, the doctors scheduled Emmy for a follow-up MRI. Emmy seemed pretty calm, so I asked if she could go without sedation. They agreed and pre-medicated her with just a small dose of clonidine. I was able to lay with her in the MRI and hold down her dancing right hand. She made it the full forty-five minutes without so much as a flinch. I was so proud of her I took her straight to the gift shop and bought a stuffed animal of her choosing. We headed home and waited for the doctor to call with the results.

The next day, the doctor called and said he didn't see anything new. Against my better judgment of staying in denial, I just had to tell him what I knew to be true. "OK, I'm not trying to freak out, but I'm scared this disease is back. She is progressively getting physically worse just like the times before new inflammation was in her brain," I said, trying to hold back the fear I had kept nicely tucked away.

"Missy, there are still no signs the disease is back. Just keep an eye on her behavior and trust that the 50 percent chimerism has proven to keep HLH from returning," he confidently told me.

Setting my worry aside, the kids and I went to our neighbor's house on June 30 for an early Fourth of July BBQ.

Kids were swimming, adults were laughing, and everything seemed to be alright again. Rebecca snapped a picture of Emmy that made Emmy look completely fine, at least to my blissfully ignorant eyes. Her eyes were clear and bright, and her smile was perfect. That party was exactly what we needed to remind ourselves to leave the past behind us.

But the next morning, it all changed. The trapdoor opened, and we all fell through. We had been down this hole before, but this time, we knew what was coming at the bottom. On July 1, Emmy woke extremely spastic and complained of an earache. I called the doctor, trying not to overreact, because I was sure it was just Swimmer's Ear. Erring on the side of caution, the neurologist said to bring her in.

Being admitted on a moment's notice seemed so normal at this point. I had a go bag, filled with overnight clothes, toiletries and phone cables. Ella would pack Emmy's bag and throw in her iPad. It was done so often, it was now second nature. I still maintained a confident attitude that this was just an earache, so I alone drove Emmy, and Randy stayed home with the kids.

HLH that only attacks the central nervous system is almost as invisible and undetectable as diseases can be. While the most common form of HLH can quickly be detected by a few markers in the blood and obviously inflamed organs, there are no obvious signs that can be quickly found in normal blood work or common tests done on spinal fluid to detect CNS-restricted HLH. The only way to know for sure CNS-restricted HLH has returned is because a new lesion was found on an MRI, which had not been the case so far, or a specialized test on the NK cells, which takes up to five days. The doctor can also send off spinal fluid to be tested for neopterin, but even that can take up to a month.

When we arrived to the hospital, the doctor decided to just fit Emmy in for an MRI and then release us to go home. Everything else would take too long to find any answers, and Emmy had been poked and drained of spinal fluid enough.

After Emmy was finished with the MRI, I met her in the outpatient recovery area. She was always pretty good at waking from sedation, so I quickly began getting her dressed and ready to leave. Just as I began loading her into her wheelchair, Emmy's neurologist came rushing through the doors, telling us to wait. I didn't like the urgency in his voice.

"Missy, we have to talk? I need to show you something." His tone shook my insides.

"Sure, but please tell me you didn't find anything? I've had such a bad feeling. You found something, didn't you?" I stuttered.

"We found another spot on the frontal lobe of her brain. We can't be sure if it's HLH or one of the side-effects from chemotherapy. I secured you a hospital room. We have to run the other tests, but we are going to have to do another biopsy to be 100% sure what it is," he said, clearly showing signs he was afraid of how I would answer.

I replied back in a whisper, realizing Emmy was sitting just feet away. "A biopsy? Are you serious? She already went through that. Why is this happening again? What are the statistics of this happening twice? I really need to call Randy".

"Let's take this one step at a time. Emmy's room is on the neuro floor, and we will figure out a plan before we decide anything. We will work together to get Emmy through this," he said, trying to keep my hopes up. Then I turned and looked at Emmy, realizing she saw the look on my face.

"Baby, you know how your body never wants to stop moving and you keep having seizures? Well, the doctor said it's because he found something in your brain again. We finally know what is causing this, and he is going to help fix it. And guess what? We get to be on the neuro floor that has the awesome playrooms with all the crafts and games!" I tried sounding excited like this was a good thing and not a death sentence.

All I saw was death before us. I already knew I could never, ever go through what we just went through, but for Emmy to do it a second time? There was no earthly way. This was the time we needed God to reveal his power, not on time like before, but before we had to walk through hell again. If CNS-restricted HLH was back or if now she had a rare brain tumor from the chemo, there was no way any of us could survive it without God carrying us all the way to the end. Once almost broke us; going through this a second time was going to be impossible to recover from. *Oh, God, please take this disease from Emmy once and for all. Spare her life. Strengthen me, according to Your Word.*

CHAPTER 20

I am the Lord, and there is no one else; there is no God except Me. I will arm you, though you have not known Me, so that people may know from the rising to the setting of the sun that there is no one besides Me.
—ISAIAH 45:5-6 (NASB2020)

Words failed me. Despair hung like a thick, heavy noose around my neck. Randy and I tried to not show our fear, but Ella, Eli and Everett were sick with worry. Randy was just as speechless as I and tried to keep his words to a minimum, in fear he would cause the inevitable to come true.

Nurses stopped by to say "hi" and check to see how Emmy was. I walked the halls, remembering our first time here. The Scooby Doo murals painted on each window made me nauseous. I tried to keep my focus on Emmy and remind myself that she was actually calm enough to enjoy this stay on the neurology floor and visit the playroom. Crafts are by far her favorite thing to do, even though she has a hard time doing them. Her smile and sweet, whispery voice could convince anyone to paint, color, cut, or glue something for her. My focus was on her, so we spent hours coloring and crafting to help the days go by, patiently waiting to see what course of action would be next.

They decided nothing would tell them exactly what was in Emmy's brain without a biopsy. The date was scheduled, so Emmy had to undergo multiple PET scans and MRIs for the perfect images. The biopsy quickly turned into a partial craniotomy. The team decided they needed a bigger window to view the cranberry-sized area in case it was a tumor, caused by the chemotherapy. If that was the case, they were going to remove the whole thing while they were in there.

Emmy was all smiles on July 11 as we waited for the partial craniotomy brain biopsy. The operating room was behind schedule, so Randy and I fasted with Emmy, trying to support her any way we could. Her appetite was still insatiable, so going the day without food was proving to be miserable, not only for Emmy, but for us, as well.

The operation took six agonizing hours, but Emmy made it through with zero complications. The neurosurgeon came to the ICU waiting room to update us with the results. All patients who undergo brain surgeries have to be monitored in the ICU before going back to the neurology floor. And I thought I would never see the ICU again.

"This was the strangest thing to see. I could see the spot on the MRI scans, but when I would look at her brain, nothing was there. It definitely is not a tumor, but I still took biopsies of the area and tried to remove the rest with guided imagery. At first glance under the microscope, we saw that it is definitely inflammation. As of now, our best guess is that HLH is back. I am so sorry to tell you this news. I heard how hard the first stay was with Emmy. I'll be praying for her," he said in a gentle, caring voice.

I stared at Emmy for hours, waiting for her to fully wake up. I expected the worst—spasms, sweating, and screaming. But when she was fully awake, they never came. The VIP suite on the neurology floor became available just as Emmy was released from the ICU, and we quickly settled in. A huge corner room, a full view of Boston, and visits from all of Emmy's favorite nurses were making this stay a thousand times better than we could have ever imagined.

A team meeting was quickly scheduled to tell us the plan of action.

"Hey, Randy and Missy. According to the biopsy, this is most likely a return of HLH, but we have to be sure. Before making any decisions, we need to wait for the blood work results and neopterin results to come back from her spinal fluid. All studies show that having a 50 percent or greater chimerism stops relapse, but that doesn't seem to be the case with Emmy. Tomorrow the NK cell function test will come back, which will be one more marker proving if this is HLH or not. The NK cells Ella gave Emmy should be holding back the rogue T-cells. We will meet as soon as I get the results and then move forward with which path to take," Emmy's primary BMT doctor said, giving us each a hug before she left.

I fell into the old routine of trying to keep the mood light, which meant I had to force myself to smile. But it was all a façade. I was in turmoil. My heart hurt so badly I thought I was having a heart attack. I didn't know if I could make it one more day just to hear about the blood test results. But the morning came, and the doctor was back to tell us the news.

"We got back Emmy's NK cell function test, and it is baffling. It shows that none of the NK cells are functioning—not Emmy's, nor Ella's donor cells. This is a sign it is HLH, but now we need Ella to come in so we can test her NK cells. We know she doesn't have CNS-restricted HLH, so why her NK cells aren't working is beyond me," she said as she tried to comfort both of us.

Randy and I were stunned, completely speechless. What did all of this mean?

Before being released to go home, the doctors scheduled Ella to come back in August, when Emmy would receive her first intrathecal chemo dose. *How is this happening again? And now we have to worry about Ella, too.*

After two days of being home, Emmy's body started becoming more and more dystonic, just like before. Her left arm was curled up into her stomach, and she slept only ten minutes at a time before waking in a shrieking cry. *This is it. I can't do this again.* I called her BMT doctor at Jimmy Fund, expressing Emmy's misery and how I was exhausted. The doctor made an appointment and said to bring her to the Jimmy Fund clinic. The neurologist was notified Emmy was coming and quickly diverted me to head to the ER first and then admitted Emmy to the neurology floor.

"Let's get Emmy on some steroids and watch her. We have already done all the tests we know to do, but I don't want you doing this at home without help," he said kindly.

The next morning, Emmy was given a high dose of steroids in hopes it would calm her brain down. The doctor then left it up to us what to do next. Did we stay in the hospital, even though there was nothing left to do, or go home? Randy and I decided, with fingers crossed, to take Emmy home where we all could be more comfortable.

Another storm was ripping straight for us, leaving desolation in its wake, yet we were completely unprepared. How could we even comprehend the magnitude of what was coming after already thinking we had seen it all? I was still not emotionally healed from the first stay and once Emmy's body became dystonic again, I found myself crying at random times, completely unlike me. I was wrestling Emmy's body day and night again, and Randy was gone during the day. The kids couldn't help, and I really didn't want them to. This was unbearable for any adult to witness, let alone a child.

Aunt Coley had left a month earlier to move back to Montana to restart her business, so I lost her help. Ella and Eli watched Everett as I took care of Emmy's ever-increasing dystonic episodes. Mimi, Randy's mom, dropped everything and came to help me with the house, but I could see this was spiraling out of control, just like before.

The brain biopsy was most likely the culprit that began the agitation in Emmy's brain. From there, it just got worse, day after day, without extra medication. The steroids didn't help, like they did in Virginia. At Boston, they used a different steroid, one specifically used for HLH, but it didn't have the same effect on her brain. The steroids actually seemed to make her worse. Emmy was in full dystonic crisis, but we decided to deal with it at home. The doctor said to add Benadryl to Emmy's daily medicine list. Nothing we did helped.

On August 2, the four of us drove to Jimmy Fund to get Ella's NK cells tested and start the first round of intrathecal chemo. The sedation and intrathecal chemo was the last straw. As Emmy woke, her body flailed out of control and she turned beet red, sweating as she hyperventilated. The doctor didn't want us to leave, but we assured him we had already been dealing with this and drove home, trying to hold Emmy's body still.

The minute we walked in the house, I gave Emmy a dose of Benadryl followed by clonidine, praying it would calm her down. Acting like the world was ending, I began crying and wondering how God could do this to us again, while Randy stayed level headed and began researching.

Within an hour, Randy found an article describing a condition called paroxysmal sympathetic hyperactivity (PSH). PSH is when the brain and motor function react adversely after brain trauma or reactions to sedation or medication. This syndrome, very similar to acute dystonic reaction, causes episodes of increased activity in the sympathetic nervous system, which causes increased movements, breathing, heart rate, and hyperthermia. Once again, God was leading us to an answer to get Emmy through another crisis. Propranolol was the medicine recommended, so I quickly called neurology and left a message to send in a prescription.

Neurology and BMT quickly convened to figure out the correct dosage of propranolol to give Emmy according to her weight and symptoms. On August 3, Emmy was in full-blown dystonic crisis, but the minute we gave her the medicine, she stayed calm for about five hours. As the spasms came back, we alternated clonidine and propranolol to keep her comfortable. I felt the undeniable dread creeping back, and I had no strength to even fight it. I seemed fine as long as Emmy was calm, but as soon as she began spasming, I lost all control of my emotions.

The schedule of events could not be altered, no matter Emmy's condition—just as before. Emmy was scheduled to have a post-biopsy MRI and have more blood work done. *Why, oh, why did everything require sedation?* If only her body would stay still, she wouldn't need anything.

On first attempt, the MRI staff allowed me to try clonidine, but it didn't work. Emmy was miserable and said it hurt to lay still. As I walked out of the room, Emmy finally still from sedation, I just cried. I knew what was going to happen. The minute she woke up, she was going to be just as bad as when we were transferred to the ICU.

Screaming, sweating and crying, Emmy looked just like a toddler throwing a tantrum as I pushed her in her wheelchair from Children's to Jimmy Fund clinic. The walk was only five minutes, but it felt like miles. Randy was covered in sweat from trying to hold her hand and then leg that would kick wildly. I knew the moment the staff saw Emmy, they would do something to help her.

Emmy was quickly given a secluded room. Her BMT doctor asked what could be done, and I asked her to order propranolol, which I'd forgotten to bring. I had already given a dose of Benadryl, but it only worked with propranolol. Once the meds kicked in, we rushed Emmy home as far away from the hospital as possible. But home became just as uncomfortable as when we lived in the ICU.

Randy and I were numb. There was *no* way that this was happening again. There was just no way. We really were living in a nightmare. But thank goodness for kind neighbors. God knew what He was doing when he moved us next to Rebecca. Comforting and wrestling Emmy during the day when the medicine didn't work was not only overwhelming, but making me go partially crazy. I reluctantly asked Rebecca if she would help, and she quickly came to my aid. I don't think she knew what she was getting into, but she graciously sat with Emmy during the periods of dystonic distress to give me a break. Her sweet words and gentle touch was exactly what Emmy needed.

Somehow, by either stubbornness or a complete miracle, I had made it this long without going on antidepressants. The thought of needing medicine seemed so foreign to me, mostly because I didn't understand how they worked. I had come to understand from a large group of holistic women, that these medicines were more harmful than helpful. But I was so wrong.

I can't remember when the initial breakdown started. But on the morning of Randy's birthday, August 7, I found myself curled-up on the floor. My sobs were so loud the whole family came running to see what happened. The wails of pain wouldn't stop. All I remember was that the night before was so awful, it threw me into complete darkness. I was trapped and couldn't see any way to escape. Screams from Emmy had echoed through the hallway from her room to ours. She wouldn't stop until I came to her bedside. Many times, she didn't need anything, just for me to be there. I should have been more comforting, but I didn't have it in me. I was tired and angry and on the fifth time she woke and screamed, I lost it.

I stopped halfway to her room and sat in the hallway, heat radiating from every inch of my skin, feeling complete and utter hatred. Fists clenched and fire filling my body, I thought about walking out the front door and leaving all of it behind and starting a new life. Every thought that crossed my mind was mean and pure evil. The darkness swallowed me whole, and I just sat in the hall crying for hours, ignoring Emmy's screams.

After I'd gained some composure the next morning after crying uncontrollably, Randy told me to call the doctor immediately. When the receptionist answered, all I could do was cry. She quickly pushed the call to the nurse practitioner as I was crying too hard to answer the initial question. "Are you suicidal?"

"What? No. I don't want to kill myself. My daughter is sick and maybe dying, and I am just so tired and angry. I can't stop crying..." I said in between the sobs. I was so embarrassed as the nurse practitioner told me to come in instantly.

The nurse practitioner was barely thirty years old. There was no way she had been out of school long enough to know how to deal with my kind of pain and hurt, but she was all I had.

"Please, tell me everything. I want to understand why you are crying so hard," she said as the floodgate of tears broke through and the last wall of defense came crumbling down.

I cried, more like bawled, for thirty minutes straight. There was no way this lady was ready for all I had to say, but it all came pouring out in between sobs and blowing my nose. The biggest issue was that Emmy's spasms were back, which made me feel like my entire world was over, once again.

"I am so very sorry this is happening to your daughter and family. I've never even heard of HLH before. You may not be able to control your daughter's situation, but there are medicines to help you control your emotions to it. There are medicines that can increase the serotonin in your brain to help you deal with what's happening," she said, her eyes filled with compassion.

She gave me the phone number to a counselor I could talk to and prescribed me some medicine. I had finally admitted that I needed help, yet I felt defeated that I needed medicine to get through the pain. I thought I was stronger than that.

Yes, a strange sense of peace came over me as I drove home. I had finally admitted I wasn't strong enough to do it all on my own, and now everyone knew. I began crying again, soaking the front of my shirt. Then came the prayers, and before I knew it, I was screaming at God for making us go through all of this again. I wasn't angry at Emmy or myself, I was angry at God. Why were we being forced to go through the same pain and agony all over again? What lesson did we miss the first time that He would think we needed to repeat the class again? *God, what did we do wrong? If I have sinned, please forgive me. Don't let us go through this again. You already know we can't possibly go through all of that again. It is impossible.*

I was so wrapped up in my thoughts and prayers that I didn't realize people were staring at me. Driving alone was still my time to pray or scream—a time of release. I was able to scream and pray and sing as loudly as I wanted. I can only imagine what people thought of me. I remember once, back in Virginia, Emmy was quickly deteriorating before our eyes and I just had to get away—drive alone to gather my thoughts. After realizing I was being stared at, while waiting for a red light, I thought back to the Old Testament story about Hannah.

Hannah went to the temple to pray for a son. She had been mocked and ridiculed by the other wife of Elkanah, who easily became pregnant and had many children. Everyone looked wide-eyed at Hannah while she silently cried and prayed before the altar to just bear one son, whom she vowed to give back to the Lord.

As I was pleading for God to save my own child's life, these onlookers probably thought I was drunk, just as the prophet Eli did when he saw Hannah. And when the prophet Eli asked Hannah if she was drunk, she quickly replied, "No, I just want a child." I think every mother can relate to the pain of a child—the pain of not being able to conceive, of watching a child suffer, or even the immense pain of losing one. There is no greater pain than what a mother experiences with her own child.

I arrogantly told God I wouldn't do this again. If He was faithful, like His Word says, why didn't the first transplant work and heal Emmy? Why did He bring us to this dry, deserted, godless land to get Emmy a cure, only to take it away and leave us abandoned? I truly didn't think that I could sit and watch Emmy go through one more minute of pain, chemotherapy, hair loss, or any more spasms. There were no churches I could turn to, no family, no local prayer warriors. I didn't understand why God had brought us to Boston to go through the most difficult battle we had ever faced with no spiritual support. Why was God doing this to us?

After going home, with prescription in hand, I finally admitted the last thing I had been trying to deny. I could no longer handle Emmy alone. As much as I wanted to keep Emmy from the hospital that scarred us for life, I knew I couldn't handle her spasms anymore. I called Emmy's neurologist and asked for help. He reserved Emmy a room and we drove Emmy to Children's the next morning. We were terrified they would over medicate her, but something had to be done to help treat her misery. I couldn't stop praying. *Please don't let them make her worse, God. Please don't let them make her worse.*

The doctors increased some of her meds, among them Ativan and clonidine, and felt sure we could go back home in a few days. As we were packing up to leave, the BMT doctor came to have a meeting with us about doing a second bone marrow transplant.

"Randy and Missy, the blood test proved Ella's NK cells not working so we need to talk about who will be the next bone marrow donor. NK cells are vital to stopping the bad T-cells, so you need to think long and hard if you want Ella to donate again. The only way Emmy would not end up with HLH again is if Ella's transplant is 100% successful. I also need you to understand that, if we go forward with a second bone marrow transplant, we will not use the same protocol of chemotherapy. If something fails the first time, I never repeat it. That means it will be stronger and harsher on Emmy's body. And from what I see, she is still pretty fragile," she asked, waiting for us to reply.

"No way. We don't want Ella to donate again. But why would her NK cells not work? Is there a test we can do? How can you increase her NK cells?" Randy added.

"We don't have a test to understand why the NK cells aren't working. And the only cure, which you will hate, is a bone marrow transplant," she calmly stated.

"Are you kidding me? A bone marrow transplant just for NK cells? Does she have to have one? Overall, if her immune system is strong, can she live without NK cells?" I questioned, hoping for a good answer.

"No, she doesn't need one. The rest of her immune system is working just fine, but NK cells are important. NK cells are the first line of defense against cancer. They can also attack viral and bacterial infections before the other cells know what's going on. But Ella has not been too sick. So right now, I don't think we should worry about it. It's Emmy that we need to focus on. Are you both willing to move forward with a second bone marrow transplant from an unrelated donor? I want you to understand this is her last chance and there is a possibility she may not make it through," Dr. Lee said, worried we may not like what she had to say.

"Of course! We were brought here for a cure, and we aren't leaving until Emmy has one. Plus, even though she is having dystonic reactions again, I think she's way better off now than in the ICU," I added. "Everyone knows her and knows what to expect!"

"Plus, we understand that this may kill Emmy, we really do, but if we don't move forward with this, her brain is going to slowly kill her anyway. That is not an option for us," Randy boldly said.

We asked if she could possibly speed up the process because Emmy couldn't keep living like this. She said they were already getting results from the donor registry "Be the Match" and it looked like there were multiple people who were perfect matches.

"What should we do about Ella? We know she has something wrong with her hormones and we really need to get her some help, at least someone to help her understand the importance of not having NK cells present, I quickly added before our meeting was over.

"I will put in a referral to a pediatric specialist. That doctor can run more tests and help Ella with her other issues," she concluded before shaking our hands and leaving

The appointment was made for two weeks later. The doctor tested Ella for all kinds of things, but the one thing that was finally confirmed was that Ella suffered from polycystic ovarian syndrome (PCOS). For some reason, Ella didn't ovulate and would develop painful cysts on her ovaries. We had known since her first cycle that her body wasn't on a normal schedule and her hormones weren't right. With PCOS, the body is high in testosterone, making it difficult to lose weight. I had a hunch something was wrong even before puberty and actually took her to the doctor when she was eight years old.

"She is completely normal for an eight-year-old. The X-ray we took proves her growth plate corresponds to her age. Excessive hair growth and early puberty at this age can be normal for some girls. Have her checked in a few years if you're still worried about her," the doctor told me.

That was all he said, not researching any further, but my intuition had been right. Once puberty did start, it was obvious something was not right. But I had no time to take her to the doctor. She hit puberty when Emmy became sick. Now the gravity of the situation struck me. We now had both daughters fighting different diseases, and both with the possibility of never having children. This felt like a preplanned, strategic attack on our daughters and future grandchildren. Our daughters were created for more than suffering and it would be their choice if they wanted children or not. A battle cry rang though my entire body and I hit my knees in prayer, the only way I knew how to fight back.

We spent days juggling medicine to keep Emmy's body comfortable. We decided to make an appointment to do Botox, but I knew better than to put her through that while she was already miserable. Making her go through the agony of laying still and enduring multiple needle pokes were only going to exasperate things. But I took her in anyway. Just as I imagined, the entire process made her body lose control and go into another full-blown storm of dystonia. We made it home in time to do propranolol and Benadryl, but now we were playing catch-up again. Her body was nowhere near calm, but Emmy was scheduled the next day for another appointment.

Months before we knew HLH was back, an orthopedic doctor had scheduled Emmy to have a consult to fully understand the damage dystonia had done to her hips. While Emmy stood, her left hip bulged and her leg appeared shorter, until I rotated her hip back into place. After the initial hospital stay enduring months of spasms, Emmy always kept her left leg bent up to her chest or sat on her knees. This appointment was added to her regular check-up at Jimmy Fund, so I didn't cancel anything for that day. I still regret not just cancelling all of them, because the turn of events not only left Emmy worse off, but Ella and I deeply embarrassed.

The days of driving alone with Emmy were gone, so I brought Ella along for help and support. The first stop was a hip X-Ray, which ignited the terrible chain of events that day. The minute we forced Emmy to lay flat on her back, which she had not done in months, caused pain to shoot through her entire body. I seriously thought her dystonia could not get any worse, but I was so wrong. Once it was done, I quickly loaded Emmy into her wheelchair and Ella pushed her to the waiting room. I held her flailing body parts; patiently waiting to find out if the picture was good. Somehow the technician took a clear picture though all of Emmys screaming and jolting. We quickly headed towards Jimmy Fund clinic, which was only a three-minute walk away, but felt like eternity with all of the screaming and swinging limbs. Everyone we passed couldn't help but stare.

As we came upon the entrance, Emmy was drawing unwanted attention, so I had Ella wait with her in the hallway. I quickly checked Emmy in and then asked if any rooms were available. The clerk was sorry and said she would let me know when one became available. I walked back to the hallway and noticed that everyone who walked by or was in eye-shot of the hallway just stared wide-eyed at Emmy. Emmy's cries were echoing off the tall ceilings and wide hallways, so we pushed her into the waiting room, praying for a room to quickly open.

This was where the most uncomfortable event took place that left me in tears. Before I go on, I will say that I am not a religion expert. My knowledge is only in Judeo-Christian theology and small details of other religions that I had picked up from my years in the Air Force. I am not familiar with Muslim customs or how they practice their religion, but on August 16, I learned firsthand how diverse the world is when reacting to someone who is miserably sick.

It isn't just Islam who teaches about specific spiritual reasons for sickness, because I had already heard my fair share of opinions from many Christians. From the one friend in Virginia who said Emmy would not get better because Randy did not "shout from the rooftops" he was the spiritual leader of our home to the well-meaning Christians who constantly blamed our unrepentance or lack of faith on her never-ending disease. Sickness and death do that to people. They try to reason and understand how anything terrible could happen in this world, especially to children. The desire to place blame on someone or something is the only thing that seems reasonable: sin, lack of faith, God, but especially the devil. I used to believe some of the same things, until we witnessed it all first hand. But on that day, to our sheer horror, Emmy was thrown into the middle of an exorcism.

I was covered in sweat and red-faced from embarrassment as I tried my hardest to keep Emmy comfortable on my lap. In the midst of all the stress, a woman came out of nowhere and sat directly next to me. Out of the corner of my eye I saw that she was going to touch Emmy, so I whipped my head around and saw an older woman, covered from head to toe in a black Muslim dress. I guessed she was an older woman by the wrinkles surrounding the only visible part of her body, her eyes. Frozen in shock and embarrassment, I turned and looked at Ella in sheer horror as the woman began chanting something in Arabic.

I didn't know what to do. I was busy wrestling Emmy and trying to stay calm, so I forced myself to ignore her. At first, I thought that maybe she felt compelled to pray for Emmy, which I didn't have the strength to stop her from doing. But then I knew something was not right as she began spitting puffs of air at Emmy. I was mortified. I knew a little about the Muslim faith but had never witnessed this in my entire life. I began telling her that we were fine and saying thank you, not wanting to be rude, but she just continued praying and spitting. The woman's daughter or possibly her granddaughter was quietly pleading with her to go back and sit next to her. Nothing could stop her from chanting, spitting and rocking back and forth.

She continued doing this forever it seemed, until Emmy's name was called. Ella and I quickly grabbed our things and ran to the room. I was so upset and confused at what had just happened, especially in front of an entire waiting room. I choked back my tears and told the nurse what we just went through.

"Oh, that happens all the time! They believe the kids who are sick are cursed or filled with evil spirits, and this is part of the way they pray for them to be delivered," he told me like it was no big deal.

I was speechless. I could never imagine walking up to a stranger and assuming that they are cursed or possessed by evil spirits, just because they are sick. The nurse quickly took Emmy's blood and the doctor came to check on her. After asking if I wanted to admit Emmy to the hospital, again, I told her that Emmy had one more appointment with the neurologist. I was hoping he could prescribe Emmy Valium, which was a last-ditch effort to keep her from being admitted. For the first time, I hated that they'd put all of Emmy's appointments together to make it "easier" on me.

Ella was utterly distraught, but she held it together better than me. It was painful to watch Emmy like this, but having people stare at her only amplified the pain. The neurology clerk sent us directly to a room after witnessing Emmy's misery. Within seconds of the door closing, the neurologist quickly opened it back up and quietly closed it behind him. He looked as defeated as us as Emmy cried and hyperventilated on the exam table. He urged me to admit her, but I wasn't going to do it—not yet. I wasn't ready for all of that again. I knew it was the only thing left that would have the power to break me.

After sending a prescription for Valium to the pharmacy for Emmy, he told me once again that we could admit Emmy anytime I felt like I couldn't handle it anymore. I nodded and thanked him and then Ella and I rushed to the car. I hated Valium and benzodiazepines. But when we'd been there just a week before, the small dose of Valium had seemed to ease her discomfort. I was at the point I was willing to try anything but Artane.

The pharmacy was perfectly distanced between Boston and Pepperell, but still thirty minutes away. Ella sat with Emmy in the back seat, while I drove as fast as possible, in bumper to bumper traffic. At first, I had no idea what was happening, but a car was swerving from our lane to the right lane. Then I noticed they were slowing down, honking and pointing at us, then speeding up to cut us off. The carload of teenagers bullied us on the two-lane highway for twenty minutes straight. The honking and erratic driving was more than Ella and I could handle while our own little chaos was happening right in our own car. What were the chances this would happen on this specific day? Did they even see a kid crying and flailing in our back seat?

Between the impromptu exorcism, full-blown dystonic storm, and reckless teenage drivers, I found myself just seconds from a panic attack. I sped off the highway exit and skidded into the pharmacy parking lot. I was in and out in under two minutes and gave Emmy 4 mg of liquid Valium. Ella held Emmy close the entire way home, and by the time we pulled into the driveway, the Valium had finally taken effect. How was it possible we were going through the exact same scenario a second time? I still believed God was merciful, but even I knew mercy didn't feel like misery. As we walked into the house, I saw Randy standing in the kitchen. I laid Emmy on the couch, looked straight into Randy's eyes without uttering a word and went straight to bed. Words could never describe how I felt after everything that I witnessed that day.

CHAPTER 21

For where two or three gather in My Name, there I am with them.
—MATTHEW 18:20 (NIV)

He says, "Be still and know that I am God, I will be exalted among the nations, I will be exalted in the earth."
—PSALM 46:10 (NIV)

If the movie *Groundhog Day* could be remade into a horror film, we would have been the main stars. Day after day, the same child in complete misery, the same parents trying to make everything better, and the same medicine having zero effect. We were back at the beginning—back to November, back to being hopeless. But this time, we knew what was causing the spasms.

We changed medicine, checked doses, prayed for sleep—day after day after day. This was all eerily similar and I just knew something had to change. We added in CBD and even THC, but nothing really helped. We needed more of something, but we just didn't know how much more her body could handle.

We called neurology to see if any medicine could be increased. Clonidine was the only medicine that Emmy was on that could be increased. Once we increased the dosage, all she did was sleep in-between dystonic storms. At least her heart and lungs could get some rest. There were no obvious difference between the day and night, except the sun. The lack of sleep was making me so sick, my insides would shake uncontrollably. Thankfully, Lexapro was doing its job, and the anger that I had once felt was completely gone.

I am so thankful for friends like Rebecca, who didn't make me feel inadequate for having the emotions and thoughts that I had. I told her everything and pretended like she was my therapist. The guilt and shame for feeling so angry and resentful for my current life were too painful to keep locked up, so she just listened as I poured my heart out. She had dealt with depression herself and was able to explain to me that not all depression comes out in the form of sadness and tears. Many people who are depressed don't even know it because they may experience exhaustion, weakness, physical pain, headaches, or even anger, which was me. I was amazed at how well Lexapro balanced my serotonin levels so that empathy now replaced my anger every time I was woken up to Emmy's cries.

Concern was still hanging over all of us as we waited to hear about the bone marrow donor. I used Emmy's Facebook page to request that everyone pray for a perfect match and healing for all of us. We needed some major help in keeping our hope lifted and our faith strong. The trauma had shut down most of my brain again, and I was no longer a mommy to four but, rather, a caretaker to one sick, miserable, dying girl. Randy was playing Mr. Mom and had to balance work and home life, making sure the other kids' needs were emotionally and physically met.

Matches for Emmy's next bone marrow transplant were finally identified, and Emmy's doctor called to give us the news.

"Missy, I have really good news. Be the Match has found ten exact matches for Emmy's bone marrow transplant. We really needed this many because we wanted the perfect donor. We filtered out all the moms and people who are adenovirus, CMV, and BK virus negative."

"Why can't Emmy use the women who are moms?" I asked in confusion.

"Many people don't know this, but pregnant women's immune systems become very complex from carrying another human being, and their immune systems are mixed in. It's just better if we can find someone who was never pregnant, but we would use a mom if we needed to," she explained.

Ten donors. What a complete blessing there were ten perfect options, and Ella didn't have to worry about being the only one. There are some people who can't find even one donor with 5 out of 10 markers, and we'd found ten people who had 10 out of 10 markers. The testing and filtering out people didn't take long. Emmy had one perfect donor—a man from Germany.

We found out that Germany has one of the largest registries in the world because of a faithful husband who was trying to find a match for his wife, Mechtid, who was dying of leukemia. There were only three thousand potential donors in 1991, but with savvy business skills and a promise made to his wife, Peter Harf helped grow DKMS German registry to what it is today.

Even knowing a bone marrow donor was willing and ready to help Emmy beat HLH a second time, I was still having a hard time convincing myself that I could live in the hospital again with Emmy so miserable. What if the side effects of the stronger chemotherapy landed Emmy in the ICU again? I tried not to think about what could happen if she got mucositis again and needed to be intubated. I tried not to imagine what could happen if she lost this transplant, knowing doctors never do more than two.

Worry weaved itself into every thought, but God was still there, listening to each and every prayer. God had never stopped working, even though I saw no signs of His handiwork. I thought He abandoned me because I hadn't heard His voice, but He was talking, it just wasn't to me. This time, God was speaking to three women who clearly heard His voice, and quickly relayed the message.

"Hello," I said as I saw the call was from a friend I hadn't talked to in months.

"Missy, how are you doing? I know you are going through a lot right now, so I'm going to keep this short. God just keeps telling me to call you and tell you that this time, you just need to be still, because He's got this," she said.

That was so unexpected. I remember praying over and over that I would hear God tell me something to help us stay calm and do what needed to be done to help Emmy through another BMT. This was my answer, but God wanted to make sure I heard him.

One more phone call and then a text message both came within twenty-four hours of the first call. The words were slightly different, but the meaning was the same. "God told me to tell you to be still! He is going to take care of Emmy and your family."

What was the probability that three women, who didn't even know each other, would contact me at the same time and tell me basically the same thing? Zero. That was God—making the impossible possible. That is how God works, so incredibly mysterious yet obvious that there is no denying it. Their obedience to God was what I needed to shake off those negative thoughts and fight another day for Emmy. My despair had completely shut out the voice of God, but now I felt the presence of God surround our family like never before.

As I sat in awe of God, I remembered back to when Emmy first became sick. One month after Emmy went through the horrific events of plasmapheresis and losing her smile, I found out that two other people had a dream that was almost identical to mine

While Emmy was undergoing plasmapheresis, chemo and steroids at CHKD, I drifted into a light sleep that allowed me to remember my dreams. I suddenly woke with a joyful hope after what I saw, but I also didn't want to tell anyone, thinking it was just wishful thinking. A couple weeks later, my friend Melissa called me to tell me about a dream she had of Emmy. It was almost exactly the same dream as I had. Then a month or so later, my mother-in-law, Linda, also told me she dreamt of Emmy. After she carefully explained the details to me, I was speechless.

The three of us all dreamt of a time when Emmy was older, walking down a road. As she walked, we could all see that she had a slight limp, like her foot was turned in. Then as she cheerfully began running around, she drew her arm up into her stomach, like it was hurt. The setting of my dream was on a road, with carnival games and rides on either side. The other two ladies couldn't remember the setting details, but they both said Emmy was in the middle of a street that was closed off to cars. It was that tiny dream given to all three of us that kept me praying and believing that God would completely restore Emmy.

The last set of tests, including a sedated MRI, had to be done before her bone marrow transplant. I hated sedated MRIs, but they had to make sure the disease hadn't spread further, or they would need to do one more intrathecal chemo. I don't remember how long she was gone, but I prayed the entire time, hoping her body was not worse after she woke up. At this point, I really couldn't imagine how she could get any worse.

The MRI was stable. And thankfully, Emmy woke up the same.

The test that really bothered me was the echocardiogram. Emmy's heart still showed cardiomyopathy. Science couldn't explain why her heart was still weak, except that deep down I knew she had to be so sad that she was still sick. So sad that the disease was still ravaging her brain, keeping her from getting stronger and relearning all the things she could no longer do. Jesus was the only One I knew who could heal the hurt and loss she had experienced.

Emmy loves Jesus more than any person I know, from a very young age. She made me read the Toddler's Bible until she memorized every word and then made me read one for older kids. Worship music that emphasized the goodness of Jesus was her favorite, and I would often find her in her room singing her own made-up songs about Him and how she loved Him so much.

I have family that prays and worships all the time, but I have never seen someone so deeply connected to Jesus as Emmy. Even after all she went though, believing Jesus would heal her the instant she asked, she never lost faith in Him when it didn't happen. On the days she was stable, we would take her to church in Virginia and she would ask me to stand her up so she could raise her hands in worship.

Emmy loved singing and praying and praising, but her love for Jesus became more intense after her stay in the ICU. As she would watch *The Bible* series, Emmy would light up whenever His name was mentioned or He was in the scene. Emmy acted like He was her best friend that she hadn't seen in a while, smiling and giggling the whole time. That's when I wondered if she had actually met Him during her fight in the hospital.

Ella and I would talk about what it could mean, but neither of us wanted to know the real answer. Had Emmy met Jesus in heaven? I knew she'd never physically died, but mentally I had no idea. During all that pain and suffering, I know He was with her, but I just don't know to what extent. I don't think she can remember the details, but I am sure she still feels His presence all around her. How else would she have survived everything she went through and still smile, even now, having to go through it all again?

From July till September, I found myself so overwhelmed that I could only pray and ask for the small things from God. I prayed that the spasms would stop or that she would stay strong enough to live through the second BMT. But after my three friends told me what God said, I began setting my sights on the bigger things. This time around, I wanted it all. I wanted a perfect transplant, no intubations, and no side effects, and I wanted Him to tell us when to intervene on her behalf. Satan was not going to control any part of this hospital stay. God was going to be in complete control.

The transplant day was finally here, again. Our bags were packed, and we checked in at outpatient surgery to have another CVL placed in Emmy's chest again. Forced smiles and silent prayers helped us through the one-hour procedure, but then fear snuck in.

Spasms were worse the minute Emmy woke from sedation. Benadryl and clonidine calmed her down a little bit, but I looked at Randy and said, "I can't do this again. I just can't. How am I going to stay with her day and night while she screams and spasms?"

"Missy, she is still better than she was before. Don't worry. I will be here as much as possible. This is why God sent us here. We already know once the sedation wears off, she will be fine."

Ying and yang—all the time. When I am on edge, he is calm. When he is upset, I am the voice of reason. We were meant for each other. And just like that, his calming words helped me get to the next day, where a small miracle fell to us like manna from heaven. Emmy was given IVIG because her IgG levels were a little too low to start chemotherapy. Within ten minutes of starting the infusion, her body slowly relaxed, and she fell asleep. We first thought it was from the Benadryl and Tylenol the doctors had premedicated her with, but after several hours, she never became dystonic. All I could say over and over was, "Thank you, Jesus! Thank you, Jesus!"

Headaches, nausea, and small bouts of crying still occurred during the ten days of chemotherapy, but thankfully those were common reactions for almost any child. Nights were filled with lots of ice cream and juice and an abnormal craving for macaroni and cheese. Emmy had everyone coloring and making crafts. This was what hospital stays should be like. Randy and I were even invited to the cafeteria for a specially prepared dinner by Tom Brady's previous vegan chef, which we were able to do with the help of Child Life. Somehow, we had made it to transplant day without losing our minds.

October 17, 2017—so many things happened to Emmy on important dates. Ella's birthday, Eli's birthday, Good Friday, and even our anniversary. But this date was a new one, though one quite easy to remember. Emmy's transplant day was during the tenth month when she was ten years old, and prime number seventeen taking center stage, as the seventeenth day of the seventeenth year. I prayed those numbers would be the last ones we had to remember. The prayer calls were sent out, and we all prayed for healing to finally be hers.

The moment the stem cells arrived from Germany, we were given the good news. The nurses were scurrying around preparing Emmy for the transplant when, all of a sudden, it was pushed back two hours.

"They harvested too much blood for Emmy's tiny body, but we never waste it. This stuff is liquid gold. If the quantity is too much for the patient to receive, we simply remove the plasma, which will easily grow back," the nurse explained.

Randy and I held our breath as the blood finally made it to her room and was hung from the IV pole. As the deep red blood pushed through her CVL tubing line, directly into her heart, I took a huge sigh of relief. This was it. This was the last chance—other than a biblical-type of miracle, for Emmy to live. There was no fluid retention, nausea, or throwing up, even with so much marrow being pushed into her body. The next day was a little harder, with headaches and stomach pain, but nothing like the first transplant. It was like we should have never done the first bone marrow transplant. It is amazing how cloudy one's judgment becomes in the face of life or death for your child.

Pills, pills, and more pills—some of the pills were converted into IV medicine to ease the stomach pain. I have never seen Emmy so discouraged when we showed her the cup full of pills. GVHD, antibiotics, antivirals, magnesium, and all of her regular meds had to be taken daily. Emmy was born with wisdom from above, and she knew to just take them and move on. She also knew that this wasn't forever, which is hard for most kids to fully understand. I am an adult and could barely look at our situation and not be overwhelmed.

With our newly acquired 6th sense, we could see every change in behavior, and every small difference in Emmy's movements when a medicine was given that her brain didn't like. The IV medicine given to prevent her body from attacking the new cells was the first we identified. Within five minutes of the medicine being administered, Emmy would turn beet red and squirm like her body was filling with lava. Thankfully, the doctors were able to switch out the medicine. Other medication still irritated her, but nothing like before.

Back in July, three months before the transplant, when I finally admitted HLH was back, I started researching ways to prevent chemotherapy side effects. I knew the stories. I saw the kids. Too much chemo meant kidneys and livers would fail; and sometimes, more often than not, the child would die. I also knew there was a possibility of Emmy getting cancer from receiving chemotherapy the first time, and now she was twice as likely. I didn't want that to happen. I couldn't go through all of this just to end up with a child filled with cancer because of a cure.

All I knew to do was research what I had already learned and new ways to help Emmy. I looked up natural methods of detoxing chemo and aiding the body during a transplant. The doctors and nurses called me "Dr. Quinn, Medicine Woman" when I pulled my essential oils and diffuser out onto the bedside table. I didn't care what anyone thought at this point. It was our job as parents to give Emmy the best chance at surviving this transplant and with the fewest complications before, during, and after.

Before the first day of chemo, I started using a variety of plant oils recommended by a doctor who helped get hundreds of cancer patients through chemo. During the week and a half of chemo, I rubbed oils over Emmy's heart, kidneys, and liver to prevent toxins from building up. I also used certain oils over her lungs to hopefully prevent adenovirus from occurring when she was immunocompromised. That simple act kept Emmy from retaining fluid and swelling up like she had during the first transplant. When post-chemo liver tests came back, her liver function had actually improved!

Around week three post-transplant, we thought things were going to take a turn for the worse. Adenovirus tested positive on a weekly blood test, but the doctors caught it just in time. Within three days of receiving the antiviral, the virus was untraceable. Mucositis also started to hurt Emmy's throat and mouth, but she never stopped drinking and eating. Dystonia tried to rear its ugly head with different antibiotics and GVHD meds, but as soon as the medicine wore off, she would balance back and find ways to calm down. Hair loss was the one thing I wish I could have changed. I hated seeing her hair fall out, but Emmy was beautiful either way. The process was so incredibly different that I wondered if I was imagining the whole thing. I felt like this transplant, this exact hospital stay, was the one Emmy was supposed to have all along. Everything was working out better than we could have imagined.

Miracle after miracle was happening right before our eyes. Emmy's ANC (new cell growth) came in on day ten post-transplant and only skyrocketed from there. The new bone marrow must have been laced with superpowers, as Emmy never had to receive a blood transfusion—no red blood cells or platelets. It was all so "by the book" that we were discharged from the hospital thirty days post-transplant. I was completely shocked yet humbled by the mercy of God the second time around.

I couldn't believe that, from the beginning of this transplant, we were warned not to get our hopes up, not to expect much, and to prepare for the worst. But what the doctors didn't fully understand was that we had already been through the worst. The statistics highlighted the likelihood of Emmy losing this battle to HLH, especially undergoing a second bone marrow transplant. Our hearts broke reading the reports, but Emmy leaving this world behind to meet her Maker was better than what we had already witnessed. Death was better than her being tortured while her brain was slowly being eaten by her own immune system. No, we were not about to let that happen. And I am so thankful we trusted God and moved forward with the second transplant. It wasn't that I had more faith this time around; it was that I never doubted once that God would work all of it out. Life or death—it was all in His hands, and I fully trusted what He chose.

CHAPTER 22

And he said: "Naked I came from my mother's womb, and naked shall I return there. The Lord gave, and the Lord has taken away; Blessed be the name of the Lord".
—JOB 1:21 (NKJV)

I guess we missed the hospital more than we realized, because we spent more time driving to and from Children's than we actually stayed during the second transplant. When we initially were discharged, we were given a room at the Boston House, just a mile from the hospital. Blood tests were done every three days, and the room was supposed to make it easier on us. The close stay kept us from having to drive so many hours each week, but the beds were uncomfortable, and the separation from our other kids made our hearts ache. We made it to our first appointment and then checked out of the Boston House right after. I soon regretted that decision, as random fevers and uncontrollable circumstances would make me think uncomfortable beds were way better than driving for so many hours each week.

The doctors left the chest CVL in so Emmy could have her blood tested without constantly being poked. I had taken care of her CVL and PICC line before, so I knew how to be extra sanitary. Somehow, with all the cleaning and sanitizing, I still allowed bacteria into her line. Back we went to the hospital, just days before Christmas. I am sure Emmy sensed Santa coming to Children's because she met him again and ended up with a room filled with gifts. The doctors were certain this infection could be treated with a common antibiotic and allowed us to give the medicine at home. We were back home in time to celebrate Christmas as a family.

I was still somewhat emotionally detached from all the trauma and found myself faking excitement on Christmas Day. We had been here before, thinking Emmy was cured. I was still waiting for the final trapdoor to swing open, the one that had no stairs to crawl back up. The kids seemed happy to be together, and I even made my Christmas Day cinnamon rolls. But it was hard to feel truly happy. We needed months, if not years, of constant healing and peace to feel comfortable in accepting that the disease was gone. Having your life turned upside down as often as we had made it difficult to trust that everything was going to be all right.

The antibiotics didn't work, so back to the hospital we went. Taking out the CVL was the next course of action, so that was scheduled on New Year's Day. A PICC line was placed in Emmy's arm because she still needed multiple blood tests monthly. Emmy was ecstatic to have the sticker off her chest. Of all the painful things Emmy went though, she only remembers the pain of having us clean her CVL line weekly. The sticker being pulled off and replaced was extremely painful. If that is the worst thing she remembers, I am forever grateful to God for that.

A few weeks of calm allowed us to relax and feel comfortable again, and then another random fever popped up and sent us driving to Children's. Tests had to be run, and a three-day course of antibiotics had to be given as a precautionary. Every stay, no matter how short or long, was the same. Residents (newer doctors) would come into the room, review all of Emmy's medicines, and then send them to the pharmacy. It was always a miracle if they got them correct, which is why the nurses always reviewed what they entered.

This time, the nurse didn't review them, and the resident accidentally put her medicine in the computer with the Ativan dose cut in half. I am usually the one to give her meds, but the nurses hated waking me in the morning, so I didn't catch the huge wean in Ativan. Then, the afternoon dose was by itself and such a small amount of liquid that the nurse would also give that one. It wasn't until the third day that I saw the nurse give the Ativan and realized the syringe was only half full. I frantically had the nurse look up all of her meds. And there it was, the amount had been entered wrong. I had the BMT doctor come in, and we made a command decision to take our chances and leave it at 50 percent of what she had been getting before. Weaning any benzodiazepine in half, instead of slowly, could cause horrible withdrawal, including seizures.

Being the parent of a medically complex child is probably the hardest role anyone could have. We have to be on top of everything that happens during the child's hospital stay because who knows our child's needs better than us? I found myself so wrapped up in Emmy's care throughout this entire disease that I rarely met other parents. I had "Emmy tunnel vision," either from depression or distrust of the doctors. But mostly I found it hard to hear stories of the other children who would either walk out of the hospital completely healed or who would pass away. I was already emotionally fragile, and staying in Emmy's room was just easier. But sometimes the doctors would ask me if I would speak to other parents of kids with HLH; I always said yes. If one parent could gain personal insight into what was happening to their child, I was willing to help.

During our first stay in the ICU, I met the mother of a little boy who'd developed HLH after a common virus. His mom told me that HLH had attacked his body so quickly that, if not for the quick reaction of the ER doctor to give steroids, he would have died. She and I were able to comfort one another, at least until they were discharged a few months later.

Another boy was placed right next to Emmy in the ICU about four months into our stay. The mother's story was one of the most heartbreaking I can remember. She wasn't married but wanted a child, so she chose in vitro fertilization. Her bouncing baby boy suddenly became ill after vaccinations; doctors finally discovered he had an autoimmune disease that needed only one mutation passed on from a parent. Most genetic mutations need two carriers, like HLH.

At first, I was angry he'd been put next to Emmy, but it was the only room left that had negative air pressure. He was fighting active chicken pox, and his immunocompromised body just couldn't take it. The doors were sealed between our two rooms with tape, and nurses had to cover up in gowns, face masks, and caps to make sure his virus wasn't transmitted to any other children, especially Emmy.

This little boy's mother was a nurse and a fierce advocate for her son. But out of everything she suggested and everything the doctors tried, his little body just couldn't take any more pain and sickness. His lungs ultimately failed. The chaplains and doctors held his mother's hand as the monitors were turned off. I could see their silhouettes through the window, and I just sat next to Emmy crying, praying she would not end up the same way.

Ultimately, it was doing one simple thing that made me realize how to truly advocate for Emmy. It was the day I gave up complete control of Emmy's outcome and gave it all to God. I believe when we hold on so tightly, trying to control the narrative and thinking that our love is enough to cure the pain, we ultimately forget that God loves them more. God created them and knew beforehand that all of this was going to happen, but He also knew how it was going to end. I also believe that God gave parents complete authority over our children and would never overstep the power He originally invested in us. God is a God of order, so we have to give Him the permission to take complete control. I finally understood the old saying, "Let go and let God."

After I felt like that one lesson helped Emmy receive the healing and help she needed, I opened up to another mom who was struggling to keep it together for her little girl who was just barely clinging to life. It all happened during a stop at the coffee pot, where all the small talk happened on the BMT floor.

This mom had spent months in the hospital helping her little girl recover from a bone marrow transplant and the destructive nature of what the chemo had done to her. This little girl also had an autoimmune disease that was killing her and went through multiple rounds of chemo and a bone marrow transplant, but her tiny body just couldn't fight back. She was in and out of procedures, in and out of the ICU, and nothing was making her better. Her devout mom walked to a nearby Catholic church in Boston and prayed for her daughter every day, without fail.

I remember the exact day we were both in the snack room, grabbing coffee, when she told me her daughter was admitted to the ICU again after a procedure and was now intubated. Her little body just kept getting weaker and weaker and she felt like the doctors were failing her. I don't know why, and sometimes I wish I never opened my mouth, but I started telling her of the day I essentially gave up all control and left Emmy's fate to God. Live or die, I knew it was His will.

"I have to tell you, when I knew we had done everything we could, and Emmy was in so much pain, I told God that I was done. I told Him that she completely belonged to Him, and He could do whatever was best for her. He had already revealed to us about propofol, but there was still something making her dystonic, and we just couldn't watch her in that kind of pain anymore. I remember right after I prayed and fasted that day, he led me to an article about Artane and we knew it was another medicine harming her. It was still a battle, but from then on, I trusted God was doing what was best for Emmy. She suffered for a few more months, even losing her first transplant, but I put all my trust in His plan. I even trust Him right now, having to put Emmy through a second transplant. I wish I would have listened to God sooner and given her completely to Him in the beginning, because she has been through too much pain for a child to bear. So much pain, that my prayers usually end by asking God to never let her remember," I told her as I gently grabbed her arm.

Two days later, her daughter was in heaven.

I ran into her the day after her daughter died, and she told me she had gone to church that day and prayed just like I had said I did. All I could do was hug her and tell her God would take care of her broken heart and her little girl.

I don't know why, but after we talked, I hid in a bathroom and just cried. I felt personally responsible for the death of her only child. I was a broken mess, so I called my friend Melissa and told her what had happened. She quickly told me I'd done the right thing in telling her to give her daughter to God. It still weighs heavy on my heart, but I know God was always in control. "Thy will be done" is more than just a saying.

The rest of January and February were tough on us. Most of the medications given for the bone marrow transplant were causing Emmy a great deal of irritability and body spasms. Pentamidine, one specifically for lung infections, had to be completely stopped, though. It turned out that Emmy was borderline allergic to it. Thankfully, her ANC was high, and the doctors felt comfortable stopping it a month early. Medicine was always the enemy. The doctors were very understanding of Emmy's sensitivity, and the minute she could safely be taken off a medication, they would do it.

Even though Emmy was reacting to the BMT medicines, Randy and I were still tasked with weaning the excessive amounts of benzodiazepines.

It was still hard telling withdrawal and medicine reaction apart. The large Ativan wean during the January hospital stay and the tiny weens we continued in February eventually did the unbearable. They caused a seizure. And with every seizure came a sedated MRI.

When the doctor said the MRI was unchanged, I was not surprised. This time, I was certain the disease was finally gone. What I really wanted the doctor to start saying was, "Wow, her MRI is so improved." But that just never happened. Emmy finally got her cure, and the disease was gone, but what she needed now was healing and restoration of all that was lost.

23

CHAPTER

To everything there is a season, a time for every purpose under heaven.
—ECCLESIASTES 3:1 (NKJV)

They say the power of life and death are in the tongue, so I refused to utter a negative word. I still believed I could control every behavior, every situation with "positive thinking," but I was wrong. Nothing good ever happened from ignoring reality and pretending everything was peachy keen. We prayed for just one thing to turn for the better, begged for it even, but the never-ending cycle of misery continued. Negative reactions to the medicine and going weeks without sleeping longer than forty minutes were still our normal. Randy and I alternated sleeping in the spare room in the basement. We were so exhausted that our emotions controlled us, and anger, nicely paired with a side of resentment, was on full display. The utter despair of not seeing the full goodness of God was ruining us. *How long will this go one, even though her bloodwork says she is healed?*

Then came the most bizarre episode of *Bosch Family Unsolved Mysteries*. Mid-April, Emmy woke with full body hives—welts bigger than my hand and hot to the touch. We gave Benadryl and called her doctor. I washed all of her bedding in hypoallergenic laundry soap, but she woke the next day even worse. Another drive to Children's ensued, just to be put on Zyrtec. The hives were relentless, and nothing helped them. We ended up going back multiple times to the doctor so Emmy could get steroids. There was no rhyme or reason for those hives, and her blood tests proved just that.

The undiagnosed batch of hives lasted an entire three months. And as quickly as they came, they were gone one morning. Once again, we had no idea what happened.

Dystonia, sleeplessness, and crying continued day and night. We spent months giving extra meds all day long. We finally decided to break down and see the new movement disorder neurologist at Children's. I am not completely sure why the previous doctor left, but I'm guessing it had something to do with the way he'd treated me and Emmy. He'd gone behind my back to tell other medics that I had "no idea what I was talking about" regarding her propofol allergy and ignored my plea to stop Artane. I still feel anger ignite in me when I think back to when I told the patient advocate all that he'd done and how he'd treated me. I truly prayed he had learned something and become a little more humble when dealing with parents of complex children.

Word must have gotten around that Emmy was an anomaly because the new doctor had already researched Emmy's case and instantly prescribed benztropine, thinking that it helped during the movements she got from the phenobarbital. At least he didn't mention Artane. We started it the next day and sadly, nothing improved.

Pill form of clonidine was changed to weekly patches, but her body seemed to drain the medicine in three to four days. Day and night, the whole family was miserable. Emmy only wanted me, so the older kids would take turns helping the new Personal Care Assistant (PCA) Jessica watch Emmy, so I could just catch my breath. Jessica was who we chose to replace Nicole when she returned to Montana. She had the patience of Job and training in occupational therapy. Another small gift from God.

It was now July 2018 and time for another MRI. I think the doctors didn't like that her body was in constant spasms, and she still couldn't sleep at night. The MRI was, as we suspected, unchanged. The chimerism test was still showing Emmy's blood greater than 97 percent donor, so we stopped worrying so much that the spasms were caused by HLH. Now we just worried that she may be like this forever—miserable and unable to control her body movements, sleepless and in never ending misery. *God didn't mean for this to be how she lived her life, did He?*

My part-time job with Young Living proved to be a blessing and a burden. I once again earned a free trip, but I wasn't sure if I should take it or hold off another year. Ella was always there to help Randy, but I was afraid we would be moving the next year and have neither Jessica nor Ella, since she was graduating high school. I decided to take my trip and pray for the best.

Randy reluctantly agreed to take off work again and let me leave for a few days away. On July 30, I headed to Spokane, Washington, and prepared myself for a few days of rest. But just like a trusty old watch, within fifteen minutes of being checked into my room, Randy called me.

"Hey, I don't want to alarm you, but Emmy just had a seizure."

"Are you serious? I knew I had a bad feeling on the plane. Did she pull out of it by herself? Should I reschedule my flight and come back home tonight?"

"Let's just see how she recovers. But if she has another one, you need to come home. I don't know why she's having seizures again," Randy sadly said.

"OK, keep me updated. I love you," I said before I hung up.

My trip was only three days long. Thankfully, Emmy didn't have any more seizures. But when I got home, I just knew it was that new medicine causing her to seize and make her dystonia worse. Once again, we started weaning her off the benztropine medicine and watched her almost seize again. Every time a medicine was started that altered the dopamine or serotonin in her brain, it only caused her to get worse. The only choice was to increase Ativan and clonidine again and start trying CBD oil more often. Medicine was obviously not going to be the answer for Emmy's movements.

Maybe things were not as bad as my extensive notes recalled, but the stars seemed to align perfectly, and Emmy was enrolled in elementary school early August of 2018. Missing years of education and having extensive brain damage allowed me to choose what grade to start her at. I felt fourth grade would be perfect, even though she was old enough to be in sixth. Plus, it was her very first time going to a classroom and the first time being purposefully taught to learn something since first grade when she became sick. Emmy's disease did one thing really well; it kept her so sick for so long that she was emotionally, physically, and educationally stunted at a six-year-old level. She never had the chance to feel well enough to do anything productive, but with help from afternoon sedatives, her body stayed relaxed enough to finally begin interacting with other kids again.

I was worried sick about Emmy being away from me longer than an hour, let alone four to six hours a day. I almost didn't let her go, but God was still working everything out. We found out her PCA Jessica was also a substitute for the elementary school, and they agreed to hire her to be Emmy's paraprofessional. Drowsiness plagued Emmy, so she only went a few hours a day, but we finally started seeing a change. She was learning how to interact with others outside our home and communicate her feelings appropriately. Her behavior also improved and quit crying all day long. The entire school knew her by name within a month.

"I am the most popular kid at the school," Emmy gleefully said.

Everything was finally settling down, and just as we were breathing a sigh of relief, the mysterious hives returned. This time, I quickly made the connection. The day before, I had stream cleaned all of the carpets. When I thought the carpets were dry, I allowed Emmy to sit on them she could look through her animal encyclopedia. Six months earlier, when the hives had first appeared, I had also cleaned the carpets. She had never been allergic to anything besides medicine. I instantly looked up the allergen levels of carpets and realized that water breaks down all of the flame-retardant chemicals, making it caustic. Not to mention, carpet is literally the grossest thing in your house, especially when you have animals.

Benadryl and a bath, followed by sleeping in a room where the carpets had not been cleaned, seemed to do the trick. Thankfully, the hives didn't last as long as before, but now we knew to keep her away from wet carpet and would never buy a house with carpet again.

Brain damage is an invisible thief. What might be unnoticeable on an MRI could be visible in a person's behavior or body movements. Reading about brain diseases, disorders, and the healing process had become all-consuming for me. I learned that many people with brain damage or traumatic brain injury never regain their personality but, rather, become someone else entirely. Some people only show physical changes, while others show nothing. No two reactions are the same to brain damage.

While Emmy's MRI was filled with scarring, holes, and pockets of inflammation, I am deeply thankful that Emmy didn't lose the personality she was born with. Emmy's emotions seemed to be changed, maybe heightened, but she was still witty and understood the entire world around her. The farther we got from the second BMT, the more we noticed

Emmy's brain activity speeding up and her dry sense of humor returning. Our family is full of jokesters, and while it had been quite a while, we used to love joking with one another.

I remember one day I needed to run some quick errands, so Eli agreed to sit with Emmy in the living room. As I was walking out, Emmy said, "You aren't going to leave me with this guy, are you?"

We all just busted up laughing! Slowly but surely, she was making her way back to the "old Emmy."

We were at our wit's end using extra meds and changing things up just to keep Emmy comfortable, so I gave in and called the movement disorder neurologist. I kept hoping there was just one magical medicine that would make her all better—just one, not to make her 100 percent normal, but one that would take away all of her muscle movements. Naive—that is what I am. Or I have a problem learning my lesson—always trusting that things will be different the next time around.

Once again, the doctor reviewed her records and decided to retry another medicine—Sinemet. It was the very first medicine the doctors had given Emmy when we'd first arrived in Boston. This time, within five days of starting Sinemet, Emmy's movements visibly became worse. We instantly called his nurse, and she said that, because Emmy was only on it for five days, it was OK to stop cold turkey. I knew better than to just stop a medicine, but I did what she said. Five days after stopping, Emmy had another seizure. Pete and repeat were on the boat; Pete fell off. Who was left? Yep, repeat. Another seizure which meant another MRI.

Emmy's body was still so bad that she had to be sedated for the MRI. The results were the same. No change. It was obvious Emmy's brain was not going to handle any new medicine and it definitely couldn't handle weaning it. I chose to stop weaning all of her medicines for a while and would pick it up after we saw her body get more comfortable. Getting her off all of the extra medicine was going to take years.

Christmas came once again, and this time, I found myself more at ease, genuinely enjoying myself. Emmy had maintained 97% donor blood cells longer than a year and each MRI had been stable. Not only was the fear of HLH gone, we were surprised with Christmas visitors and a special notification that Randy had been chosen to be a support group commander at Little Rock Air Force Base, Arkansas.

Aunt Coley and Uncle Johnny traveled from Montana and made Christmas extra special. It was so nice seeing all of the kids laughing and playing together and not having to be extra quiet because Emmy was sick or having a migraine. So many holidays had been spent in a hospital, and I felt like it was time to start reclaiming all that we had lost. I slowly felt my mind opening up to the chance of happiness again, but my heart was still locked up, trying to protect itself from the chances of "what-if."

Each decision we faced with Emmy were getting harder and harder. Every medical decision could cause Emmy to become worse, physically, if sedation were needed. But Emmy's hip was not getting better, so early in January we drove to Boston to meet with Emmy's orthopedic surgeon and discuss her hip issues and the possibility of surgery.

"Missy, Emmy needs a procedure called an osteotomy. We will literally cut her femurs and rotate them to force the joints to stay in place. We would do both, so the right one won't eventually fall out of socket. The recovery is long and painful, but if Emmy wants to do meaningful therapy, she needs it done. Should we schedule the double hip osteotomy before you move, or will you do it in Arkansas?" he asked.

"I'm afraid of doing anything with sedation in a new place, especially if she wakes up with worsening dystonia. I don't want to end up in an ICU again. I think we should plan to do it before we leave with doctors who already know what to expect," I said with uncertainty.

"Ok. She will need at least three months of recovery time before you leave. I will have my nurse fit you in the schedule and call you with a date," he said.

I really didn't want to do any type of surgery, ever again. But without this one, Emmy would never have the chance of walking again. We had to give her every possible chance to regain her motor function.

The nurse called a day later and said the surgery was scheduled for February 11, one day before Eli's fifteenth birthday. Knowing that there would be no chance of doing any big parties or traveling after the surgery, Randy and I felt like now was the time to spend some quality time with each kid. We had been worried about the emotional effects all of this caused on Ella, Eli, and Everett after missing years of relationships, guidance, and just regular kid activities. We wanted to do something special for them, so we decided to take each one on a trip. Ella would go with me, and the boys would each have a weekend alone with Randy. We had them each list a place they wanted to visit, which Ella quickly knew where she wanted to go.

Since Virginia, Ella had wanted to see *Hamilton* live on Broadway. I was able to purchase three tickets for a showing exactly on her eighteenth birthday and had her best friend Megan fly to Boston to celebrate with Ella. The play was exceptional and I knew Ella deserved so much more, but this was one thing I knew would help repay her for all she'd done for this family.

Eli's birthday always seemed to fall on huge events, just like Emmy's upcoming surgery, so Randy found the time to take him to New Hampshire to do some male bonding. Mountains and relaxing were exactly what Randy and Eli needed. Everett's trip was also last minute, but Randy and Everett had a blast driving around New Hampshire in a Slingshot three-wheeler. Those three trips definitely didn't make up for all the lost time, but we prayed they understood how important they all were. Every day was a balancing act making sure Emmy was taken care of and then meeting our other kids' emotional and physical needs. No one ever said parenting would be this hard.

From the moment we learned the date of the surgery until the morning we drove Emmy to the hospital, I prayed nonstop. This surgery scared me almost as much as the brain biopsies. Emmy was going to be in surgery for hours upon hours. The doctor would be cutting both femurs completely free, reposition them so her hips sat deeper in the sockets, and then place them back together with metal straps and screws. He would also be cutting the left side of her pelvic bone to straighten it out and then finish up by slicing the muscles in her left groin and both ankles so she would have full range of motion. It was a very large, gruesome procedure and would have a long, painful recovery. As always, we called in Randy's mom, Linda, to be our extra support. Without her, I don't think we would have made it through the past four years.

When we arrived at 7:00 a.m. to check in for surgery, we were instantly surprised by two familiar faces waiting for us in the waiting room. Randy's dad and stepmom had flown to Boston to be with us during the surgery. They showed up, once again, for us during one of Emmy's biggest surgeries. During the first bone marrow transplant having them there was such a blessing. Now today, their presence was exactly what Randy and I needed to keep our minds from thinking of the worst possible outcomes.

Emmy was in surgery for over five hours. The doctor came out to greet us and let us know everything had gone perfectly.

"Emmy's recovery is going to be hard. She has both ankles in a cast and a large triangle-shaped wedge between her knees. She will have to stay like this for six weeks or maybe longer. Right now, she will feel no pain because we have her on a spinal pain block, but that will need to come out tomorrow. I know you hate Valium, but she will need it around the clock to stop her muscles from spasming in her legs. I also have to warn you; she is going to have horrible bruising and swelling in her groin area. It is normal, but it will take you all by surprise," he finished.

"How long will she stay in the hospital?" I asked.

"Because of her sedation issues, we will keep her for at least five days. Then, if her pain is controlled with morphine and the spasms aren't bad, she can go home."

Emmy woke from the surgery spasm free but only because she had an enormous amount of pain medication being given through a spinal block. Once that was stopped, Emmy's pain was unbearable. She was still getting 4 ml of Valium once daily, but the care team increased it to every four hours. When she wasn't needing Valium, she was getting morphine. All I could worry about was the more medicine she was given now, the more we would have to wean later on. The never-ending cycle of weaning and withdrawal.

There should be a camera crew that follows special-needs parents everywhere they go for at least a week. The hoops we go through is quite amusing but also exhausting. Taking Emmy home, with a wedge between her knees, became a source of some creative thinking. After pushing the front seat down, I had to angle Emmy so bizarrely that Randy thought I was going to drop her. After layering blankets and pillows, I strapped her in and sat next to her. I had to make sure her legs were propped up and didn't move for the hour and a half drive home.

Once we arrived home, we had to carefully carry Emmy up the stairs and into the living room. Emmy's room was on the second floor, so a hospital bed was delivered and placed in the corner of our living room. A tiny commode became the centerpiece of the room. Our house was transformed into a hospital room overnight.

The next few weeks proved to be more difficult than the doctors warned. Sleeping on the couch next to her, listening to her cry in pain was the most difficult part because there was nothing we could do to make her feel better. When her casts started itching her, Linda and I had to figure out creative ways to itch her without scratching her. At one point, we had rubber spatulas poking out from the top and bottom of each cast.

Toileting was also very hard to do. We tried to convince Emmy to wear a diaper, but she refused. One person would hold her by the armpits, another by the ankles, and then we would slowly slide her down to the toilet. Everyday life became so bizarre. It was normal to be watching a movie while Emmy used the bathroom next to you. Everyone quickly became used to this new, weird reality.

Driving back to the hospital for the four-week checkup, just to hear she really needed to go at least two more weeks in the wedge was devastating. We truly hoped she could get out of those casts and wedge. Sleeping flat on her back became painful, so two of us would have to flip her on her stomach to sleep. Moving her was like trying to roll a triangle up a hill. Nothing was easy.

Two weeks post-surgery, I slowly began weaning the Valium at a slow pace. At the four-week appointment, the doctor said to also start weaning the morphine. Even though I weaned slower than the pain management team recommended, Emmy had a seizure on April 1.

CNS-restricted HLH was no longer an issue we worried about; now we worried about seizures. Diastat didn't work, so 9-1-1 was called. I took her out of the wedge, since she was close to the six-week mark, and the EMTs loaded her up. The ambulance took us to a local hospital, but they were forced to transfer us to Children's when the seizure wouldn't stop after two hours.

All I could think is that God had won the HLH war, so Satan was now trying every maneuver to keep Emmy in a constant state of spasms, misery, and epilepsy. The BMT doctors wanted to make sure this seizure had nothing to do with HLH, so they retested her for everything. As soon as she woke from the day-long sedation, she was instantly worse, but not from HLH. Sedation was getting the best of her, again.

After returning home, nothing we did could get Emmy comfortable. I just prayed for answers. "God, how will we drive Emmy across the United

States with her so spastic and miserable? Please, tell us what to do," I pleaded to God.

Two days later, I remembered the propranolol and clonidine mix and how well it had worked before Emmy's second BMT. I called her neurologist, and he put in another prescription. In just two weeks, her body was calm enough to go to school, and she showed no signs of dystonic storms. Emmy's left arm was very tight, so we waited a month and scheduled Botox. Her body continued calming down at a constant rate, just in time for the move from Massachusetts to Arkansas. I finally felt confident this season of pain was over and the season of healing was about to begin.

PART III
ARKANSAS

Then your light will break forth like the dawn, and your healing will quickly appear; then your righteousness will go before you, and the glory of the Lord will be your rear guard.
—ISAIAH 58:8 (NIV)

24

CHAPTER

And we know that all things work together for good to those who love God, to those who are called according to His purpose.
—ROMANS 8:28 (NKJV)

So many pieces had to fall perfectly in place for this gigantic move to work as we ventured from the north to the south. Trauma still blocked many of my physical abilities, especially multitasking. I was thankful I had a few hours to myself every day as the kids went off to school. Ella, who had been homeschooled from second grade to eleventh grade, was finishing her senior year at the local high school. Eli drove with her as a new freshman, and Emmy and Everett were at the local elementary school. I took those hours to pray, focus, and trust that God would work out all the details I just didn't have the ability to understand.

During those hours, Rebecca and I began walking. It was during those walks, through the picturesque landscape of Pepperell that I was able to discuss all I had been through. Holding things in and contemplating was not how I worked through any problems in my life. I have to talk it through, dissect it, and figure out the answer. Those hour-long walks were my outlet. I started to feel like myself during that time. Talking and walking became a new daily routine.

Selling our house was first on the agenda. Rebecca gathered all our friends and helped me organize, clean, and paint the house before putting it on the market. It was perfectly put together for showings, but not one person put an offer on it. We were quickly losing hope of selling until our friends, Jeremiah and Jana, offered to rent it from us. Jeremiah was taking over Randy's position at the medical squadron, and they needed a place to live. The large issues we couldn't see a way around were simple fixes for God.

Ella's high school graduation was quickly approaching, and I asked Jessica if she would run some errands with me to prepare. Emmy was home early most afternoons because she was still on a lot of sedatives and just couldn't make it to the end of the school day, so we all went together.

As we were driving through a nearby town, the car in front of me slammed on the brakes. I quickly slammed on my brakes, stopping about five feet from her bumper. Those two events set into place a perfect scenario for a triple car pileup. The truck directly behind me was able to stop without hitting me, but behind him was a newly licensed teenage driver not paying attention.

The teen girl was in a brand-new Jeep Wrangler and didn't know how to react. She didn't even brake before slamming into the F-150 truck. He was hit so hard from behind, his foot fell off the brake, and he flew directly into my van. I saw the entire event happening in slow motion in my rearview mirror. As soon as it was over, I flew around to look at Emmy and Jessica. Emmy was safely in her booster chair, but Jessica had been looking at Emmy, so her neck whiplashed.

The police were there in minutes. As we looked over the damage, I couldn't believe what I saw. My trunk was crushed, and in between the back seat and trunk was Emmy's wheelchair. That wheelchair had stopped the truck from collapsing the entire back of the van.

The trunk wouldn't open, so I had to take Emmy out to try and reach the wheelchair. As soon as the teen driver saw Emmy, she burst out in tears. She thought she had hurt a little girl who was unable to walk. We quickly set her mind at ease, and the fireman crawled over the two rows of seats and dislodged Emmy's wheelchair from the trunk. The damage was too much for me to drive it home, so Ella came to pick us up.

As soon as my car was checked out by a garage, the mechanics said it was totaled. I can't believe Emmy wasn't hurt even the slightest, yet my minivan was crushed. It reminded me of the song by Amy Grant, "Angels." They truly were watching over us.

We were down to the last three weeks in Massachusetts, and we had to find a new vehicle and a home to live in when we moved to Arkansas. With the addition of a baby chihuahua last Christmas, we now had three dogs and two cats to manage on a three-day trip. We needed a home and fast, but we'd never been to Arkansas to even know where to look.

Thankfully, the Air Force is a tight community, and we had friends from previous assignments living there. Everyone we talked with recommended Cabot because of the school system and well-funded special education programs.

Before I started house hunting, I remembered Emmy's orthopedic doctor telling us to get her in a pool as often as we could. Swimming increases the recovery rate and helps with overall coordination, especially in children with brain damage. It was a great excuse to finally have a house with a pool. Plus, Emmy still loved swimming more than anything else, and we were now going to be living with very hot, miserable summers.

We needed a house with two bedrooms on the main floor and a swimming pool. There was only one home that fit our specific needs so we put a contract on it, praying it was as nice as the pictures seemed.

The timing and location of this assignment was too good to be true. Emmy needed to be in a warmer climate after we realized the cold made her muscles very tight. Everything else about her seemed to be better overall, even though she was still waking up every forty-five minutes throughout the night. Ella had been accepted to Loyola University in New Orleans, a long six hours away from us, yet just right around the corner from Randy's mom in Harahan. The boys, who hated moving, stayed positive and didn't complain too much. Then one more blessing happened unexpectedly.

Right before we moved, we hired a new PCA, Nicole, to help cover the weekends. After hearing us discuss that we would need help in Arkansas, Nicole said she would move with us until we got settled. God placed so many amazing people in our path during this journey, and always at the perfect moment. Selfless people, who never asked for anything in return, would be the reason we never quit or gave up. People gave up their time, money, food, and even jobs to help us with Emmy's needs. From Emmy's dance teacher in Virginia, who did a huge fundraiser that helped us afford living in two different locations during our first months at Boston to our church, Harvest Fellowship Baptist, which provided prayers, meals, help with home repairs, and hours of driving to Boston just to pray over us. My sister gave up a career to live with us for a year, and now Emmy's new PCA, Nicole, gave up her life in Massachusetts to help us with our huge move to Arkansas. Just when I thought things were going to be too hard to tunnel through, trek over, or dig under, God sent us angels who made a way.

The drive from Massachusetts to Arkansas was going to be long and boring. My mom flew to Massachusetts to give us one extra driver, since we had three cars to move. We chose a route that allowed us to stop and visit my cousin, Sheri, in Maryland for our first stop. Though ten years apart, Sheri and I had become very close while we lived in Hawaii. Her family took annual vacations to O'ahu, so we would spend our annual stay-cations with them, letting our kids play and get to know each other better.

While in Virginia, we'd taken road trips to visit them, and we often swapped kids to get a kid-free break for a week. Sheri also helped me homeschool Eli while I was in the hospital with Emmy. She created zoom meetings so her son Jennings and Eli could learn together. That time created a close-knit relationship between Eli and Jennings, which is a huge blessing for military kids.

Emmy had the best time during our stop in Maryland. Gerbils, a tortoise, and four-wheelers kept her very busy. That was the most normal Emmy had felt in such a long time. The boys were able to run around, and the adults could relax before we made the last leg of our trip.

As we drove into the city we would now call home, the kids were wide-eyed, trying to figure out where we brought them. From every direction, all we could see were fields upon fields. It reminded us of our time in Oklahoma. This was a far cry from the beauty of Pepperell, but it was also so far from the horrors of Boston, I thought it was perfect.

We decided to rent an Airbnb until we could close on our new house. We spent three weeks in very close quarters, especially when everyone came for Randy's Change of Command ceremony. This would be Randy's first command at Little Rock AFB clinic, and everyone was there to support how far he had come in his career under such difficult circumstances. I don't know how he juggled both work and home, but he did it, and he did it exceedingly well.

We spent the next few weeks driving around our new little town, searching for restaurants and checking out where the kids would go to school. The kids had a sense of excitement that had been lost for a long time. The warm summer air and just weeks from owning a swimming pool were keeping us all antsy for our new life ahead. I am so thankful for those few weeks in the rental house, because once we closed on our new house, we were inundated with work we had never planned for.

CHAPTER 25

He heals the brokenhearted and binds up their wounds.
—PSALM 147:3 (NIV)

The transient life that comes with the military is hard. Being without a home, with kids and animals makes it even harder. When we left Hawaii, I didn't want to live in an apartment with four kids till we found something permanent in Virginia, so we purchased a house, sight unseen. We did have friends that accomplished multiple walk-throughs to inspect everything, and the home proved to be perfect, with no underlying issues. Sadly, most things don't happen perfectly twice. This house purchase in Arkansas was completely different than when we purchased our home in Virginia.

An in-depth walk-through couldn't happen because the family was still living in the home up until closing day. The realtors tried to video every room, but we still didn't have a good sense of the condition of the home. As military members, we had always purchased from other military members, so we had a false sense of what the home would be left like. Military members were trained from basic training, to leave something better than how you found it. When we lived in dorms or in base housing, we would have white glove inspections to make sure we were cleaning properly. So, when we sold our previous homes, we cleaned everything, repainted rooms and made sure everything was just like new. That is what we expected. But expectations can be our worst enemy.

As soon as we closed and were given the keys, we headed directly to the house so the kids could swim. We didn't notice much at first, since we hung out by the pool, but then I started noticing things weren't left as clean as I thought. As I began cleaning, I began unlocking years of neglect. It took everything in me to not cry. As we looked closer, we found holes in walls and doors, dingy carpets, and a decade of dirt and grime. A squeaky dishwasher, a refrigerator with a broken ice maker and a water heater that looked as if it would blow at any minute were obviously going to have to be replaced. I was so mad at myself. How could I be so careless in buying a house like this? This was not how we wanted to start our new life in Arkansas.

I tried to clean the house myself, but it was hopeless. I broke down and hired professionals to clean the entire house. The replacement of the new appliances was money spent that we didn't plan for. But it was the carpet that just ruined me. There was no way we could clean the carpets without making Emmy sick, so we had to replace it all. Against my better judgment, we decided to just buy new carpet instead of spending thousands more in replacing everything to match the wooden floors. The house was over ten years old and the tile and wood flooring was no longer available. It took months covering holes in walls and doors then repainting the entire house. It felt like we bought the Animal House!

The pool was this house's saving grace—until we realized the salt generator was also broken. Thankfully, we'd purchased the additional home warranty and replaced it for a fraction of the cost. Salt generator or not, the kids spent every day swimming. If not for that pool, I would have put the house right back on the market.

Swimming was exactly what Emmy needed. Muscle memory kicked in and she instantly tried to pull away from whomever was holding her, to swim on her own. She had no control of her body and would almost drown, so we bought floaties to keep her upright. After a few days, she kept trying to put her head underwater. We quickly realized she was unable to hold her breath once her face hit the water. Holding her nose closed did the trick. It was amazing seeing her hold her breath longer and longer, increasing her lung capacity. Nose plugs and a small floaty ring, and she was free as a bird. She had zero ability to swim, but she worked hard trying every single day. It was hard to watch her sink and try to move her limbs to swim, because she had been so gifted at swimming before. But Emmy didn't care. She just loved being in the water again.

Within a couple of months of being in Arkansas, Emmy was scheduled to see her new hematology/oncology doctor. When her BMT team from Boston said they would coordinate care with the Arkansas team, they really meant it. The first appointment with the new team was early August, and they exceeded all expectations I had. Besides doing the normal checkup of blood work and sending in Emmy's chimerism test, they had already scheduled Emmy with a throat specialist to look at her paralyzed vocal cord, a physiatrist to help with her movement disorders, the orthopedic surgeon to check on her hips, and an echocardiogram to monitor her heart; they'd even scheduled occupational and physical therapy evaluations. If I was going to judge this hospital on our first encounter, it was now the best children's hospital in the world!

I quickly enrolled the kids in school and prayed they would love it there. I used to love homeschooling and teaching my kids everything, but my mind was still in "lockdown" mode, and I knew they would not get a quality education from me.

Eli was now a sophomore in high school and was already plugged into the football team. He didn't enjoy football, but he told us that it was a way to get a free weight lifting program. I have to say that kid knows what he wants and figures out how to get it. Everett was going to a school just one minute from our house and would be entering the third grade. He had always hated yet loved school simultaneously, so I didn't know what to expect from him.

Ella would be entering her first year in college at Loyola New Orleans. We had so many changes happening at once, but seeing our firstborn leave for college was hard to accept. From being born six weeks early as a four-pound baby to now walking away as a woman was hard on us. But leaving home and becoming independent is part of life, and I knew God was going to use her in a mighty way. Right after we drove Ella to New Orleans to get her settled into her dorm room, I had an important meeting with the special-needs department regarding Emmy. She was still an anomaly, and I needed to make the right decision on how to get her an education without it being hard on her physically and mentally.

The special-needs department was very accommodating and instantly agreed to giving Emmy a one-on-one paraprofessional. I was so relieved knowing Emmy would be taken care of. They decided to place Emmy in a step-up classroom consisting of about ten kids who all needed extra help. I was so excited for all of our kids' new adventures, finally able to be alone for a few hours a day. I had been surrounded by kids for eleven years. Five of those years were spent trying to keep Emmy alive and comfortable. My mind, body, and soul needed solace to heal.

Restoration became my word for Arkansas. If Virginia was the state of dying and Boston was the struggle for a cure, Arkansas was going to be the place where it would all be restored. Every doctor, every specialist, and every nurse looked at Emmy with hope instead of pity. The ear, nose, and throat (ENT) doctor said it best. He listened to Emmy's story and then looked straight at me and said, "Well, all of that is over, and now is the time for healing." I was shocked as he echoed what I had been praying for over the years. I instantly felt relieved.

He videoed Emmy's vocal cord and throat during the appointment. He told us the loud noise was because the tissue around the left vocal cord was also paralyzed, and she was sucking it down her throat with every breath. Sadly, the vocal cord couldn't be fixed, but he could remove the extra tissue, making it easier for her to breathe. He also said, if she wanted to be completely silent, he could Botox her vocal cord every four months, but it could compromise her airway and possibly cause her to choke. We opted to skip that part, and we scheduled the surgery for early November.

A few days later Emmy had her follow-up echocardiogram. Miracles were unfolding before our eyes. Before we came to Arkansas, Emmy's heart had not improved. I was eager to see the results, since leaving all the trauma behind. The results were astonishing. She was just a few points from having a totally normal heart. God was mending her broken heart right before our eyes. Everything was working out, except for new symptoms that Emmy began having upon our arrival to Arkansas.

The first month in our home, we began noticing Emmy doing something very strange. While Emmy would swim, she would have to work twice as hard as everyone else, which made her breathing accelerate, almost like hyperventilating. Every time I would pull her out of the water to take a break, within five minutes, Emmy's whole body would freeze.

It was like someone pushed the pause button. I remember the first time it happened.

"Emmy are you OK? What was that? Did you just have a seizure?" I frantically said while holding her.

"I don't know. My body wouldn't move, but I could hear and see everything going on," she said confused.

They were obviously seizures, but I never knew people could be awake during them. What started out as just a few a day, quickly went to happening almost every hour. We already had an appointment set up with her new neurologist, but the first available wasn't until October. We had to pray these episodes weren't going to turn into real seizures because school was starting in August, and Emmy was excited to go.

Not only is education different in every state, so are the public programs like Medicaid. We'd had a personal care assistant in Massachusetts because Medicaid or MassHealth, paid for them. Some states have programs for the disabled and will waive the income of the parents, with zero wait time and zero premium. Sadly, many states won't waive the parents' income or they lump all disabilities, from adults to children, together in the same pool to receive a waiver. Tricare always took care of Emmy's medical needs, but it didn't cover personal care assistance unless the assistance was medically based. If Emmy had a tracheostomy, feeding tube, or needed oxygen, then we could have had help. But because she was just physically disabled, there was nothing for her. The only insurance that provided personal care assistance was Medicaid, but we soon found out Arkansas had a wait list seven years long for the waiver. I was quickly starting to question if I really liked Arkansas or not.

I was told about an insurance program for children if we paid a premium, but over and over, I was told it wouldn't provide a PCA. With no financial assistance or Medicaid, we had to send Nicole back to Massachusetts. There was just no way we could afford to pay her out of pocket. I prayed options would become available for us. Emmy was still waking every forty-five minutes during the night, gaining weight by the minute, and I just couldn't do it all on my own.

And then I remember the overwhelming presence of God surrounding our family through the darkest times. Without the dark, would we have seen the depth and fullness of God's love, grace, and mercy? Most definitely not. I wouldn't have learned anything with a "quick fix." I wouldn't have learned to completely and wholly rely on God for everything. I would have never seen how bright the goodness of God is without being blinded by the disappointments and heartache. While we were focused on God, He was focused on working out the details. It was simply amazing.

God's timing was always on time. I still can't believe all the ways God showed up, but my selfish heart still wishes He would have just healed Emmy from the start. I think of all the torture and pain and sacrifices we all went through, but especially Emmy. So much was stolen from her; so much was lost. Yet so much was restored. We have seen victory after every battle we faced. She is the living, breathing miracle, and that is enough.

CHAPTER 26

There remains therefore a rest for the people of God. For he who entered His rest has himself also ceased from his works as God did from His.
—HEBREWS 4:9-10 (NKJV)

Arkansas Children's Hospital was such a change from Boston. It was never swarming with kids; the people were incredibly nice, and the doctors did their due diligence and studied Emmy's case and hundreds of notes on everything that happened to her. Plus, there weren't a billion specialties and subspecialties like Boston, which seemed to cause more problems than not.

Neurology still scared me. The neurologist from Boston recommended an autoimmune neurologist in Arkansas, but we found out he was fresh out of his neurology fellowship. What I really wanted was someone like Dr. Toor from Virginia, a neurologist trained in many areas, who could oversee all of Emmy's issues. After reading each doctor's bio, I knew that wasn't an option. We chose an epilepsy doctor, since that seemed to be the most pressing brain issue with Emmy.

The new neurologist read over all the notes from Boston and then listened to me carry on for almost an hour. I could tell she understood what Emmy went through and also her sensitivity to medicine. After discussing medicine options, she was very cautious about putting Emmy on a seizure medicine containing a benzodiazepine, so she decided to put Emmy on Trileptal. After five days, we noticed the medicine didn't stop the episodes Emmy was having, but it did something so much more. For the first time in five whole years, Emmy started sleeping through the night. I couldn't believe it. I had all but given up on sleep, even though I quoted Hebrews 4:9–10, reminding God of His promise of rest. I don't know if the verse was talking of actual sleep, but it is all I asked for.

When we all started sleeping through the night, there was nothing that could wake us. I felt hungover every morning from sleeping so deeply and craved more and more of it. Emmy would sleep in almost daily, and thankfully, her school was sympathetic, after a note from the doctor. Emmy needed rest more than we did, especially since the body heals during sleep. I never realized how foggy my mind was until I finally slept through the night. Days were clearer, and I felt the "closed-off," traumatized parts of my mind beginning to open back up. I began feeling human again.

November quickly approached, and the anxiety was a little high when the day for Emmy's throat surgery came. I was worried that something was going to happen with the sedation, and our trip to Disney World would have to be canceled. Randy and I had just committed to going with his mom's family. Linda had been trying to plan a family getaway for three years and this was the first time we felt Emmy could handle the trip.

The surgery was quick with no sedation side effects. We took Emmy home the next day, and within a week we could hear the extra loud breathing sound gone. The vocal cord was still paralyzed in the closed position, so there was still noise with every breath, but she was much quieter. Randy and I stared at the video monitor for weeks, watching her sleep, wondering if she was alive. Her rhythmic, noisy breathing had given us comfort since Boston. It meant she was alive and not having a seizure. We needed to let that go, to move on, and to realize this was the healing we had been hoping and praying for all these years.

Sadly, the seizure episodes were relentless. The neurologist decided to have her stay a night in-patient and do an EEG with video before we left for Disney. Within an hour, they had captured her on video having five episodes. The next day, the doctor notified us that the EEG wasn't really showing seizure activity, and she wasn't too sure where they were coming from. She believed they could be so deep in her brain that the EEG just couldn't pick them up. She asked me if it was OK to start her on a very small pill called Onfi, which happened to be in the benzodiazepine family. I hated adding more and more medicine to her daily regiment, but this medicine was specific for these types of seizures. The plan was to start weaning Keppra as we increased the Onfi, since it was obvious Keppra no longer served its purpose. An MRI was also scheduled, just to make sure her brain looked stable. Just as before—stable with no change. These tests gave us enough peace of mind to take Emmy to Disney. Days after starting Emmy on Onfi, we left for Disney. This family trip was going to be the first since our road trip from Massachusetts and the first going on an actual family vacation.

Family vacations had been a pipe dream since Emmy broke her arm in April 2014, and here we were at Disneyworld. It felt so good being around family. Disney, on the other hand, was a wild mess. Christmas was not the time to visit, but it was the only time everyone could take work and school off. Shoulder to shoulder, hours waiting for rides, and nowhere to eat. Family time was great, but Disney was crowded and miserable.

Everyone seemed to be incredibly grumpy and on each other's nerves by the end of each day. The heat probably had something to do with it. Why is it still hot in Florida in December? Emmy was extremely miserable, with constant movements the entire trip and also continued to have episodes. We were not used to being around so many people, let alone around so much noise and chaos. Every night we would try to dim the lights and calm Emmy down. The trip ended up being more stressful than relaxing.

No matter what, I was bound to make this a trip Emmy would never forget. She didn't remember the last time we came, as she was only two. It was Halloween, and we'd decided to dress up as the Incredibles and go to the Hallow-Scream party. Emmy was suited up like baby Jack-Jack, Ella as Violet, Eli as Dash, and we were Bob and Helen Incredible—spandex and all. We actually won a backstage pass during that trip. But this time, I managed to get Emmy in line to meet her favorite Disney "hunk," Aladdin. Everyone clapped for Emmy as she put her head on Aladdin's shoulder and flirted. She was definitely never going to forget this trip!

The day we left, we decided to take our kids to Universal for a few hours. We had been to Orlando three times before and somehow skipped Universal. After just a few hours, we all decided we would return to Orlando to spend our entire trip at Universal. With Harry Potter wands and an experience they would never forget, we all packed in the car and headed home.

The initial trip to Orlando took us two days from New Orleans, where the entire family met before leaving. On the way to Disney, we decided to stop in Florida and visit Randy's best friend. Lawrence and Randy had been friends since junior high, and we'd all flown together on the AWACs (Airborne Early Warning and Control System) aircraft. It had been years since we'd been able to visit him, let alone any of our friends. We finally met his wife, stepdaughter, and new baby boy. I can't believe how much we'd missed out on while Emmy was so sick. Relationships, friendships, dreams, and hopes had all been put on the back burner. Disease steals so much more than health.

On the trip home, I asked if we could skip seeing our friends and go straight home. I was starting to not feel very well. It was first a tickle in my throat, and then overnight, I developed full body aches and became congested. We stopped to sleep at a hotel that evening, and I slept away from everyone. The last thing Emmy needed was to get sick. I felt like my body was bruised from head to toe. Tylenol PM didn't touch the pain. I had only been sick like this once before, and it was when I'd gotten a food-borne bacterium while deployed to Incirlik, Turkey.

After arriving back home, I went to the urgent care clinic, and they tested me for flu and strep. Both were negative, and I was sent home without any medicine. I continued to become sicker, even losing my sense of taste and smell, then suddenly couldn't get out of bed for days. I began coughing so hard I could barely breath. I went back to the clinic five days later, and the doctor tested me again, both tests still being negative. The clinic decided to X-ray my lungs, and the X-ray revealed I had acute bronchitis. I was sent home with a Z-Pack, an inhaler, and cough medicine. Two days later, I miraculously felt like a new person.

A few days later, Eli came down with the same thing. I took him to get tested, but the clinic was out of flu tests. Everyone seemed to be getting sick, but it wasn't the flu. The doctor was worried his fever was pretty high, so they gave him Motrin and made him drink Gatorade. Once his fever began lowering, they gave him a Z-Pack and sent us home. His high fever lasted a day, and his cough lasted a week, but he recovered way quicker than me.

Like clockwork, a week later, Emmy came down with whatever we were fighting. She just seemed to have a really bad cold, but it started making her cough and her breathing became more rapid. We took her to her primary care provider, and she put her on an antibiotic. But within a couple days she started having a hard time breathing. Randy and I decided she needed to go to the ER.

As we walked into Children's ER, Emmy's noisy breathing helped expedite us to the front of the line. An X-ray was quickly ordered, and her blood was drawn. Of all the things, pneumonia in the lower left part of her lung showed up, but no flu or strep. The ER staff started her on an antibiotic. After that was finished, they began another antibiotic. This seemed normal to me, since every time Emmy had a fever, the common practice was to give two antibiotics. But something went wrong when the second antibiotic entered her vein.

"My ears itch. Mom, my throat is itchy!" Emmy said so clearly the nurse overheard her.

The nurse instantly turned off the IV medication and administered Benadryl. Everyone realized that Emmy had had an allergic reaction to the clindamycin. As they discussed what to do next, they sent us up to a room to stay overnight. I expected the staff would just give the first antibiotic again or change to something else, but for some reason, they didn't.

Two doctors bombarded me that evening, requesting we try clindamycin once more. With Emmy being a post-BMT patient, they were worried the pneumonia was MRSA related. They were also quick to tell me that clindamycin was one of the only antibiotics available in oral form, which would allow us to go home sooner.

As each doctor tried to convince me it would be safe to try clindamycin again if they premedicated with Benadryl, but I adamantly refused. I stood my ground, and I thought they understood I wasn't going to budge. But at 2:00 a.m., I was rudely awakened by some resident who was still in the stages of thinking he knew more than anyone, even a very experienced parent of a medically complex child.

"Ma'am, sorry to wake you, but I need to know why you said we can't try clindamycin again. You realize we will pretreat her with Benadryl, and I am sure she won't have a reaction," he said as haughty as possible.

"She had an allergic reaction. I know all about medicine allergies, and I know that clindamycin is not the only medicine for MRSA. I don't care if we have to stay in this hospital for seven days to get the antibiotic she needs, but she will not get that one again," I said as I sat up on my bed.

"I don't think you understand. You could be here for two weeks if this pneumonia doesn't go away with a different antibiotic. Clindamycin is the best one for MRSA, and you can take it at home. We want to try again. I promise we will use Benadryl first, and Emmy will be OK," he said, still trying to convince me. "I will have the nurse hook it up, and we can get her out of here in a few days," he finished.

"I don't feel comfortable trying it again. But if you think this is the only one that will work, you can't do it tonight. If she has another reaction, I know everyone that is more qualified than you is at home. You can do it in the morning," I said angrily.

After three doctors harassed me into trying one specific antibiotic, I finally gave in. That is how I always allowed things to happen that I didn't agree with. After I was too exhausted to argue anymore.

That morning, the nurse prepped Emmy with a dose of Benadryl and then started the clindamycin. Within seconds, Emmy's ears, eyes, and throat started itching. Then she started acting like she was going to crawl out of her skin.

The daytime resident, who happened to be a brand-new doctor, was there overseeing the whole thing. Even though the nurse turned the medicine off and was calmly going through the steps of an allergic reaction, the doctor began overreacting and becoming frantic. She felt there was no time to wait for Benadryl to kick in, so she ordered epinephrine. I was so angry, I didn't say a word. It's those moments when you want to scream, "*I told you so!*"

About an hour later, the attendee in charge came to speak with me. "We are sorry this happened twice, but something must be wrong with Emmy. I have never heard of someone being allergic to clindamycin. We should really get her an allergy test done," she said, as if blaming Emmy for all of this.

"I told everyone how sensitive Emmy is to medicine. She is allergic to this medicine, so you just need to try something else. We have all had a terrible cold, and I know this is not MRSA or related to Emmy's BMT. We will stay here as long as it takes, if the only effective antibiotic is in IV form," I said, completely offended she just blamed Emmy for being allergic to something.

"OK. We'll start her on something new and watch how she responds over the next day or so," she said and walked away.

Having a medically complex child is tough. Everyone looks at Emmy's physical disability, assumes she is mentally slow, and then overreacts when they see she has had two bone marrow transplants. So many doctors jump to conclusions, and it is hard getting new doctors to understand who Emmy really is and what she can handle. But to listen to a doctor say something was wrong with Emmy because she was allergic just made me so angry. Doctors should be the experts to know that not every medicine will work with every person.

Emmy responded quickly to the new medicine and was off oxygen just two days later. They sent us home with a regular antibiotic, and she felt fine within the week. Little did we know that what all of us had experienced was most likely the first round of coronavirus-19. Disneyworld was full of foreigners. Everyone was shoulder to shoulder, and it was most definitely a hotbed for all kinds of germs.

Eli, Emmy, and I all lost our senses of taste and smell and had really high fevers. This was one of those times that I thank God the doctors weren't testing for this virus yet. I hate to imagine what would have happened if Emmy had tested positive for coronavirus, paired with having a hard time breathing. A ventilator would have been the end of her already weak diaphragm and lungs. Another thing perfectly timed by God.

Like everywhere else in the world, schools were closed down shortly after. Because Randy was privy to everything happening around the United States and world, he warned me to take extra precautions and get stocked up on food. I wasn't worried, though, because I am always prepared with Sam's Club-sized paper products and food. Having a large family seems to keep you prepared for anything.

By mid-March, all four kids were home safe and sound. Ella was sent home once New Orleans started booming with coronavirus. Plus, dorms were a petri dish for cooties. I loved having all my kids with me, but I soon found out how rough it was trying to lift, carry, and move Emmy all day long. Eli quickly became my helper and did most of the lifting. I can't tell you how thankful I was that Randy decided to buy him a weight lifting bench for Christmas. Eli was now a strong teen, who literally saved my back and arms from hurting worse than they already did.

During the mass quarantine, Eli and Ella did their schoolwork online. Emmy and I worked on her daily assignments posted by her teacher. I quickly realized just how behind her peers she was. Everett was supposed to be doing all of his third-grade work online and watching a PBS show, but he couldn't stand it. I called his teacher and asked if I could use old homeschool curriculum to keep him engaged, and she said, "Of course! Whatever you can do to keep him caught up and ready for fourth grade!" Little did I know that Everett would soon be talking me into actually homeschooling him for fourth grade. I wasn't sure I was ready to teach again, but I was willing to give it a try. I'd missed years with my youngest child, and quality time was exactly what we needed.

CHAPTER 27

For I am about to do something new. See, I have already begun! Do you not see it? I will make a pathway through the wilderness. I will create rivers in dry wasteland.
—ISAIAH 43:19 (NLT)

Emmy's new medicine, Onfi, was finally working. We were barely seeing any episodes, so it was time to start weaning Emmy off Keppra. Everything was going great until early one morning at the end of March. Emmy's scream echoed through the dark, silent house; and by the time I made it to her bedroom, she had already started puking. It was another seizure from weaning. No matter how small of a wean or how slowly I did it, for some reason, Emmy's brain couldn't stand the chemical change. Thankfully, she pulled out of it on her own, and we didn't need to give her the Diastat. Randy and I just kept thinking about how much worse it could have been if she needed to go to an ER full of kids with coronavirus.

This virus and quarantine proved to be harder than we could have ever imagined. While the pain of what we went through with Emmy was as real and painful as it got, we were now getting thrown into what every adult would have to go through—the loss of a parent. It was apparent why Randy's mom was so adamant about all of us going on a family vacation at Christmas; she probably felt a premonition she wasn't well. I am so thankful for her pushing the whole family to be together and getting to spend those wonderful days in Orlando together. Memories are forever.

What angers me the most about her death is that she died alone, without seeing any of her kids or grandkids for weeks. Even her children who lived nearby didn't get to see her. Why would medical professionals ever tell people to stay away from family, especially during such a confusing time in history? When has it ever been normal to leave our elderly parents isolated? I sometimes wonder if her death was sped up by isolation.

Another Good Friday was marked by something life altering. Emmy breaking her arm was the first Good Friday that changed the course of our family's future. The second Good Friday brought us hope of healing and a cure with Ella donating her cells to give the gift of life. This Good Friday was filled with pain, just like when Jesus was hung on the cross. Our hearts were torn. Linda meant so much to us. I had grown so close to her over the years, and Randy had such a strong relationship with her, the kind that only mothers and sons understand.

Active-duty military members were forced to strict lockdowns and could only go to work and back home. Grocery shopping, errands, or getting basic essentials were not allowed, unless they had no civilians to do it for them. Travel outside of the state was forbidden. So, when the funeral was scheduled in New Orleans, a so called "hotbed" for coronavirus, Randy almost gave up any hope of going. He was in charge of making sure people followed the rules, so he was afraid to ask for permission. I quickly urged him, maybe a little too harshly, but he finally asked if he could attend his mother's funeral.

Promising to stay out of public places and to quarantine for fourteen days after, he was given permission to go. We stayed with his stepdad, yet we couldn't even hug him or any of our family members. It was the saddest, loneliest in-person funeral I had ever been to, considering all funerals are heart-wrenching. Not being able to physically comfort one another made me realize how senseless this virus, or maybe our fear of it, actually was.

A week after we arrived back home, I received a letter that said Emmy had been approved to see a movement disorder doctor at University of Arkansas Medical Sciences (UAMS). Emmy's neurologist became aware of how much Emmy moved when she recorded her during the EEG and felt certain there just had to be something a movement doctor could do to help her. More than anything, people truly want to help Emmy. With her body always wiggling and her right hand always dancing, her neurologist really wanted to see if there was anything that could be done.

I knew better, but I like to stay hopeful, and sometimes ignorant that all had already been done. I thought this time would be different. I still thought there was a "magical" pill that would help Emmy gain back control of her body. But the medicine he prescribed made Emmy worse, and after five days, I decided to stop it. I called the doctor's office to let them know what happened and the nurse said the doctor would be in touch. He never called back. That was the last time we went to that doctor. Our daughter is far too important for someone to be too busy to return a simple phone call. I think this is when we fully realized medicine is not and will never be the answer we are looking for to solve Emmy's movement disorder.

An appointment was made with her physiatrist at Arkansas Children's to get Botox, which always provided a couple months of relief. We never used Botox in her right arm, even though it always danced, but her left arm was a must. Just releasing some of the muscle tightness allowed her to be able to use her left hand without falling over to the right. The left arm was our biggest obstacle. We saw that when her arm was loose, she could function much more easily. Plus, Trileptal began calming Emmy's muscles as well as helping with sleep. That was truly the one medicine that helped Emmy overall.

A renewed sense of wanting to help Emmy without medicinal intervention began to reignite within me. It was now obvious her brain would never accept the movement disorder medicines that the doctors continuously tried. The obvious place to start was physical and occupational therapy.

It didn't matter who the nurse, therapist, or doctor was, the minute they were greeted with Emmy's huge smile and hung out with her for just a few minutes, they instantly fell in love with her. Both therapists quickly became invested in helping Emmy gain back some independence. Soon, Emmy was fitted for a therapy seat to help her at school and a walker that would not require her to use her arms. Her current walker required both arms to help push it, but her left arm was still overly sensitive and her fingers no longer bent at the knuckles, which made holding anything impossible. Her right arm did a pretty good job holding on but would jump off unexpectedly. Emmy was always saying her arms had minds of their own.

Hyperbaric oxygen therapy (HBOT) was still a viable option in my mind. I just couldn't shake the feeling we were supposed to start trying it again. Living in Arkansas put us very close to the doctor who had spent decades dedicating his life to helping all kinds of people through oxygen therapy. After more research, I realized our goal was to see if a soft-shell chamber would be effective for her. It would be easier, more convenient, and more cost-effective to have our own instead of paying over $150 each dive somewhere else. The only problem was, we needed to know if it would be beneficial not being able to get as much pressure as a hard-shell tank.

Without clearing it with Randy, I set the appointment with Dr. Harch, author of *The Oxygen Revolution*, and decided to get his professional opinion. Randy was upset at first because we still had that feeling oxygen would "turn on" the genetic disease, but Emmy had gone years disease free and she needed relief.

The drive to New Orleans was like the mending of old wounds. I was alone with Everett and Emmy and we were heading back to the place where it all began. I showed the kids where Emmy broke her arm and then we met with Dr. Harch.

He was excited that we had done oxygen and felt like Emmy was ready to begin an oxygen journey on her own terms. She was fitted with wireless EEG machine and we both cuddled up in a single person oxygen tank while the doctor adjusted pressure and oxygen level. The verdict, was Emmy's brain showed the most improvement with no added oxygen and at the lowest pressure. The news was exciting, so we scheduled a few more dives with him so he could monitor her daily before we purchased Emmy her own oxygen tank.

The kids and I stayed at Randy's mom's house, which no longer was filled with Mimi's laughter, but her presence still lingered everywhere. The smell of old smoke, the house decorated like she left it and the sound of kids everywhere. Randy's sister stayed there before covid hit, but left when hysteria and poor judgement said older people shouldn't be around younger people. But she moved back in with her dad since the death of their mom, so the house was filled with little girls. Everett was not impressed with all the girls, so his boy cousins came and stayed a few nights to keep him sane.

The daily dives were so calm and nothing like the past. With no plastic helmet needed, Emmy could just relax, watching cartoons. We showed up for the second dive, but Emmy had woken with a snotty nose, so he checked her ears. Emmy felt good enough, so we went into the tank once more. By the third day, Emmy was completely congested, so we had to cancel. Emmy's cold didn't clear for four days, so we didn't go back until the next Monday. Four more dives, each forty-five minutes long, and it was time to head home before school started. Before we left, we looked over options for soft-shell tanks and instantly became discouraged. To own our own, we would have to pay at least $8,000 because renting was no longer an option due to coronavirus. So many therapies were available for Emmy, but money always seemed to be the limiting factor. I was still confident that, if Emmy needed oxygen therapy, God would provide.

Seven days later, a check showed up at our house for exactly $8,000. We were not expecting it. T-shirt sales, donations, and working my home business were what I had been focused on, not a check just appearing in our mailbox. God moved the obstacle, once more. Our needs were met, and we instantly ordered Emmy her very own oxygen tank. The person who donated to us refused public praise, but we know that God saw what he did.

Over the next few months, we realized how sensitive Emmy's brain actually was. Within minutes of leaving the tank, her body would stiffen, her head would rear to the left, and she would freeze. Twenty seconds later, she would loosen and tell us her head hurt, and she felt nauseous. This was how all of her episodes had been in the past. And no matter if we knew they were "healing seizures" or not, they scared us, and we didn't want to see them.

The schedule of using the tank was eventually pushed to one dive every twenty-one days for only 45 minutes. The schedule was determined by Emmy and how she felt. She would actually tell me when she felt like she needed to go in. Emmy was starting to understand her body and its needs. Not only could we see her clarity of mind and motivation in school continuously increase, she could too. For the first time, she was seeing herself get better. That was a far cry from spending hours in therapy years ago, only to lose skills, instead of gaining them. Oxygen, coupled with her newest therapy of riding horses, called hippotherapy, showed dramatic improvements in Emmy's strength.

Her underlying movements were always present. But now when we stood her up, she could self-correct, instead of just falling over to the right. The therapy tricycle donated to her back in Virginia by SMILES was finally getting used daily. Emmy was more motivated than we had seen in a long time. Using her old and new walkers, trying to use her left arm and working hard during therapy were making Emmy hopeful she would be a normal kid again. Hope was rising all around us, and with every blood test coming back at 100 percent donor cells, we began looking at our future with hopefulness.

CHAPTER 28

The Lord's acts of mercy indeed do not end, for His compassions do not fail. They are new every morning; great is Your faithfulness. "The Lord is my portion," says my soul. "Therefore, I wait for Him."
—LAMENTATIONS 3:22-24 (NASB2020)

Today as I write this, it has been seven years exactly to the day that Emmy broke her arm in New Orleans. As I crawled into bed with Emmy this morning, snuggled nose to nose, her knees curled up into my stomach, like we do every morning, I was overcome with emotion at how far she has come since Boston. I can still feel my chest tightening when I remember the deep hopelessness that suffocated me, day after day, in ICU Room 30. I often pray that I will forget those days. But if I did, then I would forget the feeling of what it was like to be in the presence of God. The intimacy I felt to God while kneeling in that sleep room, crying, and praying for help, for miracles, for answers. Nothing can replicate that feeling because it wasn't physical; it was like I lost myself, and all that was left was God.

Out of acts of desperation, I am sure I promised God so many things during the months of agony in the hospital. I would do anything to have Emmy come home spasm and disease free. Maybe I promised to become a preacher or to never sin or to sell all that I have, but in all honesty, I can't remember what I said. I do remember this though. I remember that I promised Him that I would never stop being thankful and would never stop telling people what God did for Emmy. I would tell the story where it was God who brought us to Boston at the perfect moment for a cure. It was God who revealed the reason for her spasms. It was God who allowed Ella to be a bone marrow donor so we could find out about her NK cells and PCOS. It was God and only God Who healed Emmy's broken heart and healed her of a disease that we were told had no cure in the beginning.

I didn't want to finish this book just yet, as Emmy's story is far from over. We just weaned the last of Keppra and are only on Trileptal and Onfi, with a small dose of clonidine to relax her at night. Every single wean of medicine showed a side of Emmy that has been lost. Every drop opened up her personality that made Emmy more like the real Emmy. Dropping the gigantic dose of 3000 mg of Keppra completely has been the most amazing thing to witness. While every drop brought warning signs of possible seizures, we were able to slowly decrease it without needing to go to the hospital.

Just yesterday, Emmy tapped into the creative part of her brain and told me the funniest two-minute story involving purchasing chicken, goose livers, hot sauce, and buns at the market. We haven't seen that kind of creativity since HLH happened. And now that I see her brain being restored to its full brilliance, I just know that her body is going to soon follow.

All of the doctors and therapists here in Arkansas are amazed at the progress Emmy has made physically, intellectually, and emotionally over the past two years since our first visits in 2019. Not only has she finally started growing taller, her muscles are strengthening and moving in ways we haven't seen in years. The tiniest muscles that we thought were lost from the multiple strokes are starting to work again. Emmy's eyebrows are able to correspond to her emotions, and she practices nodding her head up and down and side to side. She can even look at us with a scowl when she's trying to show us she's mad. Those simple movements in her neck and face had been lost for years.

As far as the dystonia goes, it is minor compared to even a year ago. I truly believe swimming, Trileptal, oxygen, and all her therapies have helped. But also, the farther we get from the second bone marrow transplant, the more her brain can finally recover. We have tried CBD oil and THC oil to see if her movements would improve, but THC made her right arm dance more wildly, while also making her extremely sleepy.

CBD hasn't done anything we can visually see, but we continue to give it as a supplement to help her body heal. I pray every day that her left arm will loosen up for good and stop being the source of so much discomfort for her. Anytime she uses her left arm, her entire body still reacts, pushing her to the right. We have replaced numerous right lateral guards on her wheelchair from the force of her leaning. When the left arm is no longer an issue, there is no telling what her body can accomplish.

Randy and I are also at a crossroads at this exact moment. While the Air Force has proven to be the best decision we ever made, we decided it is time to move on to the next chapter of our lives. Moving to Arkansas was very stressful, trying to retell Emmy's medical history over and over to all the new doctors. Thankfully, every one of them proved to be compassionate and caring and willing to learn her history—and not willing to repeat mistakes done in the past. None of them had ever met a child who has gone through as much as Emmy has yet still smiles like she has zero problems in the world. We could all learn so much from her.

The thing I am struggling with is that I don't want to have to keep retelling Emmy's history every two to three years. I don't want to see the look on a doctor's face when I go through every medicine and every sedation that has hurt Emmy. If Randy takes one more assignment and we don't retire there, I will have to relive and retell Emmy's medical history two more times.

Our desire now is to plant ourselves somewhere that we can grow and flourish, building actual relationships that are close and not long distant. We want doctors who will follow Emmy longer than three years and know when something just isn't right with her. We want stability. We want a place we can call home.

This crossroads has taken us through more discussions, decisions, and plans than I could have ever thought possible. Where do we take our daughter that has the resources, doctors, and environment that will benefit her, even after we have passed away? I think that is why this has been hard for us. What will happen to Emmy when we die?

Montana was my first impulse, but Montana doesn't provide Medicaid to children of parents above poverty level. Medicaid is nonnegotiable for us. Home modifications; covered co-pays; and, most of all, a personal care assistant are only provided through Medicaid. Randy and I are not getting younger, and her siblings have futures of their own they want to discover and live out. It is obvious we have to find a state that does it all, and while Massachusetts provides everything we need, I'm not sure I could handle being back at Boston Children's again. The hospital and staff eventually became like our family, but the memories still crush my heart. I don't want to be reminded of what we went through every time we walk through the front rotating doors.

We recently discovered Colorado has a great program for special-needs kids, so we have been considering moving there. Recently, Colorado's population has boomed, along with home prices. Medicaid for special-needs kids is as good as it gets, but we also want to build an accessible home for Emmy, which is costly. As we planned out the move and places we could build, we found too many roadblocks for an easy transition. The timing is all off for every place we tried to choose.

How does Randy start a new career (if there is one), sell two houses, find a rental in Colorado Springs that allows seven pets, and set up a new medical team for Emmy? Not to mention we will have to plan out college for two kids and find schools that will work with Emmy's needs. The entire thing was causing me so much agony I stopped sleeping for weeks. That should have been my warning sign. If something was meant to be, God always gave me peace, not worry.

When we first arrived in Arkansas, I knew that the state provided an insurance program for children with special needs, but I was told it wouldn't cover personal care for her. What I needed was the full Medicaid program, so I went through the entire process of putting Emmy on the waiver list for parents who earned above poverty level. Seven years is the wait time. I quickly dismissed Arkansas as anywhere we could retire—until last month.

The owner of Beyond Boundaries, where Emmy rides horses for her hippotherapy, told me that, if we would pay for the children's Medicaid insurance (referred to as TEFRA), she would instantly be referred to an outside company who provides in-home assistance. I told her the Medicaid representative told me they didn't provide personal care, but she said there was a new program that would. We quickly signed Emmy up for TEFRA. Within two weeks, Emmy was referred to a company who would assign a person to be her hands and feet a few hours a day. The absolute relief and excitement I felt to finally know that we would have help with Emmy's care has given me a hope for my own future, because I want more than to be trapped at home when I have desires outside of being a caretaker. But that was just the beginning of what God had planned for us.

Last week, after realizing there was no way we could move to Colorado next June, I just sat and asked God what we should do. As clear as the first time I'd heard Him, He simply replied, "Be still." I have finally learned to obey the voice of God. I then remembered back to when we first arrived in Cabot and Randy confidently said to me, "We are going to retire here!" While I'd quickly laughed and dismissed his carefree attitude, he was right all along.

As if everything had been planned out long ago, the housing issue and where we would plant ourselves for years to come was solved in a matter of hours. Since Emmy had become sick, I'd secretly prayed that, when Randy decided to retire, we would find a piece of land covered with trees, beautiful scenery, and water. While the mountains will always bring me joy, water brings me peace. I can sit by water for hours and just be still, which is something I don't do often, but need to.

We already knew we had to build a house, specific for Emmy's needs, but we'd never looked for land in Arkansas. I found many lots of land near us and wrote a few places down. The next day, Randy and I drove around to just get the feel of each area. After looking at lots, quite isolated from neighbors, he quickly told me that, if we stayed in Arkansas, he wanted to live on a golf course and have friends nearby for Everett and Emmy. I guess that was his secret prayer all along. He has always golfed, but when Emmy became sick, he gave it up. It was his sacrifice, which seems silly to many, but we all gave up so many things. Our kids gave up relationships, dreams, and childhoods filled with sleepovers and playdates, while Randy and I gave up our hobbies and friendships. There is nothing we can do to get those years back, but now is the best time to begin building a future that we want.

The only lots left on the golf course were located on hillsides, which doesn't work well for someone in a wheelchair. As we were driving home, a sign caught my eye—a new subdivision was being built on the golf course that we had never seen before. I quickly sent an email and asked for additional information.

The next morning, I received two separate emails telling me lots were available and to call at my earliest convenience. I quickly called for more information and was invited to drive over to the subdivision that afternoon to see if the lots were big enough and flat enough to build a modified home.

As I drove up, the builder was waiting for me. He drove me to the lots he felt would work for us. I told him that we would love a view of the golf course, and he said one had just become available. As we walked over the land, which was perfect for what we needed, he showed me the lots surrounding it. Some were steep, and some were smaller and flat, but he ended by showing me the one he'd purchased for his family to build on.

The first step I took on the lot, and it hit me like a rushing wave. I was standing on the lot that I had been secretly praying for since 2014. This wasn't an ordinary golf course lot; this was well over an acre and covered with trees. The farther back we went, the more I couldn't believe what I was seeing. Right there, as if God had painted this picture just for me, was a lake located right next to the golf course. Trees were everywhere. And curving down the center of the lot was a path directly to the lake. Randy would finally be able to teach Everett to fish. We found the place to settle down, make up for lost time, and finally feel at home. But this belonged to someone else.

"You aren't going to believe this, but this is exactly what I have been praying for. Can I buy this from you?" I boldly asked him.

"Ha! No, this was the lot that *I* had been praying for. Every time I golfed and looked up at this lot, I prayed that it would be mine," he said while laughing. "But as of right now, I am actually considering selling it. My wife isn't ready to move, and I don't want to just keep it for later. I'm willing to sell it—if you just give me an offer."

That night, I drove Randy to the lot, and the builder met us. Randy fell in love instantly, and we signed a contract the next day. I never imagined we would stay in Arkansas. But just as in the past, God had it all planned out, and we had nothing to do with it. I just can't believe how God had taken care of every single detail regarding our lives, and it didn't cause one ounce of worry.

Only God knows the future. He has plans for us to experience peace and give us a future of hope. I cling to that verse as I think about what our future will look like. I still believe the dreams of Emmy walking again will come true. I somehow have not lost all hope but, rather, found hope in God. I can plan out a future. But as I have learned, God's plans are so much better than mine; and I trust Him completely.

Ella, now twenty, is home from her second year at college, and I wonder how different her life would have been if Emmy hadn't become sick right as she transitioned from girlhood to womanhood. She was forced to grow up way too fast, but she did it without complaints. Randy and I couldn't be prouder of the woman she has become, exhibiting true compassion, empathy, and understanding to every person she meets. She will graduate college in a couple of years with an English degree, focused on writing and editing. Whatever she does with her God-given talents will do nothing but improve this broken, ugly world we live in.

In the blink of an eye, our feisty, sleepless Eli has matured into a man and scholar of sorts. At seventeen, Eli has developed wisdom well beyond his years, which for the life of Randy and me, we can't figure out where it came from. We just thank God every day that he is driven, focused, and doesn't complain (too much) when we need him to help carry Emmy all over the house. My heart aches to think two of our children will be adults. Eli is planning to become an aerospace engineer, and once again, only God knows where that kind of knowledge came from.

Too much was taken from our youngest child, Everett, during the years that should have been filled with dreams and wonder. Even with being passed between friends and family members for three years, he still exudes joy and a spirit of hopefulness that only God could have given him. There is not one ounce of resentment for what he missed out on, and he is still patiently waiting for Emmy to walk again. I always say he was born to show Emmy what unconditional love looks like.

Many people ask me if Emmy's life will be long and fulfilling, with all the damage that occurred in her brain. In truth, only God knows the number of our days. I also know that people live long lives with or without brain damage. As far as her future living conditions, Randy and I have a goal to make her as independent as possible in case she does want to live on her own or get married. But at the same time, we will always have room for her and any of our kids to live with us as long as they want.

Emmy's prognosis is full of hope and wonder. While still a noisy breather and very short for a thirteen-year-old, she could care less what the world or people think of her. She has maintained her God-given personality; she is who she is, and I love her even more for it. Everett has surpassed her short height of only fifty inches, by a whopping four inches, yet he is exactly three years younger. Who knows? Maybe God gave us another strong boy who can help me when Eli goes to college. God is pretty awesome like that.

Emmy continues to work hard on walking, and Randy and I are committed to making that happen. I find her doing squats off the side of her bed or stretching her left wrist out, all without us telling her to. Determination is her strength. The light that shines within her radiates so brightly it lights up everyone around her. She makes people want to be better, to love deeper, and to never lose faith. She makes people remember to never complain!

No matter what she has been through and the physical abilities that were stolen, she has a supernatural joy that can't be explained. It's like every place that HLH damaged her brain, God replaced with joy. Emmy is an anomaly, one that can't be explained by science or man, and she makes me so proud to be her mama.

Randy is thankful for the Air Force, especially the medical service corps, but the time has come to hang up the hat and move on. Sadness comes with leaving any life behind, especially one that has been a constant for twenty-five years. It is time to reclaim nights and weekends to spend with family without the load of work. No matter what career he chooses going forward, his new colleagues are going to be blessed by a man full of integrity, honor, and a superior work ethic. I thank God every day that He brought Randy into my life. He is the yin to my yang.

I try not to think too much about my life and what will become of spending the rest of my days caring for another human being. I planned for a fulfilling future using my degrees in the corporate world or the public sector somewhere, spending days talking with actual adults. But this life is mine now, still fulfilling in many ways, but not what I originally wanted. The old me was crushed and unrecognizable, almost to the point of unrepair. It was painful and hard, but God took those pieces and put me back together dauntless, full of hope, and confident in an unwavering faith in the Creator of the universe.

Yes, I still dream of a life of freedom and travel, never worrying about an extra-special child. I know God will work this out. Why would God give me the personality and desires I have, only to never use them? Every time my thoughts wander into the dark, unspeakable past, I quickly remember to stop and thank God for *this* day, *this* moment, *this* life that we were given. It could have turned out so much worse. But God has done more than we could have ever imagined or hoped for, even if those things are not exactly what we wanted. I still wish Emmy would have fully recovered by now. But I believe, if we will just do the difficult, God will do the impossible.

I want to finish with a quote spoken to me by my beautiful friend Rebecca. She had a way with words during my chaotic, confusing, crippling days in Pepperell. Rebecca was able to pull me out of holes I didn't realize I was in and quickly send my thoughts to the positive things that God had already accomplished. Without her, I may have never been able to fully comprehend all of the great things God had done in our lives.

"Our lives are a symphony, and God is the conductor. You may not be able to follow the melody or understand the tune or even know all the words, but when God is finished with this composition of your life, it will be the most beautiful song that you have ever heard" (Rebecca Babine).

A TIMELINE OF EVENTS THROUGH PICTURES

Bellows Beach, Hawaii, June 2010.

Ko' Olina, where Emmy fell during family photos before moving to Virginia, July 2012.

Newport News, Virginia. Our last family photo before Emmy became sick, September 2013.

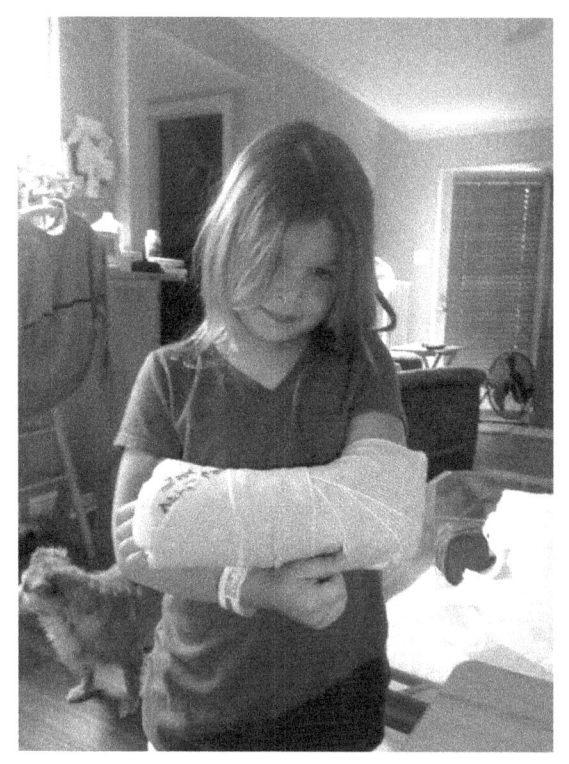

New Orleans when Emmy broke her arm on the monkey bars and turned on HLH, April 2014.

Last dance recital one month before having a seizure at the pool. Emmy was still able to do the entire dance, even though her brain was full of inflammation, June 2014.

CHKD hospital after ten days of
being sedated, July 2014.

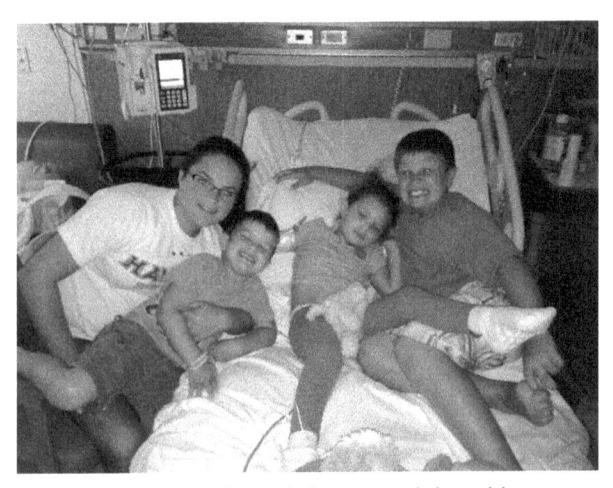

CHKD in-patient physical therapy with her siblings just
a few weeks before going home, August 2014.

At home when the HLH was still active and Emmy
became very lethargic, September 2014.

Emmy's eyes were now crossed, and she was
still very lethargic, October 2014.

Emmy's cat Bellows dies on Veteran's day—the same day Emmy has a stroke and her face becomes paralyzed on the right side, November 2014 (actual picture from September 2010).

One of the many stays at CHKD after a seizure, April 2015. So thankful for volunteers who would bring their therapy dogs to the hospitals to bring joy to so many children.

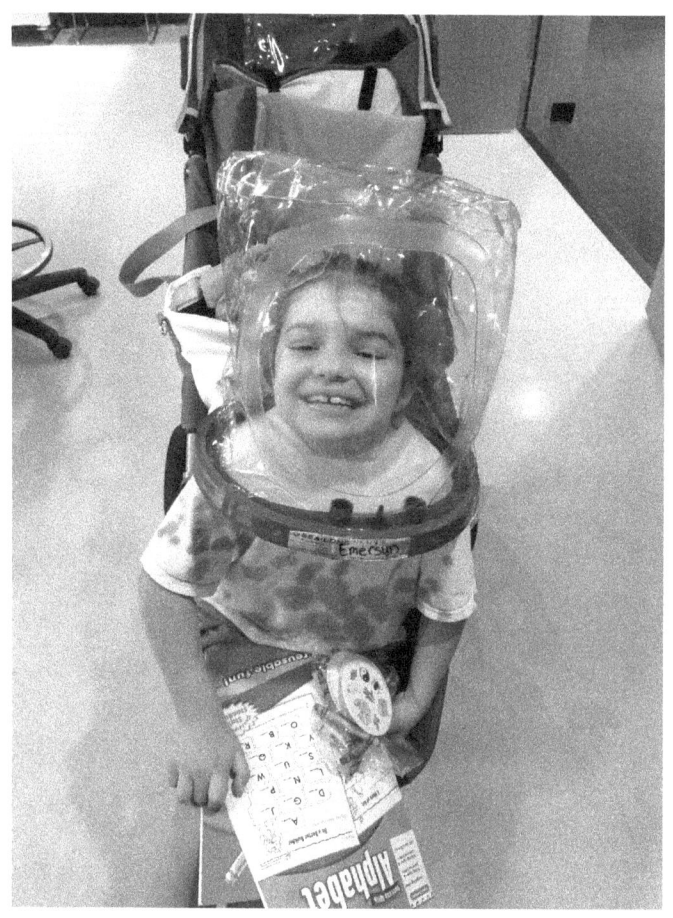

Hyperbaric oxygen therapy. The plastic helmet Emmy wore, May 2015.

Busch Gardens, August 2015. Emmy was at her strongest and best since she became sick. She stopped taking steroids shortly thereafter.

Emmy started losing many abilities and was weak
and lethargic again, October 2015.

Still having spasms after angiogram but calm enough to fly to Boston Children's Hospital for a diagnosis, November 25, 2015.

Still able to smile between spasms that lasted all day long. Pastor Randy came to Boston days before Emmy's first brain biopsy, December 4, 2015.

Day of first brain biopsy, December 8, 2015.

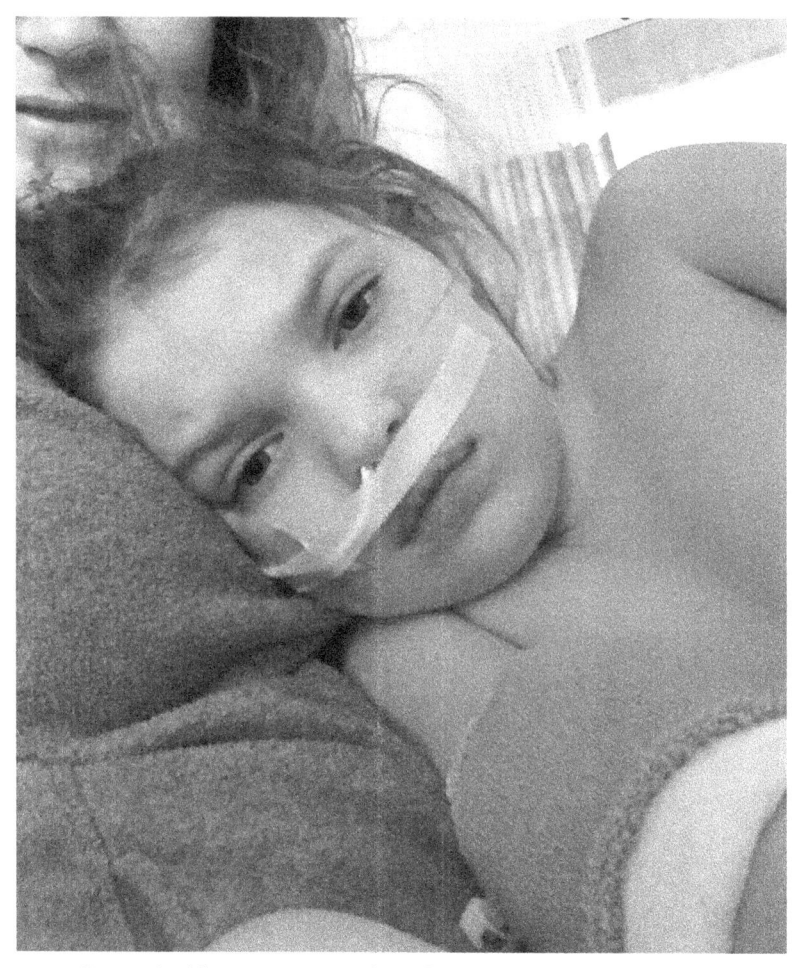

Emmy had become emotionless after month of intubation, and Artane was increased dramatically, February 2016.

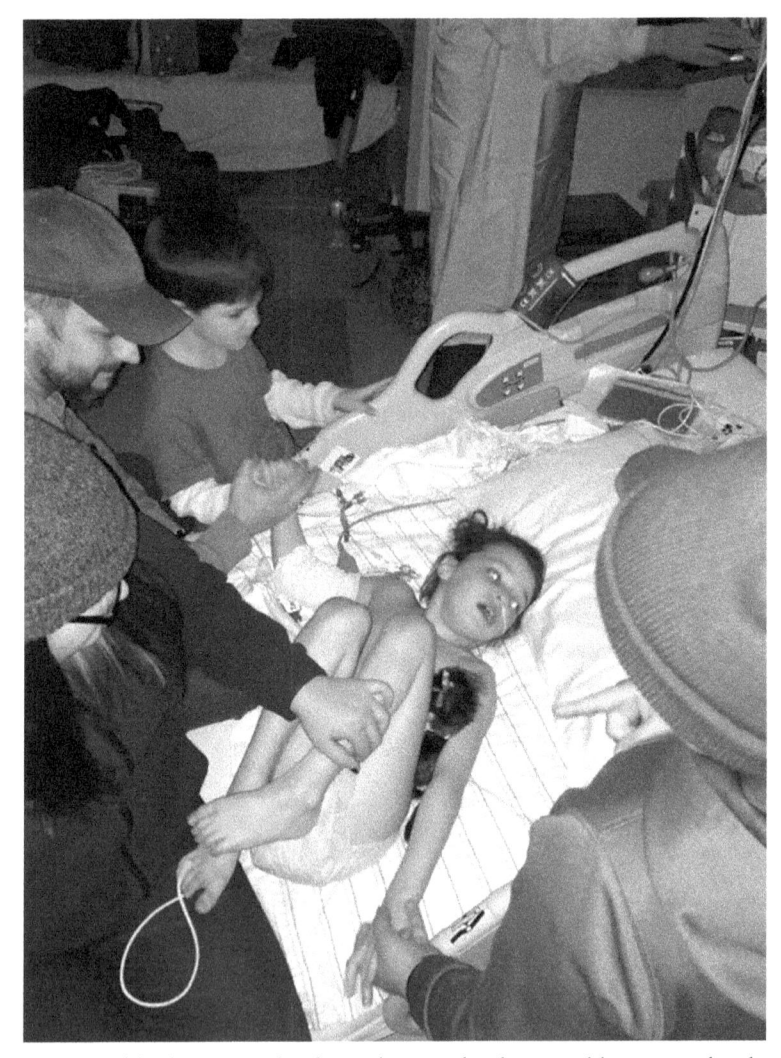

Emmy would ask to sit on her knees because her legs would spasm so hard in a straight position. This was weeks before the bone marrow transplant, and Emmy was still very distant and didn't respond to Randy, Ella, Eli, or Everett as they tried to make connections and make her smile, February 2016.

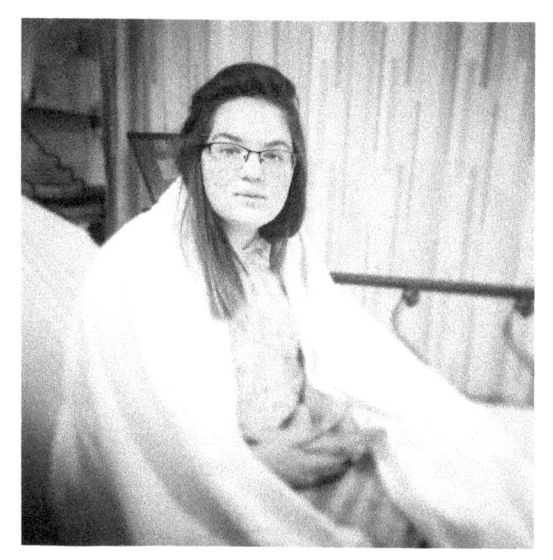

Ella before going to surgery to donate her bone marrow to Emmy, March 25, 2016.

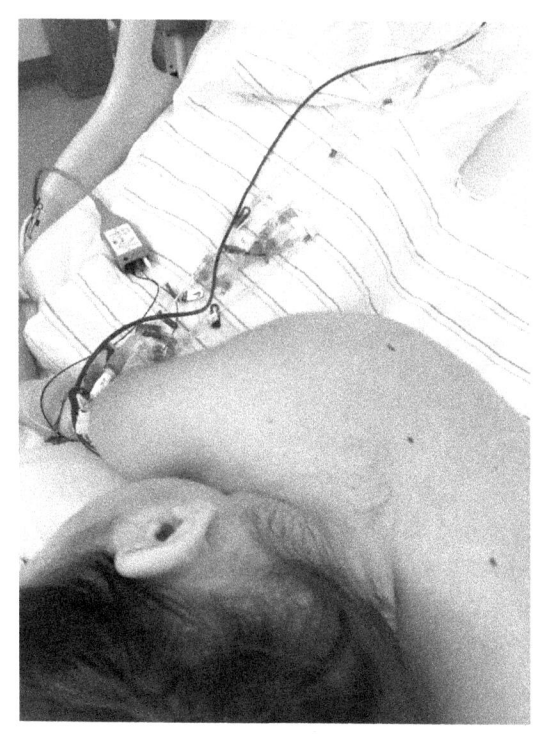

Emmy sleeping during her first bone marrow infusion, March 25, 2016.

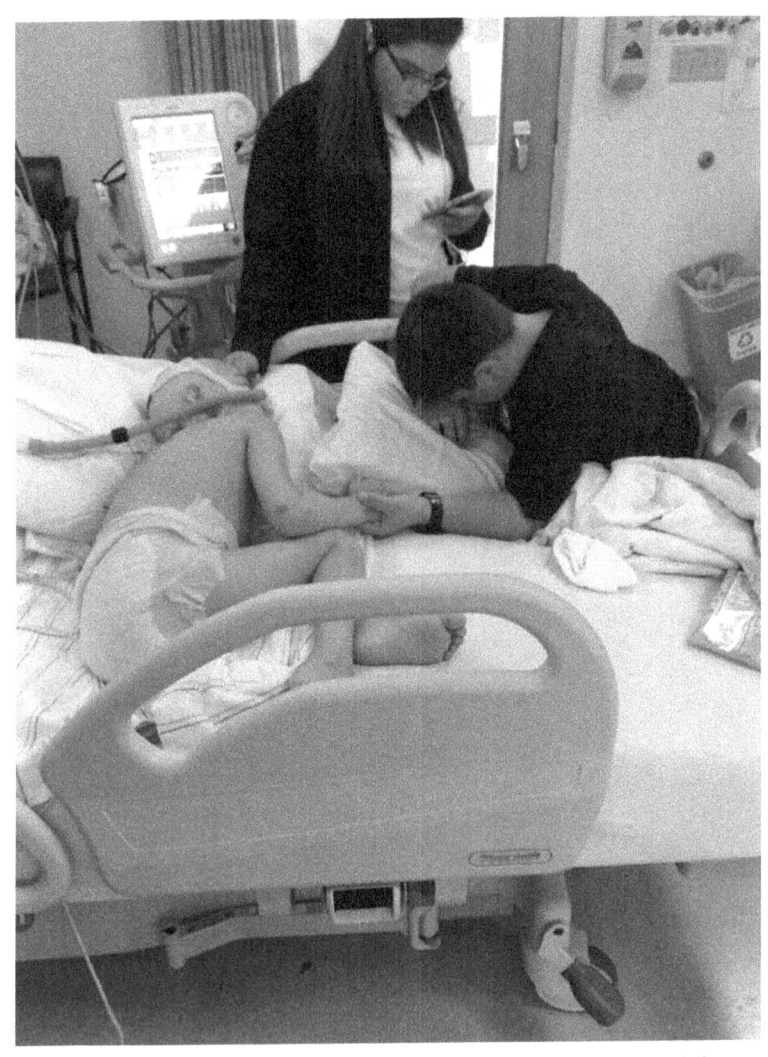

Ella and Eli comforting Emmy while in her CPAP mask, May 2016. The entire family had moved to Boston and was staying in the apartment given to us. During this time, Emmy was fighting a deadly trio of adenovirus, BK virus, and CMV.

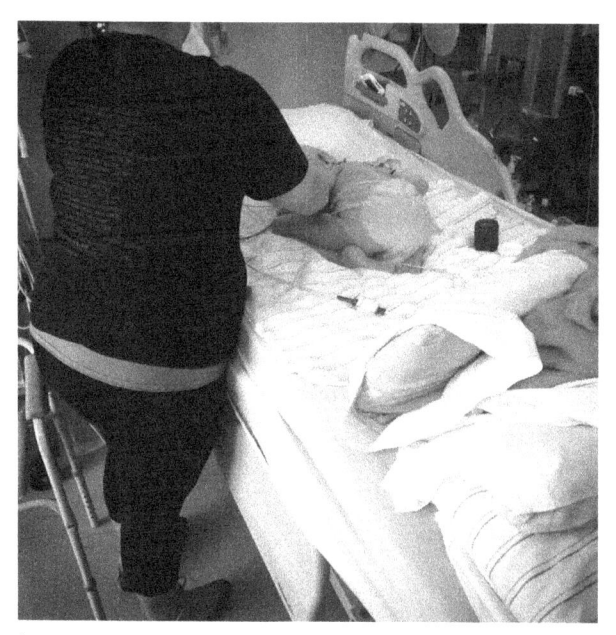

Nicole, my sister, moved to Boston in April and would spend hours massaging Emmy, June 2016. Emmy still slept in the fetal position twenty-four hours a day, which ultimately dislocated her hip.

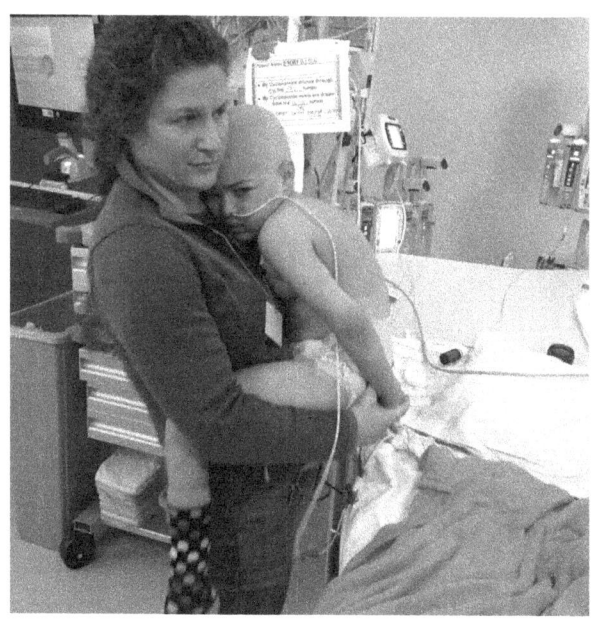

On days when Emmy was calm, I would be able to hold her. She was a mere forty pounds, July 2016.

Randy's mom, Linda, with Emmy before she was taken to inpatient rehab at Franciscans, September 2016.

Many of Emmy's Boston Children's ICU nurses came to Franciscans to surprise her before we went home. This simple swing is what kept Emmy positive and looking forward to each new day, October 2016.

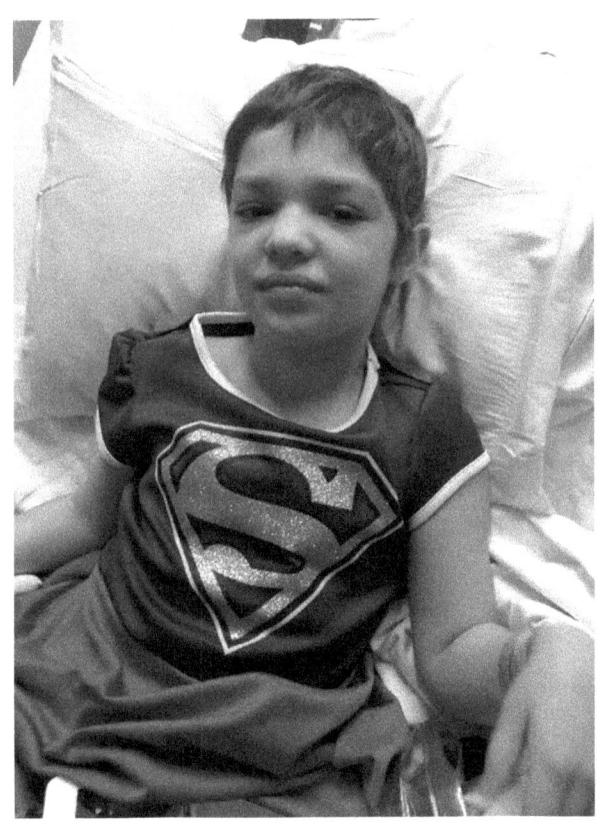

Emmy in her iconic Super Girl costume before going
home right before Halloween, October 2016.

Santa and Mrs. Claus visiting our family days before Christmas—all
orchestrated by our new neighbor, Rebecca Babine, December 2016.

Aunt Nicole spent hours with Emmy, especially doing things that made Emmy laugh, March 2017.

Emmy clothes shopping with Aunt Nicole, June 2017. Her personality and creative sense of style started to shine through. Aunt Nicole left mid-June to go back to Montana.

Celebrating an early Fourth of July at our neighbor's house, where Rebecca took this photo of Emmy, clear-eyed and so happy to be swimming with her friends, June 30, 2017.

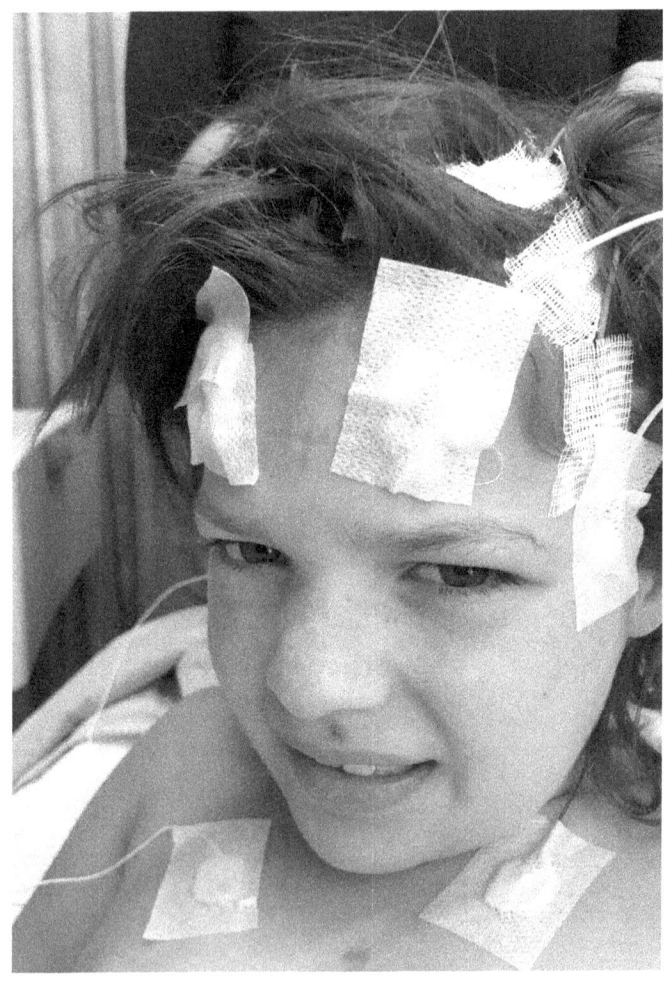

Emmy was admitted to the hospital after an MRI showed a new lesion; EEGs and more tests were done, July 3, 2017.

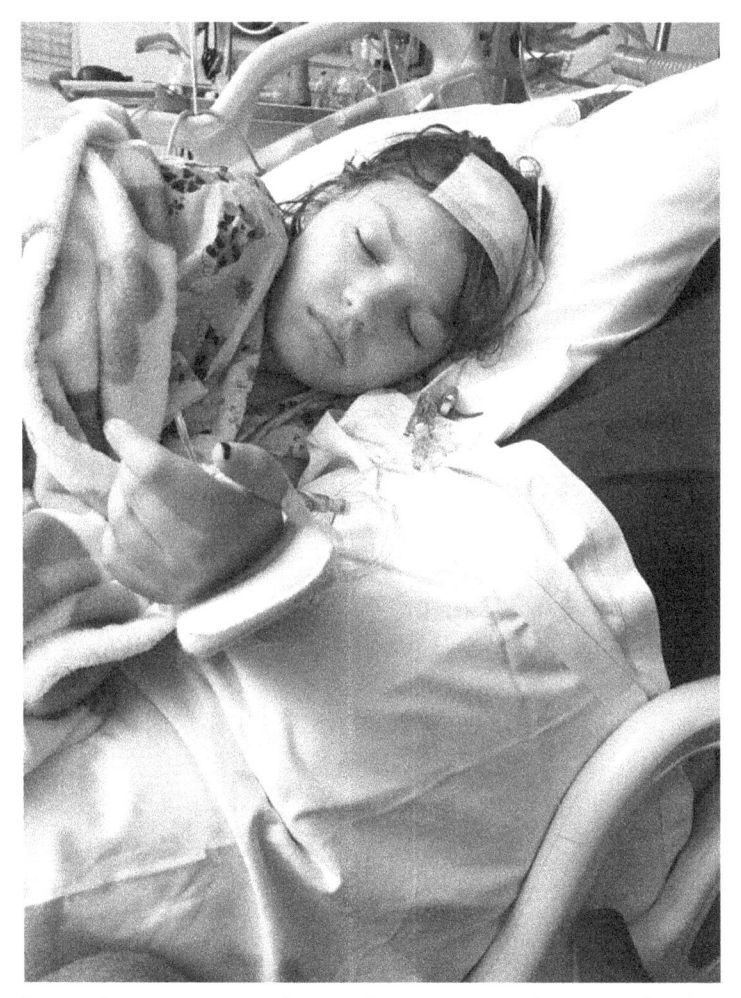

A partial craniotomy was done on Emmy to try and remove what they believed to be a tumor, not HLH. She recovered quickly, but the sedation and irritation to her brain made her body to start spasming again. Spinal fluid and biopsy proved to be the return of CNS-restricted HLH, July 11, 2017.

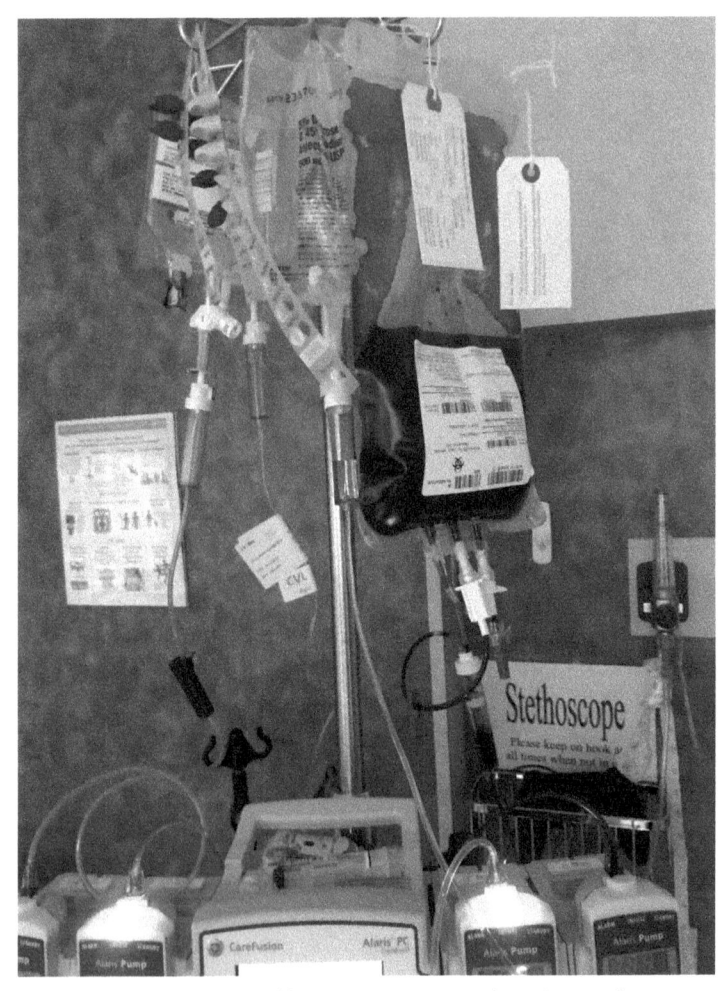

Emmy received a second bone marrow transplant from a donor in Germany. Between July and September, Emmy was once again in full body spasms, and no pictures were captured. October 17, 2017.

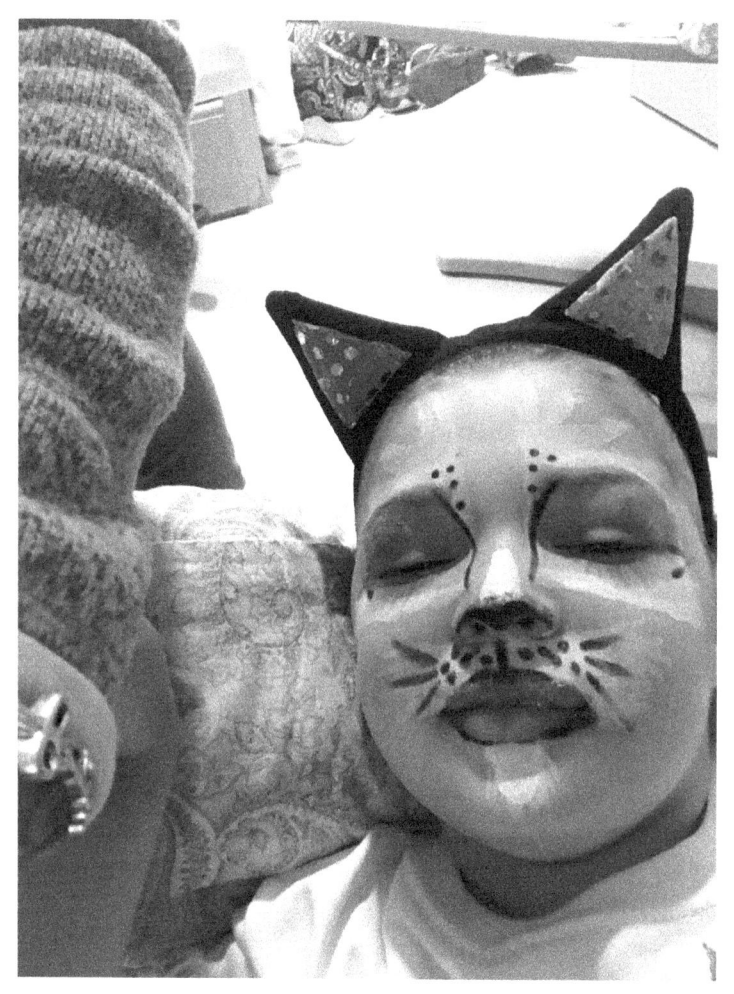

Emmy well enough to go trick-or-treating on the bone marrow floor, October 31, 2017. Such a difference from the first hospital stay. No oxygen and no intubation were ever needed.

Randy and Emmy loving on each other, November 2017. Being able to hold Emmy and comfort her through this transplant was truly a blessing from God.

Less than 30 days post-transplant, Emmy was discharged and the BMT staff through her a bubble party, November 14, 2017. The nurses on this floor made our stay as perfect as a hospital stay can be.

Everett and Emmy hanging out at one of the many times we had to drive back and forth from the hospital due to a random fever, December 2017.

Another quick trip to the hospital, where Emmy received many gifts from Santa Claus, Christmas 2017. I think she timed this perfectly! Gifts are her love language.

We started getting Emmy tested for a communication device, since her voice was still very quiet but also noisy from the paralyzed vocal cord, June 2018.

Just a typical day with our sweet neighbor friends,
Kate and Grace, September 2018.

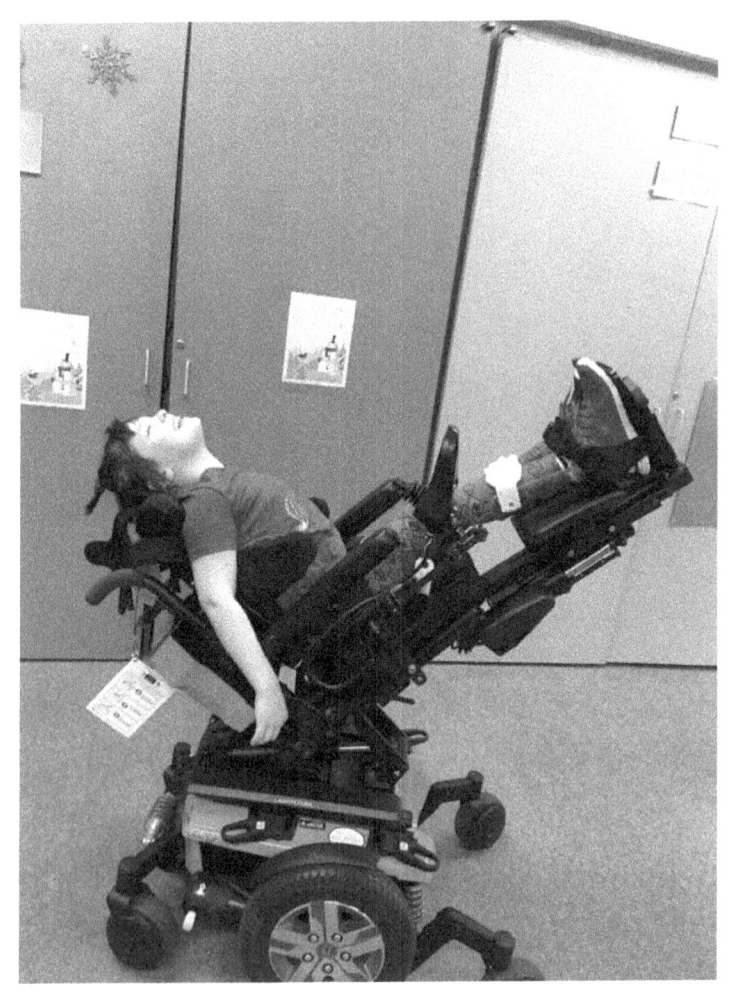

Emmy quickly became the class clown during her first year at school, January 2019. She attended fourth grade at nine years old. This was a huge turning point in our lives.

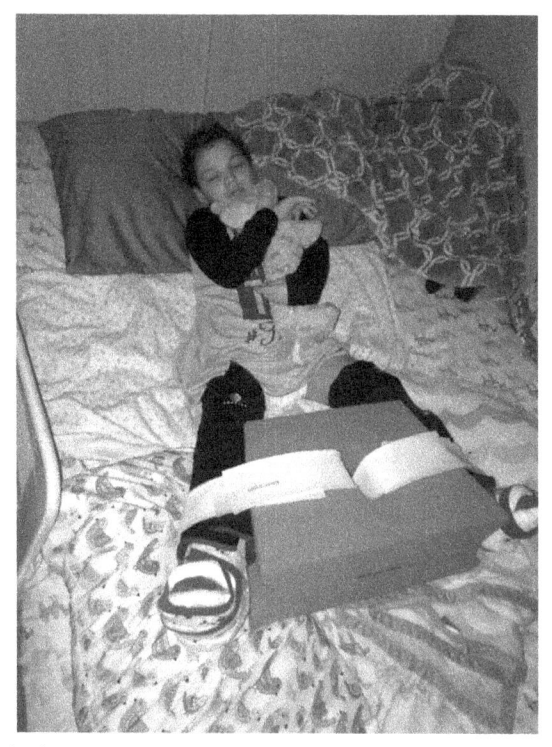

Emmy had surgery to correct her displaced hips, February 2019. She underwent a double hip osteotomy, lengthening of calf muscles and loosening of her left groin. Spasms did occur and also a seizure from weaning the Valium, but we made it through without a hospital intervention.

Emmy with her PCA Jessica, May 2019. We would have never made it without Jessica. God brought us a woman who was trained as an OT and also had a son who was born with a specific disability he had to overcome.

A quick stop in Maryland to visit our cousins during our move to Arkansas, June 2019. Jennings gave Emmy her first four-wheeler ride.

We truly believe that putting Emmy in a swimming pool jump-started the healing in her body and brain, July 2019. This was the same time we started seeing small seizure episodes.

Emmy with her PCA Nicole, who moved with us from Massachusetts, during one of our first visits to Arkansas Children's Hospital, August 2019.

Emmy's dream came true when she got to meet Aladdin and Jasmine at Disneyworld, January 2020.

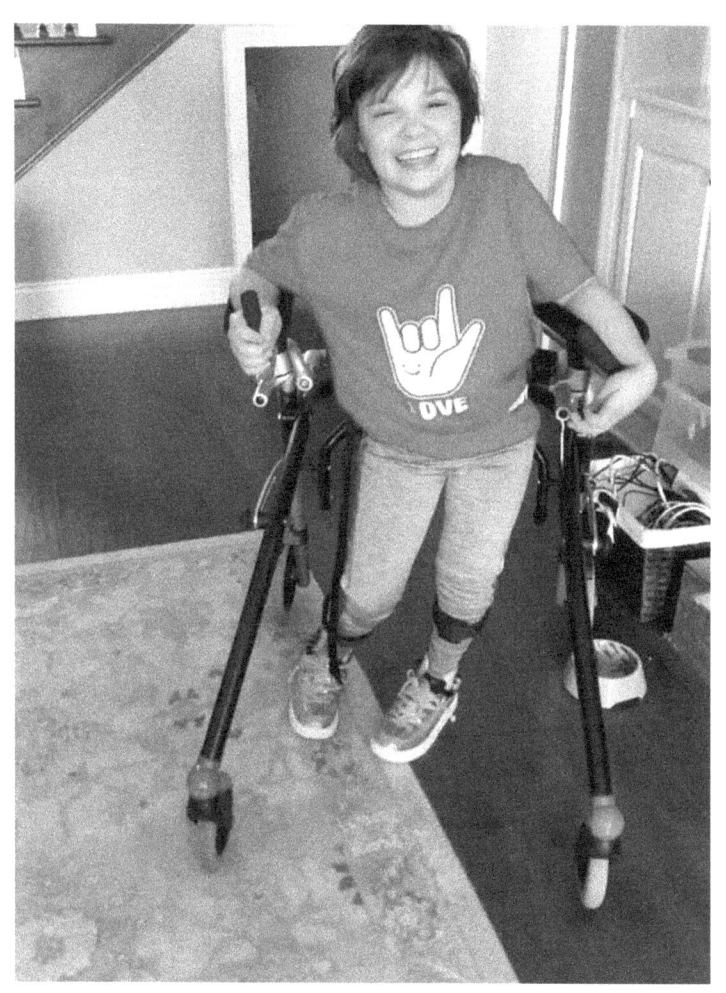

Emmy on her walker, June 2020. Her strength and
determination continue to amaze me.

Emmy snuggling outside with her three-year post-transplant
birthday present, Mr. BunBun, September 2020.

Doing HBOT at home—all because of a generous
donation from a friend, September 2020.

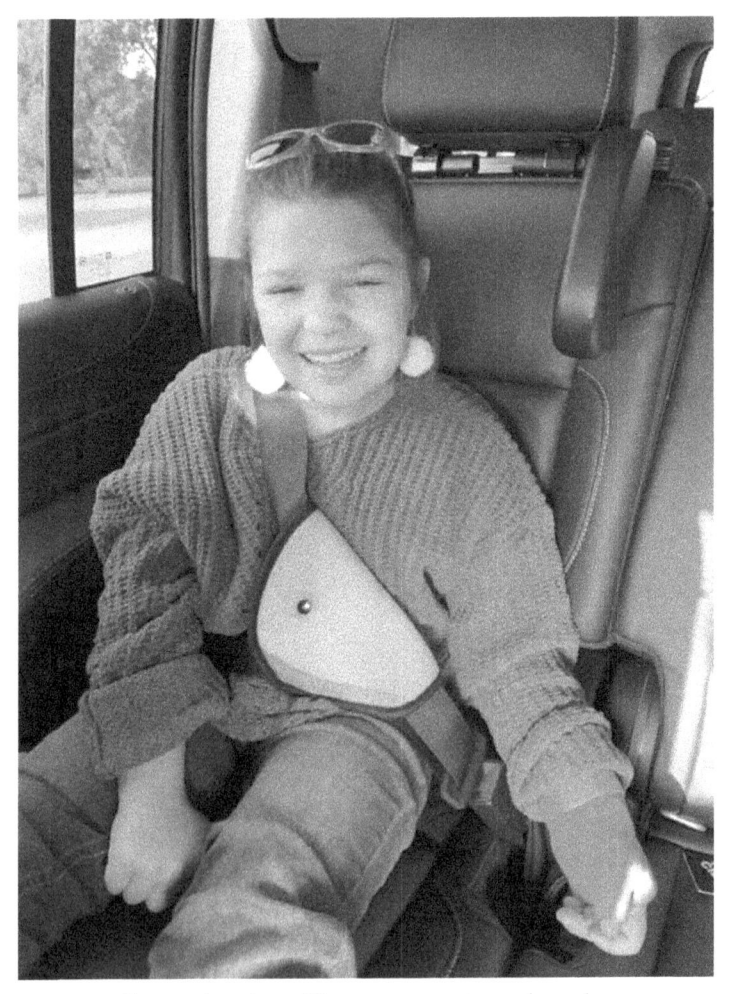

Emmy showing off her cute, creative style at the start of sixth grade, September 15, 2020.

Emmy working hard at Beyond Boundaries hippotherapy, one of the other things that has changed her entire outlook and physical strength, May 2021.

#Emmystrong symbol, worn by Emmy's very own superhero, her daddy.

ADDITIONAL INFORMATION

To learn more about HLH
https://www.cincinnatichildrens.org/service/h/hlh

CNS Restricted HLH Case Study, Emmy is patient #4
https://nn.neurology.org/content/6/3/e560

Additional CNS Restricted HLH Case Study
https://ashpublications.org/bloodadvances/article/3/4/503/246762/Central-nervous-system-restricted-familial

To learn more about parental rights
https://parentalrights.org

CPSIA information can be obtained
at www.ICGtesting.com
Printed in the USA
LVHW040818070123
736683LV00019B/192